Comments from Coworkers of the Author

Over the years, I have learned a great deal from John Rodenkirch. His rich life experience has given him a mature perspective and a volume of lessons-learned to make him the sound counselor and problem solver he has become. I am pleased now to see his life learning available to everyone through this book.

John has been gifted with a tremendous intellect, and we are fortunate to have him share it with us. When it comes to both his business life and his personal life, he understands the big picture and he sees how everything fits together. He makes connections between the seemingly unconnected, and leads us to new enlightenment in the process. With his ability to present the complicated in an easy-to-understand manner, John's style is highly engaging.

As a management peer and coworker of John, I have always valued the way he can help people be more productive. By combining his experience know-how, his critical thinking skills, and his interest in getting things accomplished, John has always set a good example. With a career's worth of important experience in both large and small companies, John has learned what it means to be a valuable employee and he teaches that to others.

John Rodenkirch's thoughts and considerations on what it takes to be successful in life are sure to make this book an important addition to its readers' own collections of guideposts.

Bob Patnaude — Director of Marketing, Federal Signal Corporation

I have had the pleasure of working at the same company as John during the last five years. Together, we have resolved various situations involving employee issues, policy implementation, benefit development, and the like. I am always interested to hear John's perspective about situations. He shares insight into looking at situations from all angles. This trait is very beneficial. Imagine if all people (not just in the workplace) would take a step back and evaluate the potential repercussions of their actions before actually taking action. John endorses pre-evaluation, showing consideration, and taking the other person's viewpoint. I read this book and noticed that John's insights are sensible and logical. He holds the reader's attention by teaching us (through his own life experiences) that there are roads that may be taken to travel from point A to point B without encountering *traffic*.

Dan Weinick — Director of Human Resources, Chicago Operations, IMI Cornelius Inc.

LIFETIME CAREER GUIDEBOOK

Having and Making the Most of a Successful Career While Raising Successful Children

John J. Rodenkirch, CPA, CMA, CFM

ISBN 978-0-9798353-5-3

Includes Index

Second Edition

Explanation Press
Carol Stream, Illinois

Dedication

This book is dedicated to Balthasar Gracian whose book THE ART OF WORLDLY WISDOM – 1637 inspired me to understand important things well enough to concisely explain them in a book.

Contents

Preface 11

BOOK ONE

GETTING ON, STAYING ON, AND RIDING THE CAREER FAST TRACK

Introduction 13

Chapter 1 **Choosing an Occupation** 15

Chapter 2 **Selecting a Potential Employer** 17

Chapter 3 **Preparing a Resume** 19

Chapter 4 **Interviewing** 25

Chapter 5 **Before Accepting a Job Offer** 31

Chapter 6 **Before Starting a New Job** 33

Chapter 7 **Starting a New Job** 35

Chapter 8 **Organizing Your Work** 39

Chapter 9 **Using Time Wisely** 41

Chapter 10 **Working Efficiently** 45

Chapter 11 **Wasting Time** 49

Chapter 12 **Handling Mistakes** 51

Chapter 13 **Learning from Others** 53

Chapter 14 **Business Writing** 55

Chapter 15 **Project Planning** 61

Chapter 16 **Projects and Tasks** 73

Chapter 17 **Presentations and Reports** 77

Chapter 18 **Business Meetings** 81

Chapter 19 **Working in Teams** 83

Chapter 20 **Being a Valuable Employee** 85

Chapter 21 **Taking Care of and Selling to Customers** 89

Chapter 22 **Negotiating** 95

Chapter 23 **Working Relationships** 97

Chapter 24 **Awkward Situations** 99

Chapter 25 **Conflicts** 103

Chapter 26 **Difficult Bosses** 107

Chapter 27 **Working Well with Your Boss** 111

Chapter 28 **Getting Promoted** 115

Chapter 29 **Supervising and Managing Others** 121

Chapter 30 **Hiring People** 127

Chapter 31 **Changing Employers** 131

Chapter 32 **Exiting an Employer** 133

BOOK TWO

EVALUATING OPPORTUNITIES TO START OR BUY A BUSINESS

Introduction 137

Chapter 1 **Evaluating an Opportunity to Start a Business** 139

Chapter 2 **Evaluating an Opportunity to Buy a Business** 169

Chapter 3 **Understanding and Analyzing Financial Statements** 183

Chapter 4 **Financial Decision Making** 195

BOOK THREE

BUILDING A SOLID FOUNDATION FOR A SUCCESSFUL CAREER

Introduction 209

Chapter 1 **Accomplishing Things** 211

Chapter 2 **Understanding Things** 213

Chapter 3 **Making Decisions** 217

Chapter 4 **Learning in General** 221

Chapter 5 **Having the Right Attitude** 225

Chapter 6 **Developing Self-Confidence** 227

Chapter 7 **Self-Improvement** 229

Chapter 8 **Interacting with Others** 235

Chapter 9 **Perceiving Reality** 241

BOOK FOUR

PRESERVING INCOME AND INVESTING FOR RETIREMENT

Introduction 247

Chapter 1 **Saving and Spending** 249

Chapter 2 **Investing** 259

Chapter 3 **Insurance** 271

Chapter 4 **Buying and Selling a Home** 275

Chapter 5 **Buying and Selling an Automobile** 279

Chapter 6 **Other Purchases** 283

Chapter 7 **Other Financial and Legal Matters** 287

Chapter 8 **Health** 291

BOOK FIVE

RAISING SUCCESSFUL CHILDREN WHO ARE PREPARED FOR THE CAREER FAST TRACK

Introduction 293

Chapter 1 **Getting on the Right Track** 295

Chapter 2 **Learning the Fundamentals of Being a Person** 299

Chapter 3 **Getting a Good Formal and Informal Education** 307

Chapter 4 **Learning to Take Responsibility for Actions Taken** 319

Chapter 5 **Becoming Hard Workers Who Understand the Value of Savings** 323

Chapter 6 **Selecting an Occupation** 327

Chapter 7 **Raising Successful Children in General** 329

Index 333

Preface

Everything people need to know about having successful careers is included in this book. The basic premise is that it is better to learn about the career fast track from other people's experiences than to learn from personal experiences. Missed opportunities and unnecessary problems can teach lessons well, if the correct lessons are learned, but the career setbacks they cause can be significant. Companies generally hire people who have the potential to advance; unfortunately, most employees take themselves out of contention for upper-level positions. This book covers every important situation an employee can be in, with an emphasis on things not taught in school. Information is related to specific situations and will enable people to manage both career opportunities and potential problems.

The goal for this book was to write an easy-to-use guidebook that has the information people need to know about having successful careers. Information in each chapter is easy to find. Explanations are concise, easy to understand, and detailed enough so readers can merge the new information with what they already know. The explanations do not use made-up acronyms that have to be memorized in order to follow the rest of the book. Conclusions are linked to the information presented and there are no unfounded assumptions.

There are five different aspects of having successful careers, each of which is a separate book in this guidebook.

Book One covers how to get on, stay on, and ride the career fast track as far and as fast as possible. The steps necessary to accomplish this are not easy to identify in advance. Learning the steps through experience is not practical because missteps usually slow people down in the pursuit of their careers. Information in here will enable people to have quick starts in their careers and to jump-start stalled careers. Companies look for employees with quick starts because it is one of the best indicators of who can quickly move up in a company.

Book Two explains how to evaluate opportunities to start or buy a business with an emphasis on the financial side of things. The accompanying information on managing a business was included to explain what business owners usually have to do in order to be successful. This information on managing a business applies to managing an owned business or someone else's business.

Book Three covers how to build a solid foundation for a successful career. The primary emphasis is on matters that need to be understood and considered when setting and pursuing goals. These matters involve how people can take necessary control of their lives and their environments, so they can make the right things happen for themselves.

Book Four explains how to preserve income and invest for retirement, both of which are often overlooked in the pursuit of income. Preserving income involves curtailing wasteful spending and getting the most from money spent. Investing involves delaying when money is spent and maximizing its purchasing power. Information in here will help people avoid the financial mistakes that many people make.

Book Five covers how to raise successful children, from early success in life through being prepared for the career fast track. The earlier children start becoming successful, the more likely they will continue to be successful throughout their lives. Children need to learn how to be successful and they need to develop the self-esteem that comes from being successful. There is a gold mine of information here for parents who want to raise successful children who are prepared for the career fast track. The right choices for parents are not always obvious and the information here will help parents make good choices. Preparation for the career fast track involves (1) understanding the importance of having a successful career; (2) being willing to work hard enough to be successful; and (3) having the skills, knowledge, and abilities to be successful. Children who are prepared for the career fast track are more likely to have successful careers.

People with successful careers do not necessarily work longer hours than people with mediocre careers. The major difference between these two groups is that people with successful careers do a better job of (1) getting more out of career opportunities and (2) avoiding unnecessary problems. This book is designed to help people identify and understand situations, so the best course of action can be taken.

This is the most comprehensive and easy-to-use book I am aware of concerning career success. Information and advice in this book is what I wish I knew and understood when I entered the work force after college.

BOOK ONE

GETTING ON, STAYING ON, AND RIDING THE CAREER FAST TRACK

Book One covers the following:

- How to get on the career fast track
- How to avoid falling off the career fast track
- How to ride the career fast track as far and as fast as possible

The steps necessary to accomplish the above are not easy to identify in advance. Learning the steps through experience is not practical because missteps usually make the above harder to accomplish. Information in here will enable people to have quick starts in their careers and to jump-start stalled careers. Companies look for employees with quick starts because it is one of the best indicators of who can quickly move up in a company.

Chapter 1

Choosing an Occupation

This chapter covers what to look for in an occupation, where to get information about possible occupations, and the importance of choosing an occupation that fits in with your long-term goals.

The ideal occupation has the following attributes, which need to be considered with a long-term perspective:

- You must enjoy the type of work involved. Confucius said something to the effect: "Choose a job you love, and you will never have to work a day in your life."
- You must be good at the work involved.
- The compensation must meet your needs.

Evaluate all occupations you consider based on these three attributes. Listen to other people's advice, but make your own choice concerning which occupation to pursue. After you make your choice, keep an open mind. You may learn or experience things that make a different occupation worth considering. You can often start pursuing a general occupation (such as being an attorney, engineer, or architect) while keeping your options open concerning a specific area of specialization within the general occupation.

Sources of information about different occupations include family members, school counselors, libraries, encyclopedias, people employed in specific occupations, and schools that prepare people for specific occupations.

Consider all occupations, not just those that others in your life have pursued. Ideally, you grew up in an environment where you were encouraged and enabled to explore whatever non-harmful things that interested you. If you have not explored everything you are interested in, try to explore it all before choosing an occupation to pursue. Take a career aptitude test, which may reveal other occupations to consider.

Generally, the more education and certifications a job requires, the more it pays, assuming someone needs the work done and has the money to pay. For the most part, physical labor is hard on your body, it often does not pay well, and experience after the first few years is not that valuable.

Choose an occupation that will make you feel good. It should be noted that prestigious occupations often pay less than you would expect; this is primarily because of the law of supply and demand.

Earn an honest living. In addition to being the right thing to do, you will have much more job satisfaction than if you earn your living by treating others less than fairly. Furthermore, you do not want to spend your life worrying about someday being embarrassed by something you did years ago.

Chapter 2

Selecting a Potential Employer

Many factors need to be considered when selecting a potential employer. This chapter concerns these factors that need to be considered.

Career Goals

Career goals need to be determined before you select a potential employer. Long-term career goals should be based on where you want your career to go. Short-term career goals are the initial steps to accomplish the long-term goals. Work backwards from the long-term goals to the present time and identify the steps that have to be taken. These steps can be broken down further into required education, experience, and the like, for each step. If there are alternative long-term goals being considered, the short-term goals for each also need to be considered. Goals should always be subject to revision based on changing circumstances and new information. Long-term goals should never be changed for short-term considerations. Do not make the mistake of valuing the short term more than the long term. In the future, the long-term goals will be more important than the short-term considerations from the past.

Your Needs

Generally, the most important factors concerning whether an employer meets your needs are as follows:

- Does the overall situation (company size, company type, job position, and advancement opportunity) fit in with your career goals?

- Do you like the type of work the company wants done?
- How much of a time commitment will be needed from you?
- Are the pay and benefits commensurate with the work you will be doing? Key benefits include medical insurance, company savings/retirement contributions, paid vacations, and educational expense reimbursement.
- Is the company profitable or otherwise financially stable?
- What is the chance that the company will be sold, closed, or will move soon?
- How long of a daily commute will you have? An extra half hour each way every day adds 250 hours a year to your travel time.
- What percent of the time will you be traveling away from home overnight?

Company's Culture

Every company has its own culture. The more you know about the company's culture, the better you can assess whether it is right for you. If any of the following questions concern matters that are important to you, ask the questions. Consider waiting to ask until after you have received the written job offer.

- Is everyone on a first-name basis? If not, who is not?
- What is the dress code?
- What are the normal work hours in the area you would be working in?
- Are open positions filled by promoting current employees whenever possible?
- Is there a company newsletter you can see? See if individual and team accomplishments are recognized.
- Is the employee turnover high or low compared to similar companies? High turnover can be okay when you are just looking for a couple years' experience and a possible promotion before moving to another company. Just be prepared to work hard and to put up with a rough work environment.

Internships

If you are still in school, try to get an internship with a company that meets your selection criteria for an employer after graduation. An internship is a great way to get your foot in the door and to get a job offer. While working as an intern, you need to keep in mind that interns are expected to work extra hard and to not treat anyone as being lower than they are in the company's pecking order. Before interning, you should understand the material in the first 28 chapters of this book.

Chapter 3

Preparing a Resume

Primary goal of a resume and cover letter is to get an interview. Secondary goal is to lay the groundwork for a good interview. This chapter covers both these goals and contains information on preparing professional looking cover letters and resumes.

The primary goal above is best accomplished as follows. Identify, as best as can be determined, all the criteria (requirements and preferred attributes) used by the company to decide whom to interview. Convey to the person reviewing resumes, in the quickest and most sure-fire way, that you meet or exceed all the criteria.

Job advertisements usually contain the main criteria that need to be met in order to get an interview. Other criteria can be surmised based on determining what a company would normally want in a candidate for the position being filled.

A cover letter is usually the best place to convey how you match up to the criteria. A bare-bones cover letter could start with, "Attached is my resume in response to…" Second paragraph could state, "Listed below are some highlights from my resume"; this is where you would concisely convey how you match up to the criteria. Third paragraph could state something to the effect, "I hope to have an opportunity to meet with you to discuss my qualifications and to learn about the __________ position at your company." If you want to have a longer cover letter, include the bare-bones items above and explain who you are, why the company is right for you, and why the company should hire you. A cover letter should be stapled to the resume, though not everyone would agree with this. If you do not use a cover letter, make sure your resume clearly shows that you meet or exceed all the criteria.

The secondary goal above is best accomplished by having a cover letter and resume that describe things in a manner that invites questions for details and explanations that you are well prepared to answer.

Rough out your resume based on the outline below; do not worry about format. Next, read your resume as if you were a hiring authority, and make changes as needed. Prepare the final draft of your resume based on the General Rules for a Finished Resume that follow the outline. You will then be ready, if needed, to select and make the most of a book that has sample cover letters and resumes for people in situations similar to yours.

It would take a whole book for me to include a sample cover letter and resume for the many different professions that college students and experienced workers could be pursuing. Fortunately, there are books that do this well. Many of these books have chapters that cover almost everything you need to know about resume formats.

RESUME OUTLINE

Your Name and Contact Information

- Nickname, in parentheses, is okay if your first name is hard to pronounce.
- Street address is better than a post office box number, unless you live very far away from the prospective employer.
- Provide personal (not work) email address in the resume.
- Provide phone number(s), other than a toll-free work number, in the resume.
- Students who live away from home while attending school may want to include their addresses for both school and home.

Profile

- This is primarily for experienced workers and is an overview of your accomplishments as detailed in the experience section of the resume.
- If you include information that is also in your cover letter, word it differently.
- Describe your accomplishments in their best light. Concisely cover scope and results in an easy to understand and believable manner. Key here is to describe the great things you did for your employers. Companies want to hire people who are going to come in and do great things for them. People who have done great things for their employers in the past have a greater chance of doing great things for future employers.

- Explain how your experience, education, career record of accomplishment, and *drive to succeed* all make you the ideal candidate for the position.
- Profile is usually in paragraph form with bullets as needed.

Objective

- This is primarily for college students who are getting ready to enter the full-time professional work force. An objective is not used when there is a profile.
- The main thing to include is something to the effect: "I am seeking a position as …where I can use my…"
- Explain how your experience, education, interest, and *drive to succeed* all make you the ideal candidate for the position.

Experience

- Experience has to support both the profile and the cover letter.
- Company name, size, dates employed, and a brief description of your responsibilities should be listed in date order starting with the most recent.
- Include dates for each position held at each company, listed in date order starting with the most recent.
- Try not to call attention to any periods of unemployment.
- The term experience as used in a resume refers to experiences and accomplishments. Experiences are usually best conveyed in terms of what you accomplished.
- Detailed experiences for each position held should be listed from the most important to the least important. Similar experiences may be best listed together. Describe what you did for the company.
- Use bullets that always begin with verbs such as developed, prepared, and administered.
- Possibly, put a short paragraph before the bullets to give an overview, but do not repeat information in the profile.
- College students may want to put this section after the education section and include jobs held while in school. Emphasize everything in the jobs that relates to the position you are applying for, such as taking care of customers, directing other employees, and saving costs. Students who had to work their way through school are often assumed by employers to be hard workers.

Education

- List work-related degrees, certifications, programs, continuing professional education, software training/proficiency, foreign languages, and anything else like this.
- Generally, list things from the most important to the least important, but try to keep similar things like college degrees together.
- College students should possibly list relevant courses taken and being taken along with information on grades, where helpful. Anticipated graduation date and name of degree should be included. Make sure the hiring authority will undoubtedly see that all the stated educational requirements to get an interview are met or exceeded.

Other Relevant Information

- Include everything else you want the hiring authority to know.
- List publications, public speaking engagements, awards, professional memberships, volunteer work, and anything else like this.
- Generally, list things from the most important to the least important, but try to keep similar things like professional memberships together.

General Rules for a Finished Resume

- Resumes should not exceed two pages, one page for college students. Second page should have your name at the top.
- Spelling errors should be eliminated.
- Grammatical errors should be eliminated.
- Format should be consistent throughout the resume. This includes capitalization, underlines, bold print, italics, tab settings, and the alignment of headings. An inconsistent format on a resume is a sign of carelessness. If you cannot get it done right on a resume, could you be counted on to put together an important communication?
- Experience and education sections should be labeled as such. Labeling other sections is optional, except the name and contact section, which should never be labeled.
- Resume needs to be concise, clear, well organized, and easy to scan for important information.
- Make sure important information jumps out when your resume is reviewed.

- Write your resume and cover letter with the mindset that you are an excellent candidate for the position.
- Make sure your resume and cover letter are designed to accomplish both goals discussed at the beginning of this chapter.
- If you are over age 40, consider leaving out dates for education and for your earliest experiences. Possibly, page two of your resume should not have any dates.
- If you are not familiar with terminology used in the profession, have someone in the profession review the terminology in your resume. Get recommended changes to your resume and decide which changes to use.
- Read your resume as if you were a person reviewing resumes for a company. Make sure everything is clear. Imagine that you are reviewing resumes and looking for reasons to put as many of them as possible into the reject pile.
- Requested salary information and your salary requirements should be put in the cover letter, not in the resume.

Chapter 4

Interviewing

When interviewing, you need to know what the company is trying to determine, how to present/sell yourself, and how to determine if the company is grossly exaggerating its employee benefits.

What the Company is trying to Determine during the Interview

When interviewing for a job, your potential new boss wants to see the following three things, and possibly the fourth, in you before you will get an offer of employment:

- First, you are technically competent.
- Second, you are eager to work hard and will do a good job.
- Third, you are the kind of employee your boss and others at the company will enjoy working with, especially when you are under a lot of pressure.
- Fourth, if applicable, you are qualified for future promotion within the company.

See the Hiring People chapter for information on how interviewers may assess you concerning these four things.

Presenting/Selling Yourself Well

General interview notes

- Act confident that you would do a good job if hired, even if you are not sure.
- Bring up subjects such as the importance of taking care of customers.
- Be a good listener. Summarize and build on what the interviewer says. This shows that if hired, you would likely listen to and learn from your boss, rather than just charge off on your own.
- Be prepared to explain in detail everything listed in your resume.
- Do not say anything negative about any former or current boss or employer.
- Do not bring up part-time jobs you have held while working full time.
- Wear a business suit, with appropriate accessories, unless advised otherwise.
- After the interview, write down everything relevant that was said and any questions or concerns the interviewer seemed to have, so you can do the following:
    - Write a follow-up letter that addresses any questions or concerns the interviewer may have.
    - Be better prepared for a second or third interview.
    - Learn from the experience.

Company-specific interview notes

- Date, time, and location of the interview should be included.
- Name and phone number of the person whom you should ask for when you arrive for the interview should be included.
- Title and name of everyone who will interview you, if known, should be included.
- Have an overview of the company and its products and services as well as the types of customers who use the products and services; review the company's website for this type of information. If necessary, ask questions during the interview in order to have an opportunity to demonstrate this knowledge.
- All the information you can gather concerning what the company is looking for in the person who will be hired. Look at the advertisement for the job. Look for clues in what was said by the person who contacted you to set up the interview. Consider what would normally be expected in a person who would be hired for the particular type of job.

- Have answers for the following; answers should take into consideration what the company is looking for in the person who will be hired:
  - Where do you see yourself in five and ten years?
  - What kind of worker would you be?
  - What are your strengths?
  - What are your weaknesses?
  - Tell me about a major project where you had to take the initiative.
  - Tell me about some major accomplishments.
  - Are you an implementer or a visionary?
  - Do you prefer to work in a team or as an individual?
  - What motivates you?
  - Why do you want to leave your current employer?
  - Why do you want to work here?
  - Why should we hire you?

  Note: Be sure to read the questions for candidates in the What to Look for in a New Hire section of the Hiring People chapter.

- When responding to requests such as those above, pause for a moment, start slowly, and do not sound as if you are reciting a memorized statement.

- If the company wants a team player, which most companies do want, talk about your involvement in team projects. Have specific examples ready to discuss.

- Have questions to ask that show you are not just looking for any company that will hire you. Questions could involve what the future plans are for the company and for the position being filled.

- Underline specific things in these notes that you want to bring up, such as answers you have ready for questions that may not be asked.

- Have answers ready in case you get asked the following questions:
  - "When could you start?"
  - "What salary level are you looking for?"

Mindset needed for interviewing

- Be relaxed, comfortable, and confident that you would do a good job if hired.

- When you shake hands, look the person in the eyes and smile. Be courteous and respectful. When you first meet people, say something like "nice to meet you." After they introduce you to someone else to interview with, say something like "nice talking with you" or "talk with you later." When you are finished talking to someone, say something like "nice meeting with you." If the person is the person who would contact you for another interview, say something like "I look forward to talking with you again."

- Get along well with the people who interview you, especially the person who would be your boss if you were hired. These people are not looking for a new best friend; rather, they want someone they would be comfortable working long hours with on a difficult project.
- Show enthusiasm and eagerness to prove yourself.
- Convey information clearly and concisely.
- Show pride in the work you have done.
- When discussing the type of work you would do if hired, say things like "I would…" not "I will…"
- When the interviewer tells you about the type of work you would be doing, be sure to indicate that it is the type of work you really enjoy, assuming it is.
- If you learn something at the interview that you may have a problem with, act like it is not a problem. If you later decide that it is not a problem, you will not want the look on your face to have shown lack of interest in working for the company. If you later decide that it is an unacceptable problem, you can always turn down the job offer.
- Do not turn your head away from the interviewer while you are explaining something, as it can be taken as a sign that you are not being truthful.

Things to bring to an interview are listed below and should be brought in as inconspicuously as possible:

- Material you may want to present or give to the company
- Everything you have sent to the company, in case it was misplaced
- Paper and a pen
- A list of references with phone numbers that is suitable to give to the company, with your name at the top

  Note: Always call your references whenever a potential employer may be calling them. If applicable, tell your references what to emphasize and what to downplay.
- Transcript for recent graduates

Before going into an interview, take care of the following so you will be as ready and prepared as possible for the interview:

- Review all the preceding material in this chapter.
- Review all specific interview notes you have gathered for the company.

- Review again the underlined parts of your specific interview notes for the company.
- Review everything you have sent to the company.
- Check your face in a mirror.
- Turn off your cell phone ringer.
- Do not be hungry or full.
- Consume some caffeine, if applicable.

Conclude the interview with both of the following, which should improve the interviewer's opinion of your qualifications for the position:

- The next to the last thing you should do at the end of an interview is ask something to the effect: "Is there anything about my education or work experience that would cause you to hesitate before making me a job offer?" If there is a problem, you want a chance to clear it up before the interview ends.
- The last thing you should say at the end of a job interview is something to the effect: "I am very interested in this position, and I know that I would do a good job," (assuming you would).

Interviewing after You Turn 40 Years Old

After you turn 40 years old, it will be harder to get interviews and harder to convince interviewers that you are not *over the hill.*

In order to help get in the door for an interview, your resume, as covered in the Preparing a Resume chapter, should possibly exclude dates for education and for your earliest experiences. Possibly, page two of your resume should not have any dates.

At the interview, you need to convince the interviewer that (1) you have a wealth of knowledge and experience and (2) you have a high level of productivity that will not start to decline for a long time.

It is very important that you convey the impression that you are very energetic and healthy, as follows:

- Be well groomed. If your hair is gray, possibly dye it. Wear good clothes that fit well.
- Sit and stand comfortably straight, avoid fidgeting. Portray yourself as being alert, attentive, and confident. Walk as if you could immediately run a 50-yard dash. Improving your exercise routine and diet will take time to improve your physique, but it will have an immediate effect on your mental energy and on how you carry yourself.

- Bring up major job-related activities that required a significant amount of extra effort on your part.
- Explain things you have done to stay up to date in your profession.
- Bring up sports you participate in and other physical activities you do.

Your energy level should not be oversold. Your potential new boss should feel confident that you would not go charging off on a project without first checking, when appropriate, with your boss. Listen carefully to what your potential new boss says and discuss the subjects and issues that are addressed to you.

Tactful Ways to Question the Company's Employee Benefits

When interviewing, be prepared to ask the following questions in response to the following statements by the interviewer:

- If the interviewer says, "we have profit sharing," you should ask "what percent of the employees' pay was put into profit sharing in the last two years and when would I be eligible to participate?"

- If the interviewer says, "we have a 401(k) savings plan," you should ask "what is the company match and when would I be eligible to join?"

- If the interviewer says, "you will be eligible for a bonus," you should ask "assuming I do a good job, what can I expect to receive the first year and then annually after that?"

If you are offered a position and want to accept, consider confirming the answers you received to these questions. Ideally, get the answers for all these questions included in the company's offer letter to you.

Chapter 5

Before Accepting a Job Offer

Before accepting a job offer, consider the six items in this chapter, where applicable.

1. Make sure you fully understand the company's and your potential new boss's expectations for you. Also, make sure you will be given the resources needed to at least meet these expectations.

2. Make sure you and your potential new boss have a clear understanding concerning advancement opportunities. Ideally, arrange for a six-month review concerning your progress toward being ready for promotion.

3. Try to determine if your potential new boss will be involved too much or too little in your work. The less job-related experience you have, the better it usually is to have a boss who did the work that you will be doing. The more job-related experience you have, the worse it usually is to have a boss who did the work that you will be doing. It is hard to determine how involved your potential new boss will be in your work, but you should try to make an assessment and determine if it is right for you.

4. When a company has made an offer to you, you will have time to think about it. Mutually pick a day that you will get back to them with your answer. Other than for an entry-level position, a company may give additional vacation or other benefits if you ask for them. When you ask for an enhanced offer, do not say "no" to the original offer, assuming you will accept it even if the company says "no" to your request. Be sure you get the offer in writing; it

should include at least the following:
- Pay and potential bonus, if applicable
- Job title
- Medical benefits, including effective date
- 401(k) type plans, including eligibility requirements
- Vacation
- Start date

5. For a higher-level position in a less than stable company, consider negotiating a written severance agreement.
6. Go back to the Selecting a Potential Employer chapter and reconsider the questions, especially those in the Your Needs section, which concern how a company fits in with your career goals.

Chapter 6

Before Starting a New Job

Before starting a new job, take an objective look at where you are with your career, where you are headed, improvements needed in your work performance, and how you can make the most of whatever career fast track opportunity exists at your new employer.

Where You Are and Where You Are Headed

Before starting a new job or new position, take at least a day off to get yourself mentally prepared. You are moving to a new plateau in life and you need to reassess your situation, as follows:

- Put your old job and position behind you.
- Review your long-term goals to see if they need revision.
- Surely, some of your short-term goals will change. Short-term goals should definitely involve accomplishing the things your new boss said you need to accomplish in order for you to be considered successful in your new position. A short-term goal may be to get three years experience with the new employer and then look for another employer. Career goals are defined at the beginning of the Selecting a Potential Employer chapter.
- Start developing an overview of your new work environment, which you can add details to after you start working. Get or rough out an organizational chart that includes your direct reports, your peers, and those in positions above you. The organizational chart should ideally have job titles and people's names. Later, you

can include the pronunciations of people's names. Add information to the organizational chart concerning the nature of significant working relationships you will have with these people, including specific issues you will need to deal with.

Note: Once you have seen your new work environment and met the people you will be primarily working with, you can build a mental picture to go with the overview. Your overview and mental picture will continually evolve.

Improving Your Work Performance

When you start with a new company, you have a rare opportunity to improve the way you function in a working environment. Identify what you could have done differently to make things work out better at your previous employers and determine if you have any work-related bad habits or traits that you need to correct. It is much easier to change how you act when you are going into a new environment as opposed to when you are still with the people who knew the old you. Keep in mind that people usually form lasting first impressions based on the first few things they see you do, so have a strong, quick start in your new job. This is an excellent opportunity to jump-start a stalled career.

Being on the Career Fast Track

Now that you have positioned yourself in a new job, you need to solidify yourself in the position and keep working on your career goals, as covered at the beginning of the Selecting a Potential Employer chapter. When you first enter the work force, promotion opportunities are greater than later in your career. Your long-term financial reward from working hard is usually greater when you work hard at the beginning of your career as opposed to later in your career. Later in your career, a strong start in a new job can put you on a mini fast track with the employer. Always remember that slackers quickly fall off the career fast track.

Keep your career goals in mind when you plan how to tackle your new work responsibilities. Read the rest of this book so you can have a better chance of accomplishing your career goals.

You should already know your advancement opportunities from the interview. The key here is to be the person the company will want to promote into the positions you are seeking.

People sometimes have trouble working hard enough to accomplish their goals because they do not consider the future to be as important as the current time period. The future has to get equal consideration with the current time period. Someday the future will be the current time period and things from the past will most likely not be as important as they once seemed.

Chapter 7

Starting a New Job

When you start a new job, consider the 11 thoughts in this chapter.

1. First impressions of you are critical. Many people at your work will form their opinions of you based on the first one or two things they see or hear about you. Once their opinions are formed, they are very hard to change. Ideal first impression is that you are a hard worker, you do quality work, and you are cooperative and friendly. Generally, it is easier to break a favorable first impression than it is to break an unfavorable first impression.

2. When you start with a company, management usually views you as someone who can move up to higher levels. Do not do anything to take yourself out of contention. If you do make a mistake, just keep in mind that everyone is allowed to make mistakes. Just work hard to offset the mistake, and do not repeat it.

3. New employees often have a tendency to not ask enough questions. It is usually better to re-ask a question for clarification than to guess which course of action to take. Start re-asked questions by stating the part of the answer you know. Always be ready in case your boss asks you what you think the answer is. Be specific when you ask a question and make sure you fully understand the answer before you end the discussion. Write down the answer, if applicable.

4. When you first start with a company, you are on a honeymoon where your coworkers are expected to be more accommodating than they normally are.

During your honeymoon, you can develop good long-term working relationships with these people by being just as accommodating as they are to you.

5. When you start a new job, with a new employer or after a promotion, make sure you fully understand your boss's expectations.

   If your boss's expectations, including the expected completion dates, are not reasonable, review with your boss the details of what needs to be done. The review should accomplish at least some of the following:
   - The scope and timing of the expectations will be scaled back.
   - It will be easier to get additional resources to meet the expectations.
   - The significance of the accomplishments will be enhanced in the eyes of your boss.

   Meet your boss's expectations. If you determine that you will not make a due date, meet with your boss as soon as possible and work out a solution. After meeting your boss's expectations, subtly verify with your boss that your work met the expectations.

6. When a new boss gives you a great deal of freedom to do things your own way, think of it as follows. Possibly, you are being given enough rope to prove yourself or hang yourself.

7. Make sure you get the training and education needed to do your job and to be promoted, as described below:
   - Thoroughly learn the computer software you will be using. Go to class, if necessary. If you ask in advance, your employer will most likely pay for the necessary training. Do not make the mistake of thinking that all you need to learn about the computer software is *enough to get by*. If all you know is just *enough to get by*, it will be hard to take your work performance to the next level. In addition, being proficient with the software will be a strong indication to others that you are capable of handling higher-level responsibilities.
   - Learn how to do things like operate the audio and visual equipment used in meetings, and how to make a conference call without hanging up on your boss or a customer.
   - Keep up with changes in your profession, so you can make sure your employer is aware of applicable new business ideas and trends. In addition, keeping up with changes in your profession will enhance your employability.

8. Often when you are hired as a replacement for someone who has left the company, some people will assume that you are the same as the person who left. You may or may not want to change this perception of you. This same phenomenon may occur when you buy a previously occupied home in an established neighborhood.

9. When you take a new job, watch out for people who feel that they should have been promoted into your job, and watch out for people previously in your job who were demoted or moved to another area. Deal with both these types of people as follows:
   - Watch out for any sign that they are trying to sabotage your work and politely ask them what they are doing. Ideally, get them to say that they have no hard feelings toward you for getting the job, after which you should say something like "of course not, what was I thinking." If you have concrete evidence that anyone is sabotaging your work, consider sharing it diplomatically with your boss and ask your boss for advice on how to handle the situation.
   - Be extremely careful about confiding in people who are in either of these situations.

10. If you start a new job and your predecessor had the same workload but more direct reports than you, possibly you have a problem that needs to be resolved. Make sure you understand your boss's rationale for your predecessor having extra direct reports. Possibly, the extra direct reports were necessitated by your predecessor's incompetence, or your boss wants you to upgrade your direct reports.

11. Make sure there is no gap between when your health insurance from the old employer ends and the health insurance from the new employer begins. If necessary, contact the Human Resources Department at the old employer and ask about COBRA coverage to keep you insured until the new employer's coverage is in effect.

Chapter 8

Organizing Your Work

The ten items in this chapter concern organizing your work so it can be done as efficiently as possible. Organizing work is explained and stressed throughout this book because time spent organizing work is usually time well spent.

1. Usually the sooner you get organized, the better. Ideally, get organized before there is any work that has to be undone.

2. Only organize work to the extent that time spent organizing the work is less than the resulting expected total reduction in time spent doing the work now and in the future. Getting organized is a short-term cost with a long-term benefit.

3. Have a separate area on your desk for work that has to be done before the end of the day, and a separate area for work you would like to have done before the end of the day. Do not mix these two groups because the work that has to be done can easily be overlooked if it is combined with the work you would like to have done.

4. Use all the applicable features of your email system for things like scheduled meetings, follow-up emails, and tasks. Keep a list of things you do periodically that you can use when setting up your calendar. An appointment book with hand written entries should only be used if there is no available email system.

   Using one calendar for personal and business matters can help avoid conflicts when the two could overlap; for example, a dentist appointment scheduled for right after work.

5. Consider setting up a file folder for each person you have significant interaction with, such as your boss, as follows:

   - Include questions you have to ask. Complicated questions should be concisely written with copies of supporting documents attached.
   - Include items you need to have reviewed and approved.
   - Include answers to questions you have been asked.

   Always check the folder when you have a chance to meet with the person. When something in the folder has to be addressed by a certain date, write the date on the front of the folder and get it taken care of by the date. Beware, it is very easy to put something into a folder and forget about it.

6. Rather than organize a disorganized computer or paper file, set up an organized file for all new material. Add something like "- before July 09" to the name of the disorganized file.

7. Set up and maintain a good PC and paper filing system. When it comes to deciding whether to break a subject into separate files, keep the following in mind. In the future, if needed, it will be much easier to combine separate files than to break a combined file into separate files.

8. Organize and name computer files so you can easily find them. Store your files where they will automatically be backed up; if not, make your own back-up copies.

9. Whenever you put paper files into boxes to be stored, clearly label each box with your name, the box's contents, and a destroy date, where applicable. In addition, number each box and keep a list of box numbers and their contents.

10. If you make lists of things to do, the following may be helpful:
    - Include required completion dates, where applicable.
    - Review the lists daily, at least check the required completion dates.
    - Do not give up on keeping lists just because you stopped looking at them daily.
    - If you come out of a meeting with a list of things to do, put the name of the meeting and the date on the list.
    - Try to minimize the number of lists you maintain. If you find yourself with multiple lists, keep them all together.

Chapter 9

Using Time Wisely

Time is an invisible resource that is constantly being consumed. As Benjamin Franklin put it, "Do not squander time for that is the stuff life is made of." This chapter explains nine ways to use time wisely.

1. Recognize and take advantage of situations where spending a relatively small amount of time will result in a larger time savings, as in the following examples:
   - Sometimes resources (people, machine time, and the like) that are not always available become available on short notice. Consider rearranging your work plans to use these resources when they become available.
   - If you will soon need approval or guidance from someone who is easily available now but who will not be easily available when needed later, consider doing what needs to be done to get the approval or guidance while the person is easily available.
   - Often, the sooner you get others working on something for you, the greater the chance they will have the time to get it done.
   - Often, the sooner you request information from others, the greater the chance they will get it to you.
   - Meetings to get people started on work should be held as soon as possible, so the people can get started on the work as soon as possible.
   - Get people's commitments to attend meetings as far in advance as possible. The farther something is in the future, the more likely that people will agree to do it.

- When you do something that you will be doing repetitively in the future, you may be able to spend extra time organizing things the first time to save more time in the future.
- Suppose you are working on a project where you need to get information from a disorganized file. If you will be using the file again in the future, consider organizing the file before you use it.

2. If you find yourself buried in work and you do not know what to work on next, start by listing the different things you need to do. Then determine their priority order and do them one at a time. The benefit of doing this is that you will be able to concentrate on each item in priority order without thinking about the remaining work on the list.

3. You will continually get work to do while you continually complete work you previously received. At times you will fall behind when it comes to meeting due dates. No matter how far you are behind, always take time to review the new work that you get. Often there are quick things you can do when you first get work that will simplify the work in the future, as follows:
   - Request information from others
   - Set up a meeting
   - Notify someone about something
   - Ask questions about what you received
   - Give work to a direct report or to others
   - Initiate long lead-time items

4. When you have identified some files and other things needed to work at home or take on a business trip, check the following to ensure that you have everything needed. List everything you will have access to and mentally go through all the work you plan to do, making sure everything needed is listed. As an alternative, consider everything you will have access to and determine what work you can do with it all.

5. Sometimes you have to put work aside to complete in the future. If applicable, organize and summarize the work so you can start up where you were when you set it aside. Possibly, complete some sections of the work that would take much longer to complete in the future.

6. When faced with a problem that needs to be fixed, avoid charging off toward the first fix that occurs to you. Analyze the problem and determine the best way to fix it.

7. If you are asking someone for information, make sure you are asking for everything you need, as it is hard to go back and ask for something else you should have asked for in the first place. When you receive the information, check it as soon as possible to make sure it is everything you need.

8. If people have already gone home for the evening and you want them to do some work for you first thing in the morning, leave it for them as follows. For direct reports, give them whatever they need to complete the work. For peers, give them the work with a note explaining why it needs to be done now and why you could not have asked for it earlier. For your boss, explain the situation in a note and offer to help with the work as needed.

9. The best way to get overloaded people to do some work for you is to simplify it and get it ready for them to do. Gather the information they will need and make the necessary assumptions. Be sure to explain why advance notice was not possible and why the work needs to be done right away. This is an example of where good working relationships are important.

   Ideally, wait for a lull in the person's work before presenting the requirements. This may be hard to do because you should not delay telling someone about the needed work.

Chapter 10

Working Efficiently

By working more efficiently, you will increase the quantity and quality of what you can accomplish in a given amount of time. This chapter explains 20 ways to work efficiently.

1. In order to manage many ongoing projects at the same time, you have to be able to focus on each one individually without being distracted by the others. To keep other ongoing projects from distracting you, you need to put them aside physically and mentally. Ongoing projects can be put aside by determining the next steps to be taken and putting plans into effect to have the steps taken. The steps may include completion dates for things that go in your email system's tasks list or may include email follow-up flags for steps to be taken by others. The key here is that you do not have to think about the other projects until it is time to take the next steps.

   It is a bad career move to acknowledge that you are distracted by things you should have put aside in your mind. The higher you go in a company, the more projects you will need to manage simultaneously.

2. If you find yourself with too many projects to complete, your options are as follows:
   - Get some of the due dates extended.
   - Get more resources to help you.
   - Get a reduction in some of the projects' scopes.

- For the hardest project, get an agreement to do a preliminary job by the due date and finalize the project later.

It is usually better to pursue getting relief from too many projects than to rush through the projects and do a poor job.

3. Never leave loose ends to be cleaned up the next day. Loose ends include the following:
   - Reports and documents that need to be filed
   - Meeting notes to be acted on or put on a list of things to do
   - Information that needs to be communicated to others
   - Information that needs to be requested from others

   Productivity is usually reduced significantly on days you have to clean up loose ends from the previous day.

4. All employees are allowed to make a limited number of mistakes that they do not catch in time to correct before problems result. Do not let yourself get to the point of making so many mistakes that you have to conceal them. The time it takes to conceal mistakes is usually greater than the extra time it would have taken to hold mistakes to an acceptable level. The number and type of acceptable mistakes varies widely, based on the type of mistake, your position, and your occupation.

5. Straightening out bureaucratic red tape can be very difficult. It is best to avoid problems in the first place by doing the following:
   - Meet due dates.
   - Properly complete everything you submit.
   - Get names, with dates contacted, of everyone who gave information to you.
   - Possibly, follow up to make sure everything you submit is in order.

6. Some problems that you have to fix involve both correcting what is causing the problem and fixing the damage caused by the problem. If you do not have time to take care of both, consider correcting what is causing the problem now and fixing the damage later. At least you will be keeping the problem from getting worse.

7. If you are researching something you may need to research again, take good notes so the work you have completed will not have to be repeated. In addition, the source (person or file) you are getting information from may not be as available in the future.

8. Do your work as if you plan to be with the company for the indefinite future, even if you plan to start looking for a new job. The reason for this is that it is always best to keep your options open.

9. Trying to be the best at everything you have to do, may result in wasting the effort spent after you reach the point of being good enough. This extra effort may be better spent getting good enough at something else you have to do.

10. Sometimes the way you have done things in the past does not work anymore. When your employer is having a good year financially, you may be expected to overstate expenses in your budget. When your employer is having a bad year financially, overstating expenses in your budget may no longer be the expected thing to do. Other things that can change the way you do your work include having a new boss and structural changes in the company. The important thing here is, do not assume that the way things were done in the past is the way to do them in the future.

11. Do not lose sight of the big picture. If corporate headquarters is going to cut headcounts in anticipation of high expenses and you have significantly overstated costs in your budget, tell your boss about your overstated budget.

12. Determine your objectives before you go into a situation. Set a course with steps to follow that lead to your objectives. Make sure none of the steps involves doing anything you will later regret.

13. For routine tasks, set up steps to follow so that the entire process does not have to be thought out every time the task is completed. The risk in doing this is that needed changes in the steps may be missed because the process is not being thought out each time. There are a couple ways to keep the steps for routine tasks up to date, as follows:
    - Whenever a routine task is to be done, take a moment to think about the purpose of the task and the steps that are to be taken.
    - Whenever anything changes within a company, take the time to consider what else is affected, such as routine tasks.

14. When you first learn how to do something, take the sure path to completion even though it takes more time. As you become proficient, the shortcuts will become sure paths.

15. If you want to work fast and accurately, go as slow as necessary in order to maintain accuracy. The more you do the work, the faster you will get. For example, think of people who are learning how to write cursively. If they want to write fast and neat, they should not start writing fast with the idea of getting neat later. I tried it and it still has not worked.

16. When you proofread/check your own work, do it as if someone else did the work; otherwise, you can make the following two mistakes:
    - You see what you meant to write, not what you actually wrote.
    - You start checking the details without making sure they fit in with the overview.

17. Suppose someone who has never misled you in the past tells you (1) "people sometimes make the mistake of getting too involved with the details, which causes them to take too long to complete their work" or (2) "sometimes people need to take the initiative to get promoted." If the person commenting about either of the matters above is in a position to have heard managerial comments about you, take the hint seriously.

18. Working excessive overtime and not taking vacations may be perceived as an inability to get your job done in a reasonable amount of time.

    When you have already decided to work late or come in on the weekend, you may be more likely to put off doing things you could have done during normal working hours by working harder.

19. The less time spent thinking about unimportant things, the more time available to think about important things.

20. If you call someone who is not available and are forwarded to voice mail, hang up if you are not ready to leave a concise message.

Chapter 11

Wasting Time

It is easy to waste time without even realizing it. This chapter explains how to deal with four major causes of wasted time.

1. Do not waste time being angry with others. For every situation you encounter in life, your goal should be to accomplish what you want to accomplish with a minimal effort on your part. Carrying around anger after you are out of a situation only keeps adding to the effort you made concerning the situation.

   You will encounter people who seem to enjoy causing problems. If the person causing a problem is someone you will probably never see again, such as a discourteous driver on the road, forget about it. If the person causing a problem is someone whom will likely cause problems for you again in the future, such as a coworker, talk to the person about how you both benefit from good working relationships. Assume that the person gets your message and forget about it unless the person causes problems again in the future.

2. It is a waste of time to worry about a future situation for which there is nothing else you can currently do to get prepared. Situations such as these can be set aside in your mind by doing the following:
   - Identify and do everything you can currently do to accomplish your goals concerning the future situation.
   - Identify the date or event when the current situation will change such that you will have to get back into the subject and do everything you can do to accomplish your goals concerning the future situation.

- Whenever you think about the subject, tell yourself that it is a waste of time to think about it because there is nothing else you can do until the current situation changes.

The above procedure is how successful business executives are able to focus on difficult situations without being distracted by other difficult situations they have to manage.

3. Avoid being drawn into a discussion about gossip or non-work-related things you do not have time to discuss. Tell the person that you do not have the time to talk or think about the subject, or just keep working while you talk. If necessary, ask the person to explain things again because you were "thinking about something else" or "working."

   Do not waste time thinking about gossip you heard. Whenever there is uncertainty at work about the future, people assume the worst and their assumptions often turn into gossip. It is a waste of time worrying about what may happen to you; just prepare yourself, where applicable.

   Do not repeat gossip. You may later be told the facts by your boss and be asked not to repeat it.

4. Do not waste time envying others. What does it matter to you if someone was born into money or has other good fortune? Good for them, we should all be so fortunate.

   Your concern should be to improve your *absolute* level in life. Your *relative* level in life, where you are relative to others, should only be used as a benchmark to assess how your plans for improving your *absolute* level in life are progressing.

Chapter 12

Handling Mistakes

Everyone makes mistakes. This chapter has seven keys concerning how to best handle mistakes, in terms of correcting them and minimizing them in the future.

1. When you are the first person to uncover a problem caused by work you did, your immediate goals are to do the following:
   - Minimize the effect of the problem and keep it from getting worse.
   - Determine the best solution for the problem and implement it right away.
   - Determine what caused the problem so you can take steps to keep it from happening again and assess your own culpability. Possibly, you were given bad information. Examining how a problem occurred and developed is necessary to make sure you fully understand the problem's magnitude.
   - Reveal the problem as soon as possible to everyone who needs to know, and explain how you are fixing it. Also, explain the problem's remaining effect and explain how long it will take to clear it up. For those who need to know, tactfully state the limit of your responsibility for the problem; do not state anything that is not true.

   You do not want to be accused of hiding a problem that others need to know about. In addition, you do not want a coworker to discover and announce your error before you reveal it, as your opportunity to minimize the problem will be diminished and your coworker may appear more knowledgeable about your job than you are.

2. Learn from your mistakes. Everyone makes mistakes. Smart people learn where they erred so they can avoid making the same mistakes in the future. Some people keep making the same mistakes repeatedly. People who do not admit that they make mistakes, even to themselves, cannot learn from their mistakes.

   Whenever you recall a previous mistake, remind yourself of what you should have done differently. Your mind may be bringing up the past mistakes in order to make sure you know what to do differently in the future.

   Do not be too hard on yourself for making mistakes. The more you do, the more chances of making a mistake. It should be noted that proper planning can significantly reduce both the chance of mistakes and their magnitude.

3. If you are only 10% at fault for a mistake and someone else is 90% at fault, do not keep thinking about the other person's 90%. Just focus on your 10% and how you can avoid the mistake in the future. Possibly, the next time you have to work with the person, you should send an email confirmation of exactly what the person committed to do.

4. Sometimes you have to fix mistakes and problems that you do not have time to fully understand. In these types of instances, you need to be cautious, especially if there is a lot that can go wrong. You may want to keep copies of how things were before your changes, in case your changes have unanticipated consequences. In addition, before implementation, you may want to have your corrective action plan reviewed by others who are familiar with the situation and by others who could criticize your plan if it does not work.

5. For many mistakes people make, there was a *red flag* in the past that they ignored. If you missed a *red flag*, determine how it happened so you can take steps to not miss *red flags* in the future. *Red flag* as used here refers to a conscious thought, while doing some work, that something is not right.

6. If you bury or conceal a mistake caused by someone else, you may end up taking ownership of the mistake. The way to avoid getting into this situation is to determine the mistake's cause before you bury or conceal it.

7. Sometimes the longer that people have been making a mistake, the less likely they are to stop. The reason for this is that the longer they have been making the mistake, the larger the mistake they will have to admit to themselves that they have made. If you are possibly making a mistake like this, just remind yourself that the past is the past and everyone makes mistakes. The only thing that is important is what you do in the future.

Chapter 13

Learning from Others

When you are learning from others, make sure they clearly convey all relevant information they know. It is a big mistake to assume that others will just tell you everything you need to know. The four thoughts in this chapter concern getting all relevant information you need to learn from others.

1. When people explain things to you and you cannot see the connection between different parts they have explained, ask questions so you see the overview, as follows:
   - If they are explaining some work that you will need to do, make sure you know what the end-result is and what will be done with it. Possibly, there is a better way to accomplish the same thing.
   - If they are explaining how something works, make sure you understand what the inputs and outputs are, as well as the reason/purpose of the work.

   If two parts of an explanation appear to be in conflict, consider stopping the explanation. Ideally, get the conflict resolved before you learn more about the things being explained. Possibly, the person who is doing the explaining has not adequately thought out the subject, in which case you want this discrepancy resolved or at least acknowledged.

   If it is important for you to get the facts straight, email them to the person who provided the explanation and ask the person to email any corrections to you. When people explain things, they often oversimplify the things they do not fully understand. After implying that these things are easy to understand, they may ask if you understand them. Do not feel intimidated and agree.

2. If you are taking over responsibility for work, ask for a copy of the written procedures. If none exists, write down everything you are told, step by step. Get the source of all needed information. Get a copy of what was done the last time the work was completed; this will be a good guide and it may come in handy if you have to defend your work after you take over this responsibility. If part of the work was being done poorly, start doing it correctly, before it becomes a shortcoming in your work.

   Often people give up work that they did not do thoroughly themselves, though they will usually be reluctant to admit it. If the work involves maintaining up-to-date, accurate information, document any information you are given to maintain that is not up to date and accurate. Otherwise, the bad information could become your problem.

   Understand the purpose of the work you are taking over, so you can improve it, as needed. If you plan to change the method used to do the work, possibly use your new method to re-create the last version issued. All differences between your re-created last version and the actual last version should be reconciled. Any errors in the actual last version should be reviewed with the person who prepared it, so you can make sure your new method works correctly.

3. If you are getting an explanation that does not fit with your understanding of other related things, identify the disconnection and ask how it all fits together. Whenever you learn new information, you need to reconcile it with what you already know about the subject so you can fit it all together.

4. Often you will meet with someone who has information to tell you. You should have a list of questions to ask. Listen carefully to the person and ask for more details as needed. Do not feel as if you need to talk as much as the person doing the explaining.

Chapter 14

Business Writing

Writing is an art. Often people who cannot write well are unaware of how this deficiency is limiting their career growth. The ten steps in this chapter cover how to write a business email.

1. Establish the goals of the communication, which usually involve one or more of the following:
   - Get permission
   - Confirm something
   - Explain something
   - Answer someone
   - Inform someone
   - Ask for a decision
   - Get someone to do something
2. Make sure an email is the best method to accomplish the goals. Possibly, a phone call or visit to the person would be better than an email. Talking to a person is usually better when you need questions answered before you can finish the communication. In addition, talking can be a quicker way to communicate something. You can always later use an email to confirm matters agreed upon verbally.
3. Determine the subject that goes at the top of the email. It should be a concise overview of the email's main subject matter. It is a good place to get information conveyed such as "Revised Budget Timetable with Earlier Due

Dates." Information in the subject should also be included in the text of the email, usually at the beginning.

4. Determine who should be copied on the email. Plan to send a copy of your email to everyone who needs or would want to be informed. Put yourself in the shoes of the following people and determine if you would want to be copied on the email:
   - Your boss
   - The recipient's boss
   - Others involved with the subject matter of the email
   - Others whom you make comments about in the email, such as what they said or did

   Before copying anyone, make sure there is no confidential information in your email or in any emails you are replying to or forwarding.

5. Explain the current situation:
   - You should give the recipient any background information needed to understand the current situation. Give the information either right after or before you state your goals.
   - Where applicable, your explanation may need to discretely clear up any doubts concerning whether you made any mistakes.

6. Explain the changes you want made to the current situation. Explain the changes as they relate to the current situation. Where applicable, your explanation needs to explain why the changes should be made.

7. Write a concise, easy-to-understand email:
   - Try to start the email with your goal such as the following:
     - I would like to get your permission/agreement/approval to proceed …
     - I would like to confirm…
     - I would like to explain…
     - In response to your question about…
     - I thought you would like to know…
     - I need/would like/would appreciate your decision concerning…
     - I need/would like/would appreciate your help on…
   - Avoid needlessly repeating information the recipient already knows about the subject. Make sure you include all relevant information the recipient may not know or may not have readily available. Also, include other information you want the recipient to know about.
   - Write the email as if you were writing a script you would read to the person, where the person cannot respond or ask a question. Make sure the person would easily understand what you read.
   - Look at the subject of the email from the recipient's point of view.

- Rough out an outline that includes all the material you need to cover. Break up the material into main thoughts that convey your message (accomplishes your goal). Each main thought should ideally become a paragraph in the email. The first sentence of each paragraph should contain the main thought and be supported by the rest of the paragraph; this helps make the email easy to scan. Add an introduction and a summary, where applicable. Recipient needs to be able to scan the email and know what to do, as follows: read it, toss it, file it, forward it, reply to it, or put it away for later.
- Organize the sections of your email. Sections that are more important should usually go first. Similar and related sections should usually go together. Keep in mind that *accomplishing your goal* is the most important factor concerning how the sections are organized.
- Write to the point. The more words you use to say something, the harder the recipient has to work to get your point.
- Make sure you answer any questions, objections, or criticisms that may occur to the recipient while reading your email.
- Avoid sarcasm.
- Use short sentences along with words the recipient will understand.
- Suppose you write about an "ABC Report." Later in the same paragraph, refer to it as the "report" or the "ABC Report" not the "study" or "analysis" or "presentation."
- Whenever you use words that have more than one meaning, like "incorporate," only use one of the meanings for the word throughout your email.
- Underline key points or use bold print, as appropriate.
- Try to avoid having two consecutive sentences or paragraphs that start with the same word.
- Be sensitive to people's feelings. Replace words like *manpower* with *staffing requirement* and avoid all generalizations, even if you think they are favorable.
- Be grammatically correct as listed below. Generally, only the first six or seven items below apply to most business emails. Use the spelling and grammar tool available in your email program.
  - Use plural and singular verbs to go with plural and singular nouns, respectively, as follows: "Jack and Tom are…" and "Jack or Tom is…"
  - Generally, use the word *good* when referring to a *noun* and use the word *well* when referring to a *verb*. Note that the second letter of *good* and *noun* are the same, and that the second letter of *well* and *verb* are the same.
  - Never start a sentence with "And" at the beginning.
  - Never start a sentence with "Because" when you are finishing a thought in the preceding sentence. The following sentence is acceptable: "Because it rained, we canceled the picnic." I would recommend replacing "Because" with "Since" in the sentence.

- Sentences that begin with "When" or "If" should have the resulting consequence after a comma.
- Sentences should read correctly when all words enclosed in parentheses are ignored.
- Do not end a sentence with a preposition, such as above, across, after, between, beyond, down, for, in, near, out, past, to, up, and with.
- For sentences that have an "or" or "and," make sure they read correctly when the "or" or "and" is deleted along with either of the two things separated by the "or" or "and." For example, the need for the italicized words in the two following sentences is clear, when the underlined words are deleted:
  - I have never *done* <u>or even considered doing</u> it.
  - I know someone *who has* <u>and have read about people who have</u> this ability.
- Use plural and singular pronouns to go with plural and singular antecedent nouns, respectively, as follows: "An intern must work hard if he/she (not they) want to get hired for a full-time position."
- A sentence should only be first person (I), second person (you), or third person (he, she, and they). Never change between first, second, or third person within a sentence.
- Try to write using active verbs rather than passive verbs. With active verbs, the subject does the verb action. With passive verbs, the subject receives the verb action. For example, "the car hit the tree" is better than "the tree was hit by the car."
- Try to reword sentences that have nouns ending in ance, ion, ment, and ship. For example, instead of "John's goal was advancement" write "John's goal was to advance."

Note: A style manual, which is available at most bookstores, will have an answer for just about every question concerning grammar, punctuation, and writing in general.

8. Treat recipients appropriately:
   - Make sure the tone of the email is correct. Do not *tell* a customer or a boss to do anything. In general, consideration and politeness are almost always appreciated by everyone.
   - Never send an email telling someone at your level in the company to do something, especially if you are copying others on the email. It will appear that you are trying to put yourself into a position of authority over someone at your level. It is best to discuss with the person at your level what needs to be done and confirm it in an email, if necessary.
9. Make sure the email accomplishes your goals. Read the email as if you were the recipient and see if any changes are needed to accomplish your goals.

10. Proofread before sending:
    - After writing the email, see if you need to revise whom you are copying.
    - Before sending, read the email as though you were the recipient and each person you are sending a copy to, such as your boss. Make sure there is nothing you may later regret not revising. Be sure you are clearly conveying everything you want to convey.
    - Slowly read the email word by word to catch errors. Others will form opinions of your work based on your emails, especially when you first start working at a company.
    - When proofreading anything you write, keep in mind that you are building a picture in the reader's mind. The key to building a clear picture is to apply the following rules:
        - Where applicable, start with an overview of the information you are conveying.
        - State things in the order they occurred, are occurring, or will occur. For example, do not write, "The power went out when I was almost done with the project." When the readers read that the power went out, they should already know that you were almost done with the project.
        - The readers should not be misled. For example, after reading four words into the following sentence, the readers think Joe felt the sign. "Joe felt the sign was appropriate." This misleading sentence can be cleared up by inserting the word *that* after the word *felt*.
        - Do not leave gaps in the picture readers are building in their mind by raising questions that go unanswered. For example, do not state, "His opinion was the same as Mary's opinion," unless you are providing, or ideally have already provided, sufficient information on Mary or her opinion. Another example is the use of technical terms the readers may not understand.
        - If you are leading a reader from one thought to another, such as "since this is true the following is true," make sure the connection is clear to the reader; provide an explanation, if necessary.
    - Remember that once you send an email or fax something, it may be irretrievable. Others, including people outside your company, can end up seeing anything you send.

Chapter 15

Project Planning

The more complicated a project is, the more important it is to properly plan the project so it can be completed as efficiently as possible. This chapter covers two widely used planning methods, has a simplified version of the second method, and lists some general thoughts on project planning.

GANTT Chart

The basic information necessary to prepare a GANTT Chart is (1) a list of the project's activities and (2) each activity's forecasted start and end dates. A GANTT Chart can be set up as shown below.

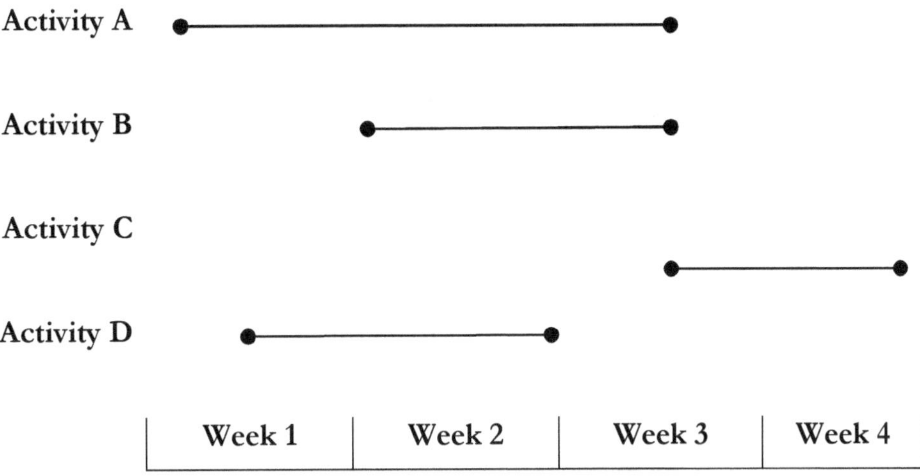

Actual activity times can be included in the chart along with the originally forecasted times.

Forecasted and actual costs for each activity should be determined so they can be compared. The forecasted costs can also be used for budgeting the project's costs and for planning the cash flow.

The more complex a GANTT Chart is, the harder it is to see the current and forecasted activities that need to be started and completed as soon as possible.

PERT (Program Evaluation and Review Technique)

PERT can be thought of as being similar to a GANTT Chart with one major modification. PERT requires that you determine which activities have to be completed before other specified activities can begin. This determination allows you to identify all the different paths (sequences of activities) that must be taken in order to complete the project. PERT uses activity lines the same as the GANTT Charts, but identifies an *event* that occurs at the end of each activity. The event is the completion of whatever the activity is to complete. In PERT, all activity lines for activities that can only begin once other events have occurred, are each shown as coming out of their required preceding event and leading to their own event. As shown in the following example, activities B–F and B–D can only begin after event B occurs.

PERT Chart

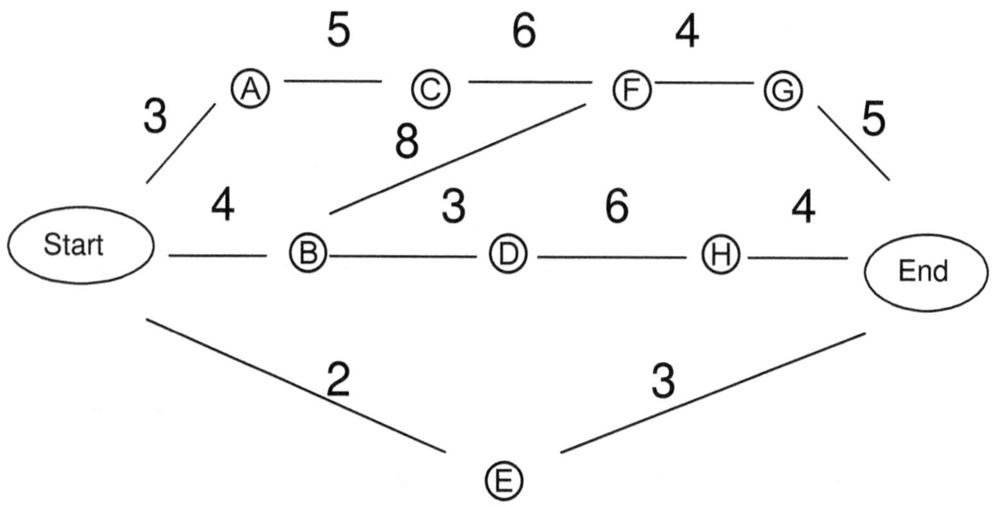

Events and their Forecasted Activity Times

In PERT Chart Above

Event	Forecasted Activity Time In PERT Chart Above (To Accomplish the Event)
Start	
A	3 weeks after event Start
B	4 weeks after event Start
C	5 weeks after event A
D	3 weeks after event B
E	2 weeks after event Start
F	6 weeks after event C
F	8 weeks after event B
G	4 weeks after event F
H	6 weeks after event D
End	5 weeks after event G
End	4 weeks after event H
End	3 weeks after event E

All Paths That Must Be Taken In PERT Chart Above	Time To Take Path
Start–A–C–F–G–End	23 Weeks: Critical Path (Longest Time)
Start–B–F–G–End	21 Weeks
Start–B–D–H–End	17 Weeks
Start–E–End	5 Weeks

The PERT Chart above was constructed as follows:

- All events that did not have a preceding event other than Start (events A, B & E) were linked directly to Start.
- All events that did not have an event after them other than End (events E, G, & H) were linked directly to End.
- Both these sets of events (A, B & E and E, G & H) were linked through the other events that have to occur after one or more of A, B & E and before one or more of E, G & H.

Events occur at the end of an activity and make it possible for the next event's activity to begin. Instead of naming an event "Receive parts," consider naming it "Order, receive, & check parts."

Your identified events may change when you figure out how to fit them into the PERT chart, as shown in the following two examples. Suppose you have an event such as "Land cleared for construction" that is required before two other events — "Building A constructed" and "Building B constructed." If building A has to be completed as soon as possible and building B can wait, you may want to split the "Land cleared for construction" event into two separate events, one for each building's land. By splitting the event, construction of building A can begin before the land is cleared for building B. The second example can have the opposite effect. Two events can possibly be combined when completion of both will enable the activity for another event to begin but completion of either one alone will not enable the activity for another event to begin.

Costs for activities can be included, as described in the preceding information on GANTT Charts.

The critical path is the path with the longest total time. The critical path's time is the time it will take to complete the project as planned. You can work with the critical path as follows:

- Look for ways to shorten each activity on the critical path. An activity's *crash time* is the shortest time to complete the activity given that you devote all available resources to it. The decision to crash the project is based on the cost to crash versus the benefit of the earlier completion time for the entire project. For example, spending an extra $20,000 on overtime pay is worth it if it results in a $25,000 bonus for completing the entire project early. Note the effect in the PERT example above of reducing activity C–F by 3 days. The project's critical path only goes down by 2 days because path Start–B–F–G–End would then become the critical path.
- Look for ways to work around the critical path. Suppose you are having a building constructed and are buying production equipment to produce a new

product in the building. If the building is on your critical path, consider temporarily renting a building. If the production equipment is on your critical path, consider temporarily outsourcing part of the work. Suppose you are building a resort and the administrative building, which is separate from the rental units, is on your critical path. Consider using one of the rental units for your administrative office on a temporary basis so you can build all the rental units and start collecting rent before the administrative building gets started. The key in all these examples is to look for ways to profitably modify the critical path to achieve some of the project's goals before the entire project is completed.

- Manage all activities on the critical path so they are done as quickly as possible. Other paths can take longer than planned, as long as the extra time does not exceed the path's slack time. A path's slack time is the difference between the sum of its activity times and the project's critical path time. Cash flow can be improved by delaying high cost activities on non-critical paths. Do not waste a path's slack time to a point where the path becomes your critical path. If there are two paths with slack time and changing circumstances have created a situation where one will have to be delayed, delay the path that has the least chance of becoming the critical path.

Simplified PERT

Simplified PERT is a simplified way to identify and manage all paths (all activities and their events) that have to be taken for projects that are not large enough to require regular PERT planning. This simplified method can also be used to rough out a project plan to see if there are any long lead-time items that should be started before the formal project plan is prepared.

Simplified PERT planning involves the following steps that were taken to construct the table shown in Exhibit 15-1.

While following the steps below, be sure to consider the information in the preceding PERT section of this chapter about combining events, splitting events, and managing the paths that have to be taken. Keep in mind that a project is complete when all its required events have occurred. Each event occurs when its activity is complete.

1. Identify all events that have to occur in order for the project to be completed. This can be done by either or both of the following:
   - List events that had to occur when a similar project was completed
   - Start with the end-result (completion of the project) and work backwards, identifying all required events

   Your identified events will most likely change, possibly even after you start work on the project.

2. For each event, identify the length of time from when its activity begins to when the event occurs. Build in an adequate cushion to cover uncertainty, such as for lead-time on purchased parts. Be sure to reduce the cushion when you learn more about how long an activity will take.

3. Make each event a column heading on a spreadsheet, and sort from the most likely first event on the left to the most likely last event on the right.

4. Add a date column to the left side of the worksheet that starts with the project's start date and keeps going until when the project will most likely be completed.

5. Identify all events whose activities can begin as soon as the project begins. Put these events' activities on the spreadsheet in the column for their event. Put the start date for each activity at the earliest possible date, which for these activities is when the overall project begins. Put the end date for each activity at the point in time when its event occurs, based on the identified length of time for the activity. Draw a line from the start date to the end date.

6. Identify all events whose activities can begin as soon as the events identified in the preceding step have occurred. Put these events' activities on the spreadsheet the same as in preceding step. The earliest possible start date for each of these activities is when the event(s) that has to occur first has occurred. For each of the events started in this step, draw a horizontal line from its start date to the end date of the event(s) that has to occur first.

7. Keep adding layers of events, following the procedures in step 6, until all events have their activities' start dates and end dates on the spreadsheet.

8. Identify all paths that have to be taken to accomplish the last event. These paths include all the horizontal lines on the spreadsheet that link activities that have to be done one after the other.

9. List all the paths and include their time from start to finish. The following is elaborated on in the preceding PERT section of this chapter. The longest path is the critical path. Delays and early completion of events on the critical path will delay or speed up, respectively, completion of the project. All paths, other than the critical path, have slack time, which is the difference between the path's time and the critical path's time. The less slack time a path has, the more it usually has to be monitored. If a non-critical path is delayed for a period of time that is longer than its slack time, this path becomes the new critical path. The simplified PERT example in Exhibit 15-1 makes the slack time easy to identify.

General Thoughts on Project Planning

1. If you are managing two or more projects at the same time, you need a way to minimize time spent keeping track of the next steps on each project. Having project plans, even roughed-out project plans, can help take care of this. You can simply look at the project plans any time and determine what needs to be done to keep all the projects on plan.
2. Manage each project as if it is your only project. If your top two projects are going great, do no let any of your other projects slip.
3. Your goal for each project is to do everything realistically possible so you will not fail due to missing something that should have been done or caught in time to fix.
4. Be sure to notify others who need to know when (1) you change your project plans or (2) your project's progress deviates from plan, especially when you fall behind.
5. Compare completing a project to building a house. You need to start with a good foundation. If you start by building walls, it may look like you are quickly making progress, but you will end up being inefficient.
6. There is a major difference between *jumping the gun* on a project and *procrastination.* Often you may feel compelled to start working on a project even though you have not properly planned the work. On the other hand, do not spend half a day planning a project you could have completed in half a day with minimal planning.
7. It takes less total time to do a project right in the first place than to do a careless job and then later redo the project the right way. You may not think you have enough time to do the project right in the first place, but you will always be able to find the time to redo it.
8. Before you start a difficult task, gather and analyze enough information so you can make sure there is not a better way to complete the task.
9. Do not rely on luck to help get a job done correctly. Luck is no substitute for, and is not nearly as reliable as, proper planning and completion of the work.
10. The more important it is for something to work, the more important it is to have back-up systems or other plans for things that could go wrong.
11. Determine the required accuracy for a project before you plan the work. Accuracy of 60% to 70% may be all that is needed for a rough estimate. Accuracy of 100% may be required if you are determining minimum and maximum tolerances for machined parts. A five-percentage point gain in accuracy is usually harder to get than the preceding five-percentage point gain in accuracy, due to the law of diminishing returns.

Exhibit 15-1 (part 1 of 2) Electric Device Project Plan (using Simplified PERT)

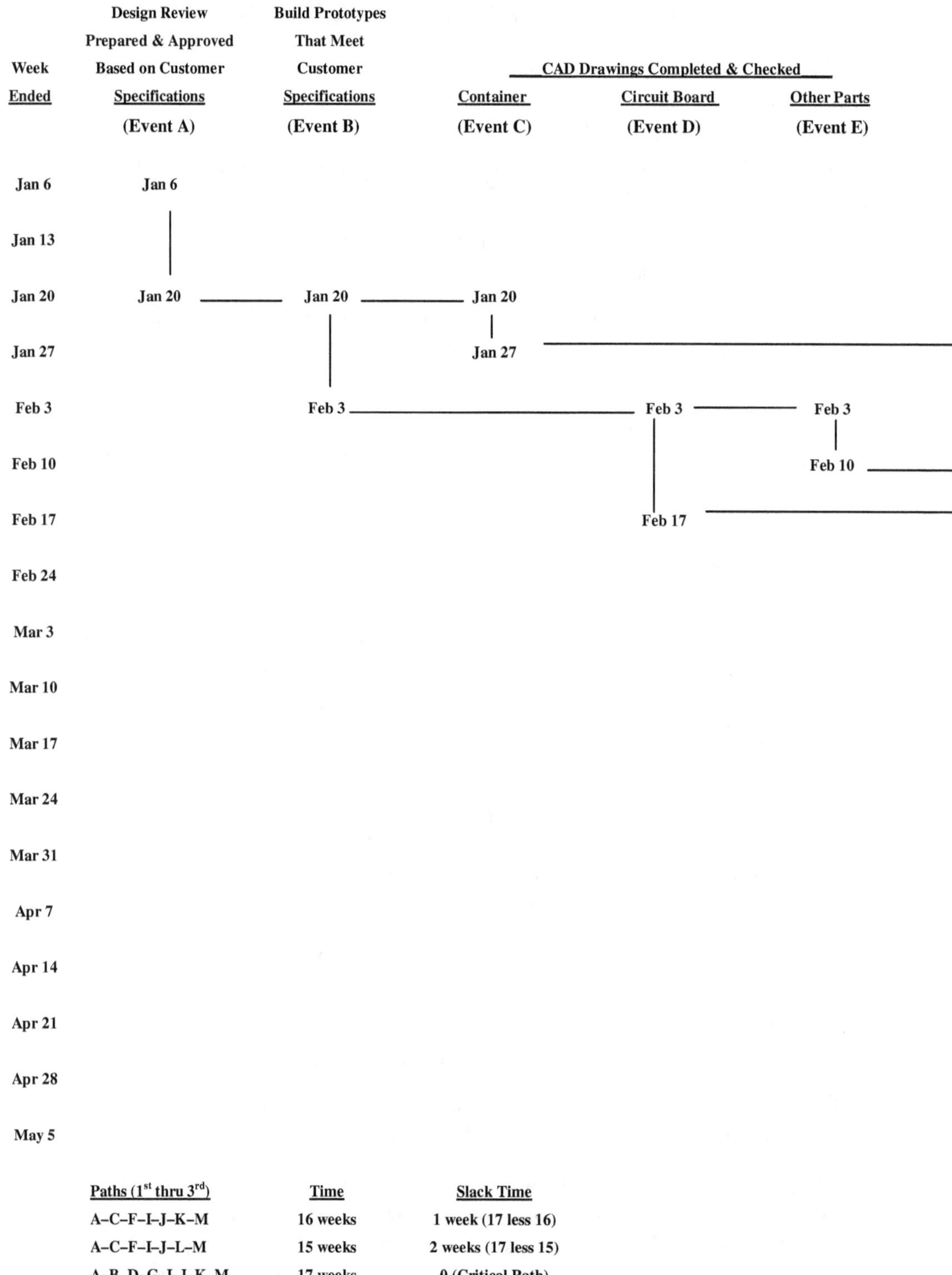

Paths (1st thru 3rd)	Time	Slack Time
A–C–F–I–J–K–M	16 weeks	1 week (17 less 16)
A–C–F–I–J–L–M	15 weeks	2 weeks (17 less 15)
A–B–D–G–I–J–K–M	17 weeks	0 (Critical Path)

Exhibit 15-1 (part 2 of 2) Electric Device Project Plan (using Simplified PERT)

Order, Receive, & Check			Assemble Product as Specified in Design	Send to Customer & Receive Customer Approval of		Mfgr. Test Fixture	
Container	Circuit Board	Other Parts	Review	Product & Drawing	Acceptance Test Procedure	Order & Set up Equipment	Write Instructions for Equipment
(Event F)	(Event G)	(Event H)	(Event I)	(Event J)	(Event K)	(Event L)	(Event M)

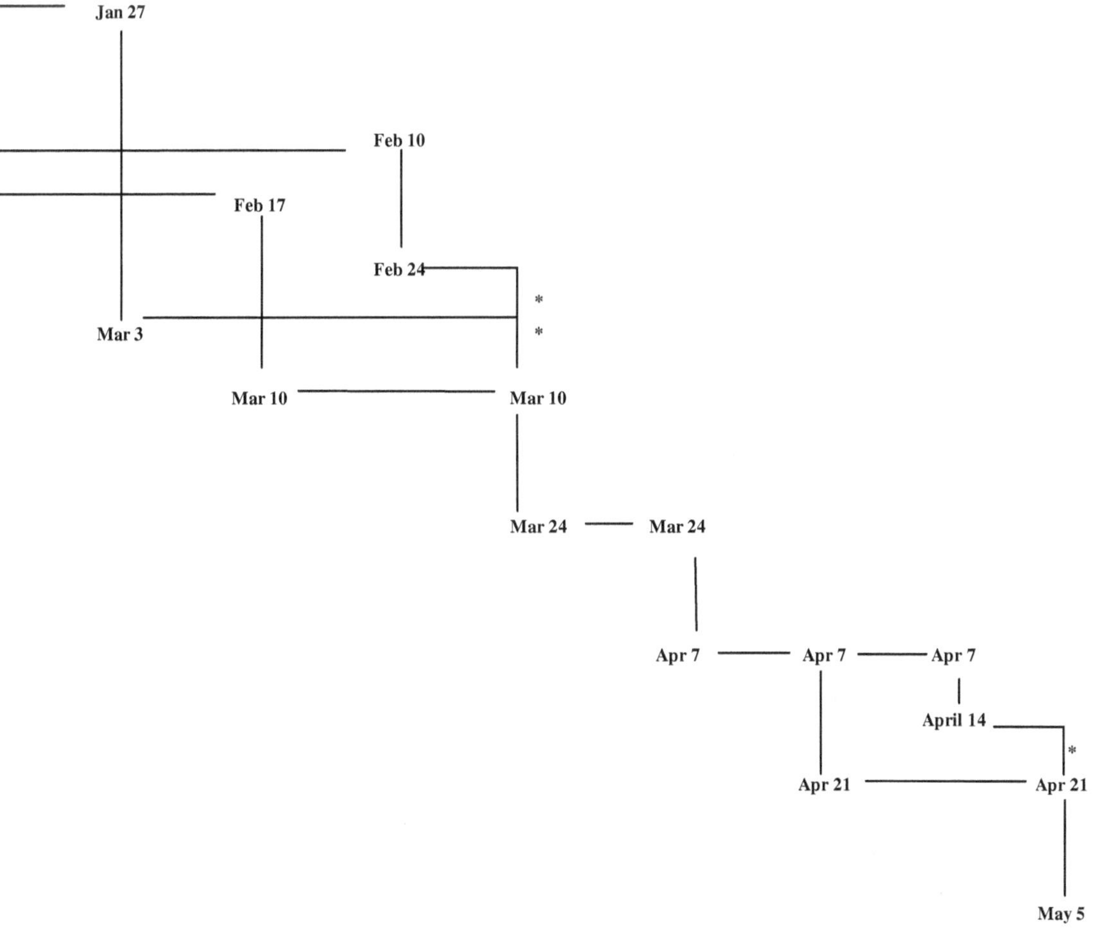

Paths (4th thru 6th)	Time	Slack Time
A–B–D–G–I–J–L–M	16 weeks	1 week (17 less 16)
A–B–E–H–I–J–K–M	15 weeks	2 weeks (17 less 15)
A–B–E–H–I–J–L–M	14 weeks	3 weeks (17 less 14)

*Denotes One Week Slack Time

12. The expression "a chain is only as strong as its weakest link" can be applied to many projects. The chain represents the total project and each link of the chain represents an activity that needs to be completed. Time spent making one link stronger than the planned strength of other links can be wasted effort. For example, you probably should not do an extremely in-depth analysis of unreliable information you could have easily made reliable but decided not to do so.

13. If work does not go as planned, be willing to change the plan as needed. For example, suppose you have six hours to study six equally difficult chapters for a test. If after two hours of studying, you have only finished the first chapter, you probably need to study the last five chapters in less detail than the first chapter rather than to continue at the same pace and skip or minimally review the last few chapters.

14. When you take responsibility for a project to be completed in the future, do all the required advanced planning right away. Imagine yourself in the future sitting down to work on the project. Identify the things you will need in order to complete the project. Of these things, determine which you should request and order immediately. Request and order the needed things right away. Due dates should include extra time to allow for a late delivery.

    Put the due dates in your email calendar or flag your emails so you can follow up immediately if the requested and ordered things are not received by the due dates. When you receive the things requested and ordered, examine them right away in case they are not everything you need them to be. Make sure you receive reasonable answers to any questions you asked. Possibly, the person submitting the answers did not understand your questions and the sooner you re-ask the better.

15. Try to never promise more than you are sure you can deliver. Failing to meet expectations will diminish your accomplishment's value in the minds of others. For a given accomplishment, the perceived value will be greater if you had set lower expectations and exceeded them versus having set higher expectations and not achieved them.

16. Try to avoid saying that you are going to take a project further than you are sure you want to go with it. If changing circumstances make it not worth doing something you said you were going to do, let it be known to people who matter such as your boss, why you changed your plans.

17. It is not enough to have a plan and just follow the steps; you need to make sure the steps fit together. For example, you do not just go to college and get a job; you need to make sure you get the degree needed for the job you want. If you want to start a retail business, you do not just buy products and resell them; you have to buy products you can resell at a price that generates a sufficient profit.

18. When you complete a task you will be doing again, write down the following to make it easier the next time you do it:
    - Things to be done in advance
    - Plan you followed to complete the task, with any modifications you can think of to simplify the task
    - Mistakes you made and how you can avoid making them again
    - Better ways to do things next time

Chapter 16

Projects and Tasks

Everything worth doing is worth doing well. The preceding chapter, Project Planning, should be read before reading this chapter. The 17 thoughts in this chapter concern doing projects and tasks well.

1. If you are going for the gold, get the best equipment and best assistance. Having the best equipment and best assistance rarely diminishes the recognition you get for the completed project, just like having bad equipment and bad assistance rarely enhances the recognition you get.

2. Do not turn a project into a bigger project than it needs to be, unless you are also taking care of another project. The bigger a combined project is, the longer it usually takes to complete, so make sure each of the individual projects' due dates and other objectives are met.

3. When you work on a project, do not let a roadblock stop you. Figure out a way to get around the roadblock. Your goal is to complete the project, not to be able to say, "I tried, but…"

4. With most projects you do, excess quantity does not make up for poor quality. Poor quality can be defined as actual quality that is below the quality level required to properly complete the project.

5. It is sometimes difficult to deal with both the details and the overview of a project at the same time. Get too involved with the details and you may lose sight of what you are trying to accomplish. Get too involved with the overview and you may lose sight of the details. A good way to pull together

the overview and the details is to set goals based on the overview and develop strategies, with their own plans of action, to accomplish the goals. The detail work on the project will just be whatever is required by the strategies' plans of action. Keep an open mind concerning the goals, as you will usually learn new information or gain new insight as you move closer to accomplishing your goals.

6. Even for small tasks, make sure your answer is reasonable. For example, suppose you are asked for the gallon to liter conversion rate. You look at a conversion table and see 3.7853, so you are about to answer 3.7853 gallons per liter. A quick test of reasonableness would reveal that gallons are bigger than liters so it must be 3.7853 liters per gallon, not gallons per liter.

7. If you are working on a project and your frustration level gets to the point where you are about to *lose it*, stop before you damage what you have done so far. Before you resume work on the project, you should recognize and accept that progress through the particular part of the project will be slow and require more work than anticipated.

8. If part of your task involves methods and assumptions that could be criticized, avoid needlessly exposing those parts. If applicable, ask others for the information you do not have so you can defend your assumptions by saying, "the information is not available." Your boss should always be made aware of any significant assumptions you make concerning your work.

9. If information needed to complete a project is flawed, tell the project's intended recipient; possibly, the request will then be withdrawn. Also, note the flaw in your written report on the project. Failure to take these two steps could result in you taking responsibility for the flawed information.

10. When you work on a project with others, keep an overview of the project in mind, even if your involvement is a small part. You may come up with a unique insight that is worth sharing with the others. Ideally, send the insight in an email.

11. When you are asked for information by someone you want to help, provide the requested information and provide, or at least offer to provide, other information you feel may be needed. Do not provide information that is both not requested and not needed.

12. If a project involves risks, to yourself or your employer, take steps to minimize them. Inform others who need to know.

13. Sometimes you get verbal information from people who may *forget* what they told you. In these situations, you should write the information down along with who told you, the date, and time you were told. Ideally, confirm the information in an email to whoever provided it.

14. If a task turns out to be much harder than others thought it would be, it is all right to let others know. In the opposite instance, do not needlessly expose the circumstances so you can use the freed up time to get other work done.

15. Before you take on work to win praise, remember both of the following:
    - Praise for taking on a project will be more than offset by criticism if you do not deliver.
    - The lasting praise goes to the person who got the job done correctly.

16. With any project or task, follow through until you achieve your goal. Do not drop a project after you have made *some progress.* Goals should only be dropped or otherwise changed based on long-term considerations.

17. Often projects move from department to department as they are completed. For instance, marketing gets a project approved, engineering designs it, accounting gets the money approved, and purchasing places the purchase order. You should never hold up the process; get your part of the project done and pass it along as soon as possible.

    If you are responsible for getting an entire project done, follow up with everyone involved to make sure no one is needlessly holding up your project.

Chapter 17

Presentations and Reports

Most presentations and reports involve written information you will give to your audience. The 15 items in this chapter cover presentations and reports that are all written, all verbal, and a combination of both written and verbal information.

1. The advantage of putting a presentation or report in writing is that you have a record of exactly what was included. The possible disadvantage is that those who receive your report will have a record of exactly what was included.

   Sometimes you may want to exclude sensitive information from a written presentation or report and convey the sensitive information verbally.

2. Many presentations of information involve pages your audience can follow. Your audience should get copies of the pages and/or the pages should be displayed so your audience can see them. On your copy of each page, write out everything you plan to say. Sequentially number your comments in the order you plan to mention them. For example, write "1" by the first thing you plan to mention and start your presentation by reading the comment by "1" such as "if you look at the total variance for the month at the bottom of the page…"

3. Do not present information to anyone at your boss's level or higher without first reviewing with your boss any of the information that could be sensitive.

4. When presenting a project you worked on, the following should usually be included:
   - Why the project was undertaken

- Overview of the project's scope
- Concise description of the project's end-result
- Assumptions you made, rarely will all required facts be available
- Information and directions received from others for which you do not want to take responsibility
- Information that is better disclosed in the report than disclosed later
- Schedules detailing your work
- Your recommended plan of action, if applicable
- Your summary/conclusion that is based on the project's end-result

5. The first page of a report should have the end-result without much detail. The supporting detail should be organized and easy to find in the rest of the report.

6. If you are trying to explain something new to people, start with what they already know. This will make it much easier for your audience to understand and retain the new information. For example, your presentation could start by briefly covering what was presented last time concerning the subject, and then explain what has changed.

7. Your presentation should only include information your audience needs and wants to know. Generally, the more concise your message is, the greater the chance your message will be conveyed.

8. Be prepared for questions whenever you present information. Answer the obvious questions during your presentation, before they are asked. Some answers are better left unsaid, unless you are asked, such as those that concern errors that have been corrected.

   Consider holding back the most detailed parts of your explanations. Often you will encounter people in your audience who will ask for the next level of detail, no matter how detailed your explanation is.

   Do not guess when you do not have the answer. If you say something that is not correct, you will need to correct it later.

   For questions you cannot answer, tell the questioners that you will get back to them with an answer; be sure to get back to them in a timely manner. Consider copying the other members of your audience with your answer, though you should always be careful with sensitive information.

9. Mentally rehearse for important presentations as well as for presentations to less than friendly audiences. Try to anticipate the different subjects your audience could question you on, and have your answers ready.

10. If you are going to be sending a report or analysis to someone, determine if the recipient may have a third party review your work. If yes, possibly have this third party review the questionable sections of your draft. Write a note along the lines of the following and send it with the questionable sections of the

draft to the third party: "This is a partial draft of a report Chuck Welsh requested. Is there anything here you feel could be explained more clearly? If yes, let me know by this Friday." Never send the draft to the third party unless you are sure the intended recipient of your final report or analysis would consider your third-party review to be nothing more than just being thorough.

11. The main disadvantage of distributing advanced copies of your presentation is that it makes it too easy for people who like to ask questions. Some people like to ask questions during presentations in order to impress others in the audience.

12. Suppose you are putting together a presentation, and a particular person in the audience may challenge some of your assumptions and conclusions. Consider reviewing the applicable assumptions and conclusions with this person in advance.

13. Sometimes when you are writing or talking, you need to refer to someone whom your audience does not know. Be sure to provide the necessary background information concerning this person, either before or when you first mention the person's name.

14. A complete outline is sometimes better for conveying information than putting the information in paragraphs. A complete outline is easier for the reader to skim and to see how all the parts fit together. An outline is more like a picture.

15. Flow charts are usually the best way to show how a process works.

Chapter 18

Business Meetings

Well-run business meetings can be very productive. Unorganized business meetings can be a huge waste of time. This chapter covers seven ways to help make meetings productive.

1. If you are in charge of a meeting, use an agenda to keep the meeting on track and to make sure all topics are covered. Make sure everyone's ideas are considered. Brainstorming at the beginning of a meeting is a good way to get everyone's ideas captured for discussion during the meeting. Have someone write down all the ideas that everyone comes up with, ideally where everyone can read them. During the brainstorming session, no one should be allowed to criticize another person's idea.

2. Before going into a meeting, you should know what you want to accomplish, as follows:
   - Convey or receive certain information
   - Get the group working on a particular project
   - Get time and work commitments from others
   - Steer certain projects toward or away from you

   Use cooperation, not confrontation, to achieve your objectives. Cooperation may seem to take longer, but in the long term, it builds the working relationships that make future work go more smoothly.

3. When you go into a meeting, be prepared for any questions you may be asked. Also, be prepared to contribute any relevant information that you feel should be considered.

Where applicable, tell your boss about the information you are planning to bring up at the meeting, so you can avoid the following:

- Disclosing information that should not be disclosed, possibly because it is too preliminary
- Making your boss look bad, maybe your boss previously said something contrary

4. In most meetings, it is important to get everyone's ideas expressed so the group can consider each idea. Watch out for meeting participants who interrupt others and try to change the idea being discussed by bringing up their own ideas. Do not let participants like this control what ideas are discussed, unless this offending participant is your boss. To get the meeting back on track, ask everyone who was interrupted to complete their thoughts and then complete the discussion of any ideas that were not adequately considered.

5. At the end of a meeting, write down the following:
   - Conclusions that were reached
   - Decisions that were made
   - Any work you and others agreed to do and the due dates

   Before the meeting adjourns, it may be appropriate to summarize the above so there are no misunderstandings. Possibly, put the summary in an email to all the meeting's participants. If someone in the meeting is going to provide you with needed information not summarized above, get a commitment from the person concerning what will be provided to you and when it will be provided, consider confirming the commitment in an email.

6. Do not be late for meetings. People who are late for meetings are wasting and showing lack of respect for other people's time.

7. For a phone meeting with a customer, you need the following in front of you:
   - List of things to say
   - List of things to avoid saying unless asked directly
   - Answers to possible questions
   - Material possibly needed for the meeting, such as problem notifications, corrective actions, test results, and correspondences

   Before and after putting all the above together, consider the following:
   - What are your and your company's objectives?
   - What does the customer want to know about?
   - What is the purpose of the phone conversation?

   If you meet with your boss before the meeting, bring the following so you can better prepare yourself for the customer meeting:
   - All of the above, to review what you think should be said and not said
   - A list of things you want your boss to be aware of

Chapter 19

Working in Teams

The seven items in this chapter concern how teams should be set up, how their performance should be measured, and how team members should work together.

1. Teams should be established to achieve worthwhile company objectives that an individual could not achieve as efficiently. Members of the team should be selected so that collectively the team will be able to (1) thoroughly understand the current situation, (2) determine the objectives, and (3) find and implement the best way to achieve the objectives.

2. Teams need time-based goals that can be compared against future actual performance. The first step in establishing goals is to determine a valid method for measuring the things the team is to improve. This method would then be used to determine the base line (situation when the team was established), for the things that the team is to improve. Goals would be established based on improvements above the base line. The goals would specify how much of an improvement is required by set dates.

3. Teams within a company should not be competing against each other because it takes the focus off everyone working together on the common goal of taking care of customers. It is good to have teams compete against industry and competitor benchmarks, if they can be determined.

4. Be the kind of team member others enjoy working with in a team environment. In return, most of your fellow team members will make an effort to be someone you enjoy working with in a team environment.

5. You can measure how well people are functioning together by looking at how much progress they make toward achieving their goals and objectives.

   You should look for opportunities to get into teamwork type relationships with others where you help each other. When you see something that will be a problem for others, inform them, especially if it is something that probably would not have been seen early enough to deal with properly. In addition, if you can spend 15 minutes doing something that will save someone else an hour, offer to do it. After noticing either of the above, most people will start returning the favor to you at the first chance they get.

   Also concerning the above, if you are in the position of the person who could have been warned about a problem or saved an hour of time, and someone fails to help you, politely ask why. Tell the person that if the situation were reversed, you would have provided the help. People with reputations for "only looking out for themselves" will get little help from those around them.

6. Do not let people take credit for other people's ideas. The best way to get team members to contribute ideas is to make sure everyone knows that they will get credit for good ideas they contribute.

   There are people who will meet with you prior to a meeting to discuss the information you *both* have for discussion at the meeting. If you think this person may state your information at the meeting before you say it, hold back key details you can add to what this person says.

   If you are bringing a new idea to a group meeting, consider emailing the idea to meeting participants before the meeting.

7. When working with others, make them do their share of the work.

Chapter 20

Being a Valuable Employee

Your value to your employer is the amount that your compensation is less than what the company would have to pay someone else to do your work as you would have done it. Your value has nothing to do with the effect on the company caused by your work not being done. Value created by combining resources (people, material, and facilities) is created by the person who is paying for the resources.

You can increase your value by working well with your boss, consistently doing a good job, and being willing to take on higher levels of responsibility. This increased value should lead to increased compensation with your current or a new employer. There are many factors affecting your level of compensation in a company. Increasing your value is usually the best thing you can do to increase your compensation. It is hard for companies to find valuable employees; consequently, companies are usually willing to pay premium wages to hire and keep valuable employees. Do not make the mistake of being very valuable in a critical area of the company and hinting about quitting if you do not get a big pay increase. You may get the raise, but your job will be in jeopardy as soon as the company gets an opportunity to lessen its dependency on you. This is especially true if you work directly for the owner of the company.

Make sure you understand where your employer needs value created; a good place to start looking is in your company's vision, mission, and strategies, as follows:

- Vision — A long-term, broad inspirational picture of where the company is going

- Mission — Time-specific and measurable goals that will bring the company closer to its vision
- Strategies — Specifics involved with how to accomplish the goals in the mission

  Note: Your efforts in the company should be in direct support of the company's strategies. If you do not fully understand how your job fits in with the strategies, ask your boss.

Things That Can Be Done to Support Strategies that Most Companies Have in One Form or Another

- Do all aspects of your work in a manner that meets or exceeds expectations.
- Help the company benefit the most from customers, as covered in the Taking Care of and Selling to Customers chapter.
- Identify areas within the company where operational efficiencies can be improved. Rate these improvement opportunities based on their financial benefit in relationship to their implementation time and cost. Easily implemented opportunities with relatively high returns usually belong on top of the priority list. Make sure improvements in one area do not cause problems in another area, as in the following examples:
  - Fixing excessive material stock outages by increasing inventory too much
  - Reducing bad debts by not shipping to anyone with less than perfect credit
  - Reducing late shipments to customers by quoting excessively long lead-times on deliveries

  Balanced scorecard measures the four key areas of the business so that the full impact of improvements gets measured. These four key areas are (1) employee development, (2) operational efficiency, (3) customer satisfaction, and (4) profitability.

  Lean thinking uses KPIs (Key Performance Indicators) focused on its five principles. These five principles are (1) customer value, (2) value stream, (3) flow and pull, (4) empowerment, and (5) perfection.

  Present your list of improvement opportunities and accompanying analysis to your boss and others, if applicable. Volunteer to pursue the improvement opportunities, if you are given the necessary resources such as team members.

- Work to reduce or eliminate non-value-added activities. Non-value-added activities are activities the customer does not want to pay for, such as moving product from the end of one production line to the beginning of the next production line.
- Look for ways to lower costs, such as strategic partnering with suppliers.

- Help others in your company be more productive. Remember, you are all on the same team.
- Offer advice when others are having trouble with their work.
- Let others know when you think they did a good job. This will increase their sense of accomplishment, which is a great motivator.
- Do your part to make the work environment enjoyable so no one dreads going to work each day.
- Follow your company's policies and procedures.

Chapter 21

Taking Care of and Selling to Customers

One way or another, everyone's job, directly and/or indirectly, is to help their employer get, keep, and benefit the most from customers.

Taking Care of Customers

Help your company take care of customers better than your competition does in as many of the following areas as possible:

- Understand customers' needs, which are not necessarily what is first asked for.
- Lower the cost to meet or exceed customer expectations.
- Reduce lead-times from ordering to delivery.
- Accurately forecast delivery dates.
- Be reliable, so customers know they can count on your company for on-time delivery and consistent quality.
- Be easy to do business with in all areas of sales and service. This involves, among other things, ordering, checking on an order's status, being told of late shipments, payment arrangements, and service after the sale.

- Be a strategic partner with your customers, which may result in them making you the preferred or possibly the only supplier for the products you provide. Strategic partnering begins with understanding what your customers do with the product you sell to them. For example, suppose you find an opportunity to add $20 to your product's cost that will save a customer $30 in other costs. The two of you can split the $10 savings by increasing the selling price between $20 and $30. Try not to reveal to the customer any proprietary information that your customer's other suppliers of the products you supply could use to lower their costs.

Selling to Customers

In order to sell, you need your own interpretation and understanding of the following 17 sales matters.

1. Use market research to determine where you have the greatest potential to sell products and make profits. Prospective customers who currently buy the type of products you sell are usually the best prospects. Converting prospective customers from a different type of product to yours, such as vacuum forming to injection molding, can be difficult and time consuming and may not be worth your effort unless the potential sales are large.

2. Develop a sales and marketing plan that starts with identifying prospective customers and ends with ongoing sales arrangements. Keep prospective customers moving through the steps in your plan. Asking questions to prospective customers that assume they agree to the next step in your plan can keep things on track. Rather than ask for a meeting, possibly ask if a certain day to meet is convenient for them. If they say no, ask what date would be convenient. As another example, if a prospective customer is noncommittal about agreeing to a sale (not giving you a purchase order or not signing your sales agreement/contract), consider asking how the delivery should be scheduled or other specifics of the sale.

   Questions can be used to get prospective customers to agree that your product is the best solution for their needs. If prospective customers do not express agreement with your calculation of dollar benefits, ask if they see any flaws in it. If they do not point out any flaws, proceed as if they agree. Similarly, suppose a prospective customer brings up your competitor's product or brings up alternative solutions to their needs that do not involve the type of products you sell. In these types of instances, you need to present your best analysis that explains how your product is the best solution for the prospective customer's needs. If the prospective customers do not express agreement with your analysis, ask if they see any flaws in it. If they do not point out any flaws, proceed as if they agree.

3. Make your sales presentation directly to the decision maker. Consider the five following items, where applicable, when planning your presentation:
   - Determine your objective. Be prepared to conclude the sale; for example, have the sales agreement ready for signature. Verify your assessment of needs during the sales presentation and make changes to your objective during the presentation where applicable.
   - Have questions to ask so you will properly understand the prospective customer's needs.
   - Calculate the dollar benefit to the prospective customer of buying your product. Be ready to make modifications to your calculations based on information you get during the sales presentation. The focus of your presentation should be to convince the decision maker that (1) the benefits of purchasing your product exceed the selling price by as much as possible, and (2) your product is the best solution for the decision maker's company's needs.
   - Have answers for possible questions or concerns that the prospective customer may raise such as advantages of your product versus competitors' products. Do not bring up the name of competitors your customer may not have thought about contacting. If the customer brings up the name of competitors, ask if you should explain differences between the competitors' products and yours. Your explanation could be used to arrange a follow-up sales call. If the customer does not ask for the explanation of differences, proceed as if the customer agrees that your product is the best.
   - Plan to avoid bringing up subjects for discussion that are unrelated to your sales presentation. You need to maximize the amount of time your prospective customer listens and pays attention to your presentation.
4. Remember that your goal is to get the sale. Make the most of every opportunity to close the deal as in the following three instances:
   - Get a commitment for an order based on something you know you can do, such as a cost benefit analysis with a short pay back period.
   - If the customer asks for a demonstration of your product, get a commitment for an order contingent upon a successful demonstration. Rehearse your demonstration completely. You want the demonstration to go smoothly and you want to make sure the product operates properly.
   - When you give advice that helps a prospective customer with a big problem, ask for the sales order at the first opportunity you get after the customer expresses, or should have expressed, appreciation for your advice.

Take advantage of good opportunities to ask for the sales order rather than wait for the *perfect time*, which may never come. If you ask and the prospective customer is not ready to make a decision, find out whatever else you need to do. Try to get a commitment for an order based on you doing whatever else you need to do.

5. As soon as possible, explain all your reasons why the decision maker should say "yes," because once the decision maker says "no" to a meeting or a sale, you will have the additional burden of getting the decision maker to lose face by changing the decision, especially if others are aware. If you are told "no," you will have to present new information that ideally the prospective customer would not have even thought about considering.

   Remember, you are selling a product and your customer is fulfilling a need. The prospective customer will not be interested in talking to you unless there is a good chance that the cost of your product is less than the benefit of fulfilling the need. In order to get the customer's attention, you may need to roughly estimate the benefit of fulfilling the need.

6. In addition to fulfilling the company's needs, the decision maker is also concerned about getting credit for doing a good job. For the most part, finding the best solution for the company's needs will make the decision maker look good but there are other factors you need to consider, as listed below:
   - You and your company must look and act professionally when you meet others at the decision maker's company.
   - Decision maker needs to feel that you are honest, trustworthy, and a friend who will never do or say anything that would discredit the decision maker.
   - By negotiating a better deal from you, such as a delayed price increase or lead-time reduction, the decision maker will look good.
   - It is hard to get people to buy something that will make them look bad. For example, it is hard to sell a service that audits freight bills paid, for overpayments, to people in charge of approving freight bills for payment. You need to either sell your service to someone above these people in the company or convince these people that they will not be blamed for the overpayments.

7. Put yourself in the decision maker's shoes and try to identify what it will take to make the sale.

8. Be the kind of person you would want to do business with if you were the decision maker.

9. The more you believe that the products you are selling are good for your prospective customers, the easier it will be to sell.

10. Develop customers for the long term. Do not promise things you cannot deliver. Anticipate your customers' needs and look into different products you can sell to them.

11. Help customers identify exactly what they need and explain how your products best meet their needs.

12. Try to price your product so its cost to the customer is just below the benefit your customer gets. Make sure your customer agrees with your benefit calculation. Do not lower the selling price below your cost.

13. Deal with customer complaints promptly. When customers complain, you are being notified that their needs are not being fulfilled as they expected. Unhappy customers want a reasonable solution, from their point of view. Sometimes you need to explain to customers how their expectations should be modified to make them more reasonable. Work with customers to identify how the problem should be solved and follow through with the identified solution. Never criticize your company in front of customers, such as by saying "the shipping manager is an idiot." You should explain that errors caused by your company are the result of procedures not being followed. Also, explain the steps being taken to ensure that the procedures are followed in the future.

14. The greater the percentage that one customer is of your company's total sales, the more leverage the customer will have to get a lower selling price from you. The more your company invests in overhead, such as equipment and facilities, to service a customer, the more it costs to stop selling to the customer.

15. If your company is much smaller than your prospective customer's other suppliers, avoid pointing out this difference. If this difference comes up, explain why it will not be a problem. Your explanation can mention that your company has other customers the size of the prospective customer and there are no problems

16. Never tell a prospective customer you "need a sale" for a quota, contest, or to pay your bills because you will seriously damage your credibility. In addition, you will be putting the person in an awkward position that could end up terminating your access to the prospective customer.

17. Always view your company's products in terms of what your customer is buying from you, not what you are selling to them. If the railroad industry had realized that its customers were buying transportation, the railroad industry would probably own a big piece of the airline industry today.

Chapter 22

Negotiating

This chapter deals with pursuing your objectives and negotiating with others.

Pursuing Your Objectives

Before you go into a situation, know your objectives and have a plan to achieve them. Make sure your objectives are attainable and make sure they are what you really want. Do not blindly pursue objectives; you may gain new insights that could change them. On the other hand, do not change long-term objectives based on short-term considerations.

Conceal your objectives from those who may be inclined to make it difficult for you to achieve them. If your objectives are in conflict with someone else's objectives, first try to come up with a compromise. Make sure you fully understand the other person's objectives. If it comes down to negotiations, consider adding less important items to your objectives that make it harder for others to achieve their complete objectives. You can then negotiate away these added items for things you want. Do not overplay your hand to the point where the other person proposes a compromise that gives you the added objectives you do not really want. Remember, when you propose a compromise, you should ask for more than you will accept, in order to leave room for negotiations.

Negotiating with Others

When you begin negotiations with someone, start by focusing on the things where you both agree. Possibly, the only thing you initially agree on is that the conflict needs to be resolved.

Always keep negotiations on a business level, never personal. Once negotiations get personal, people often act irrationally, which makes it harder to negotiate. In addition, you do not want to end up with either of you having a personal grudge against the other, especially if you two may have to negotiate with each other in the future. Gloating after you get what you want in a dispute can also lead to a personal grudge.

Saving face (not looking bad) is usually important to all parties in a negotiation. If you propose a deal that makes the other party in the negotiations look bad, this other party will usually be less likely to accept. Try to structure what you want in a way that makes the other party in the negotiations look as good as possible. Ideally, structure your deal so that the other party views it as a win-win situation for both of you.

If you are trying to talk someone into something and you get an "okay," then immediately you should say "thanks," even if the person is in the middle of a sentence, and change the subject at the first opportunity you get. Do not give any more reasons for the person to say "okay," because it will just open the door for the person to retract the "okay" or attach conditions. Once you get an "okay" and you say thanks, the matter is closed.

Individuals often display peculiar tendencies whenever they misrepresent, conceal, or try to discourage others from bringing up a subject. For example, people may raise their voice in anger whenever they say something that they do not want others to question. If you identify these tendencies in someone, keep it to yourself. Similarly, when you are discussing something with someone one on one, and the person starts looking away while saying something that you have no way to verify, there is a better than even chance that the person is being less than truthful.

Chapter 23

Working Relationships

A good working relationship is in the best interests of those in the relationship. The 13 thoughts in this chapter concern working relationships.

1. Be the type of coworker that you would like to have as a coworker.
2. If you are helpful and cooperative with others, others will generally be helpful and cooperative with you.

   You will encounter some coworkers who seem to expect more help and cooperation from you than they are willing to provide to you. As a rule, the help and cooperation you provide to coworkers like this should not be reduced below what they provide to you because a little bit of help and cooperation is much better than getting into an adversarial relationship. If you get into a conflict concerning helpfulness and cooperation with this type of coworker, remember that this coworker probably has similar conflicts with others.
3. Make sure the value of your work is recognized and acknowledged by the recipient. Perceived value is what counts in the mind of the recipient. On the other hand, do not be a person who goes around *tooting his/her own horn.*
4. Suppose someone does you a favor by doing good work on something the person did not have to do. You can return part of the favor by complimenting the work in front of others whose opinions are important to the person.
5. The more you are respected for your character, the more that people will want to work with you. You want people to know that they can trust your motives.

There will be times when pursuing your goals, long- and short-term, may seem to be in conflict with maintaining the high regard that others have concerning your character. In these situations, just make sure the things you do are the things that other people in your position would be expected to do. For example, never turn down a promotion you want just because you and some of your coworkers feel that the second-choice candidate is better qualified than you are. In this example, if needed, make sure other people do not think you did anything to make the second-choice candidate look unqualified.

6. The better your reputation for honesty, the less your analyses and opinions will be questioned.

7. If you are in a position of being respected, the less you act like you expect respect from others, the more respect you will generally get.

8. Make more of an effort to get along with people whom you depend on.

9. Never exploit another person's dependency upon you; always provide the appropriate level of assistance. If appropriate, help the person become self-sufficient.

   If you are a department manager with a direct report who is helping another department manager, the other department manager will most likely be more accommodating to you in return. If you make a company change so that your direct report also reports to the other department manager, this other department manager's accommodation to you will most likely decline.

10. The more a person complains about others, the less credibility the person's criticisms will usually have. The less a person complains about others, the more credibility the person's criticisms will usually have.

11. If someone at your level or below is in your office and starts reading things that are on your desk, consider turning over the things that are being read.

12. Never say, especially in an email, that people said or did something unless you are sure they said or did it.

13. Avoid misspelling and mispronouncing people's names. For uncommon names, try to figure out the pronunciation based on how it sounds, not based on how it is spelled. To hear pronunciations of people's names, try calling the people at work when you know they are not there so you can listen to their voice mail greeting.

Chapter 24

Awkward Situations

Not everything goes smoothly at work; occasionally, you will find yourself in an awkward situation. This chapter has 11 ways to deal with awkward situations at work.

1. If a coworker starts complaining to you about the company or about someone higher than you in the company, ignore what the person says and get the person to stop. If you disagree with the complaints, let the person know. The longer you listen to the person's complaints without disagreeing, the more likely the person will tell others at work that you agree with the complaints.

2. If you see a problem coming for someone that is partially the result of your actions, or lack of actions, contact the person right away. Explain how you are fixing the problem and ask, if applicable, for any suggestions on what else can be done. Usually, the longer you wait to notify the person, the worse your mistake becomes. It is a tough call on whether to tell someone, when you still have a chance to correct the situation before the problem arises. If others were also involved in causing the problem, tactfully make sure you are not blamed for their errors.

3. If during a conversation you agree to something you realize you should not have agreed to, pause for a moment before you make any more decisions or comments. Ask yourself, was it carelessness on your part or did you misunderstand something that was said. If you misunderstood something, you may be able to get out of what you agreed to do by discussing how you misunderstood the situation. The sooner you get out of it the better.

4. If someone asks for your approval on something when you are too busy to give it adequate thought, either hold off deciding whether to approve it or stop what you are doing and give the decision adequate consideration. As part of your consideration, you should try to determine whether the person might have purposely waited to ask until you were too busy to adequately consider the request.

5. If someone talks to you about a matter for the first time and implies that you two have talked about it before, you may want to say that this is the first time you recall the two of you talking about it. There is no harm in saying this, other than the credibility of your memory if you are wrong. This is your best time to clear up the misunderstanding. If you did discuss it previously, you need to recall the discussion in order to discuss it now. If you did not discuss it previously, you need to determine why the person said you did.

6. Sometimes people cause problems by getting off track and making changes to things that should not have been changed. They may try to shift some or all of the blame to you by coming up to you and saying something like the following:
   - "I am working on __________, like we talked about."
   - "I am taking care of __________, like you wanted me to do."

   A bold person may say the above to you in front of others while you are distracted. Comments that do not really fit in with the current conversation need to be considered when you first hear them. Asking the person to repeat what was said will give you enough time to determine if you should state that this is the first time you heard about the matter. Ask what work has been done on the matter. If you can figure out what particular problems may have occurred, mention how the particular problems need to be avoided.

7. If a person slips in a comment that is not really related to the conversation such as "I am really not interested in how Project A gets completed," ignore the comment. If the person repeats it, especially word for word, it very likely is something the person was planning to say to you and to others who may have been listening. Try to observe if the person waited until a particular person, or group of people, was listening. Ask yourself why the person would make this comment in front of whoever was present.

8. Sometimes a person will bring up a false criticism of you or of someone who works for you, then quickly say it is no big deal and change the subject. If you do not challenge this false criticism, the person can later say or write something to the effect, "I mentioned it [to you], and there was no reply."

9. Watch out for people who bend the truth and try to get away with saying that you said something you did not actually say. After you stop them with the facts, they will be less likely to do it again. If they get away with it and you later recall the facts, go tell them what you remember. Information received from people like this should ideally always be in writing.

10. Be wary of people who talk to you differently in front of others than how they talk to you when no one else is around to listen. Possibly, the way you are talked to in front of others is designed to convey a message to the other people who are there at the time. Do not let someone unfairly criticize your work in front of others and get away with it by being extra friendly and cooperative later when it will go unnoticed by the people who heard the criticism.

11. Do not tell anything to anyone at work that you do not want others at work to know about, for the following two reasons. First, you may not be on friendly terms with the person in the future. Second, the person may accidentally tell someone else; some people talk faster than they think. If you feel that you have to talk about something that should not be discussed with anyone work related, call a family member or other friend who has no connection to your work.

Chapter 25

Conflicts

Conflicts are inevitable, primarily because the goals pursued by different people are rarely 100% compatible.

Avoiding Conflicts

Be proactive. Anticipate problems that could cause conflicts between you and others. If it is within your means, correct any problems before they create conflicts. Always remember that you and your coworkers are teammates with the ultimate goal of taking care of the customer.

When two people are headed for a conflict, the person who sees it first has more time to prepare in advance. For example, suppose you see something coming up that you and a coworker will have conflicting ideas concerning how to handle. You can start putting things in place so your idea will be a more logical choice. Another possibility would be to formalize your plan and get it approved before your coworker's plan is formalized. Just make sure your boss does not feel misled by you.

Avoid getting into conflicts you cannot win. Losing conflicts can be a major detriment concerning advancement within a company.

Try to avoid getting into conflicts with people who have less to lose and/or more to gain from the conflict than you.

Dealing with Conflicts

Conflicts should ideally only occur because different people have different ideas concerning what is best for the company. If what is best for the company is not readily apparent, refer to the company's mission, vision, and strategies. See the Being a Valuable Employee chapter for the definition of a company's mission, vision, and strategies. Conflicts will occur for other reasons as well. The rest of this chapter has 12 ways to deal with conflicts.

1. Suppose you and a peer have different ideas on how to accomplish something that needs to be done. Consequently, you both decide to present your ideas together to someone higher in the company for a decision concerning whose idea will be followed.

   Both of you should agree to present your ideas to the decision maker at the same meeting. Start your joint presentation by explaining the overview of what you are both trying to accomplish and why it needs to be done. Then each of you will just have to explain why you feel your idea is the best way to accomplish it. If your peer has already met with the decision maker about the different ideas before the three of you meet, then ideally the decision maker has not already made an irrevocable decision. If applicable, mention that you and your peer had agreed to meet with the decision maker together and present your ideas at the same time. Also, possibly ask the decision maker if the decision has already been made concerning the matter.

2. Resolve conflicts without needlessly involving others. It is best to have a reputation for working well with others rather than for getting into conflicts.

3. If your work is criticized and you feel it is necessary to respond, start by fully understanding the criticism. If the criticism is correct, fix your work. If the criticism is not correct, get the facts and set the record straight with whomever you deem necessary.

4. For any conflict that could end up in the Human Resources Department, write down everything that was said by all parties including you. Note the date, time, and sequence of events. Also, securely keep all documents and other information that the Human Resources Department may need now and in the future.

5. Before disciplining or confronting someone about something, get the facts straight. Possibly, put yourself in the person's shoes to better understand what happened. Start your discussion by presenting the facts you have gathered and asking for an explanation about what happened. Anticipate the person's response, so you can have questions and comments ready. If the person has lied to you in the past, consider not saying what you already know before asking for the person's side of the story.

6. If someone in your company is causing needless problems for you, deal with the person as follows:
   - For direct reports, give them a verbal warning and inform them that the next instance will be written up and put into their personnel file with Human Resources.
   - For peers, talk to them and explain how two coworkers are both better off if each helps the other rather than hinders the other.
   - For a boss, make sure it is known that you are trying to do the best job possible. When a problem arises, caused by your boss, sincerely ask what you could have done to avoid the problem.
   - For a peer of your boss, wait until you have a good example. Document it and tell your boss, explaining, if applicable, how the problem affects your work. You need to give your boss everything needed for your boss's discussion with the person who is causing problems for you.
7. Before you react to something in anger, make sure you are not over reacting. Usually if you sleep on it, you will moderate your response. View your planned reaction in a long-term context.
8. Avoid getting angry at the other person during conflict resolution, for the following reasons:
   - The angrier you are, the less you can concentrate on the important things to consider.
   - Anger often causes conflicts to get somewhat personal, which makes rational decision making more difficult and hurts working relationships.
9. Where applicable, take the following steps to keep conflicts from becoming personal:
   - Refer to "procedures you followed" rather than "you did."
   - Keep the focus on doing what is best for the company.
10. If you are having a disagreement with a peer or a direct report and the person's version of the facts changes, immediately point out the inconsistency. Do not let the person change the subject or act as if your comment is not understood. Usually a person in a disagreement only changes the story if it is necessary to support a planned misrepresentation of the facts. The sooner you point out the inconsistency, ideally immediately and in front of others, the less of a chance the person will have to get away with misrepresenting the facts.
11. Do not carry on disputes using email. What you send via email can easily be forwarded to others and taken out of context, the same as having an argument in front of others.
12. When others are having a conflict that does not involve you, avoid taking sides. If they settle their differences, you could end up in an awkward situation.

Chapter 26

Difficult Bosses

If your boss is *difficult* because you are expected to work hard all day, keep in mind that your boss is expected to get as much as possible from resources, like you, the company pays for and uses. This chapter covers four types of bosses who are difficult because their management skills are lacking in one way or another.

1. It is difficult having a boss who will give verbal or implied approval for something and later act like it was not approved. The most likely explanation is that when the original approval was given, the boss did not adequately consider the matter. There is the possibility that after making the decision, the boss acquired some new information that cannot be shared with you.

   Seeking your boss's approval for something is different than trying to sell something to someone. All possible negative consequences of the boss's approval should be covered, so your boss can make the best decision for the company; always remember that you and your boss are on the same team.

2. Watch out for a boss who feels threatened by others knowing how good a worker you are. If your boss is like this and is likely planning to stay in the current position for the near future, start looking for advancement opportunities elsewhere in the company or with a different employer.

3. Some bosses consciously and/or unconsciously let their administrative assistants take on more authority and control over others who work for the boss than is appropriate. Most of the boss's direct reports will put up with this because the administrative assistant can easily influence the boss's perception

of their work. If your boss's administrative assistant is like this, the following may help ease the situation:

- If your boss says or implies something that can only be the result of the administrative assistant's unfavorable misrepresentation of your work, challenge it. Ask to have an opportunity to defend yourself in the future whenever the administrative assistant says anything negative about your work.
- If you can work it into a conversation with your boss, ask if your boss has ever been in or seen any situations where bosses' administrative assistants misused their position to the extent that it lowered productivity and morale. Be prepared, in case you are asked, with examples of how the boss's administrative assistant is causing problems. Possibly, your boss is not aware of the problem's magnitude, or that there is a problem at all.
- The ideal time to talk to your boss about something like this is when your boss is happier than normal with your work and less happy than normal with the administrative assistant's work.
- Never turn against your coworkers in order to keep the boss's administrative assistant on your side.

Be careful, you may have a boss who is extremely loyal to the administrative assistant and consequently will get extremely irritated at the mere mention of any shortcomings. If you have any inclination of this being the case, do not talk to the boss about this unless you know that your employment is valued more than the administrative assistant's employment.

4. Some bosses are just bad supervisors/managers, but will be reluctant to acknowledge or discuss it in your presence. If you have a boss like this, read the Supervising and Managing Others chapter and identify what your boss is doing wrong. Try to improve your situation by fixing what your boss is doing wrong, as follows:
   - If you need internal and/or external training, put together a good justification and ask for the training.
   - If your boss gives you something to do that is unorganized, ask for an opportunity to review it with your boss after you have organized what needs to be done.
   - Whenever you ask a question, provide your suggested answer with an explanation, if necessary.
   - If you are given an unreasonable completion date for something, explain why it is unreasonable.
   - Make sure you understand how your work supports the company's strategies that support the company's mission and vision. See the Being a Valuable Employee chapter for the definition of a company's mission, vision, and strategies.
   - Ask for feedback concerning your work.

- Ask what you need to accomplish in order to get a good raise.
- Maintain up-to-date procedures for the work you do.
- When you take time off, make sure your boss knows what has to be done in your absence.
- Be the kind of employee you would want working for you if you were the boss.
- If your boss manages you by creating an atmosphere where you are afraid to make mistakes, explain how it is very unproductive for you to be worrying about getting into trouble.

Chapter 27

Working Well with Your Boss

Being employed involves having a boss. Bosses can have tremendous impact, good and bad, on your career. This chapter includes 22 thoughts on how to work well with your boss.

1. Remember, your boss is your boss.

   If your boss asks you to do some work that you feel should be done differently or not done at all, make sure you fully understand what your boss is trying to accomplish and how your boss wants it accomplished. If still applicable, suggest improvements concerning what your boss is trying to accomplish and/or more efficient ways to accomplish it. If your boss understands and disagrees with your suggestions, it is time to start planning how and when to complete the work your boss wants done.

   If your boss wants you to arrive at work every day on time, be there every day on time, even if you regularly work late and feel it should not really matter when you arrive. Bosses often have *pet peeves.* Avoid violating the pet peeves and you will probably get a lot of leeway in other areas. Bosses who regularly arrive at work on time every day often have a pet peeve concerning their employees who come in late.

2. Be the type of employee you would want working for you if you were the boss.

3. Be the type of employee who looks for ways to get things done, rather than looks for reasons why things should not be done.

4. Be willing to take on additional responsibility, as time permits.
5. Be productive and try to never look like you are wasting time.
6. Understand the limits of your authority and exercise them fully when needed.
7. Sometimes you cannot get all your work done on time, in which case you should tell your boss in advance as soon as possible and have an alternative plan you can accomplish. Your boss should not have to keep a list of work that was given to you.
8. Sometimes your boss will ask if you can get something done by a particular date, which you are not sure you can accomplish. It is better to say "let me get back to you on that" and get back to your boss rather than to say "yes" and then later tell your boss you cannot get it done.

   If your boss wants you to do more than time allows, make sure your boss knows everything else you need to do and how long it takes to get it done.
9. When your boss asks you for information, give the facts and, if applicable, explain how you determined them. Clearly identify any assumptions you make. If the only thing you have to present is a best guess/theory, because facts are unavailable, clearly identify your presentation as your best guess/theory and, if applicable, explain why the facts are unavailable. Also, explain the logic behind your best guess/theory. Whenever you give information to your boss in response to a question asked earlier, always start by mentioning the question.
10. If your boss asks you to check something that you feel does not need to be checked, check it before you say it is okay. Your boss may have heard, seen, or thought of something you do not know.
11. If your boss says something in error to someone else in your presence, quickly decide if and when you need to let your boss know. If it is insignificant to the discussion, wait until later. If it is an exaggeration or a deliberate bending of the truth, let it go. If it is an error that will cause problems for your boss later, glance at your boss's face apprehensively if you can do it without anyone else noticing. If you feel that your boss would want you to speak up and correct the error, do it as discreetly as possible. Later, explain why you felt that it was best to speak up, rather than to wait until later. If in doubt about speaking up, do not do it. If you do not speak up, always tell you boss about the error as soon as no one else is around. Be extra careful when your boss is talking to a customer.
12. When you tell your boss about a problem, also explain your recommended solution and alternative solutions, where applicable.
13. If you are not happy with your pay rate, tell your boss. Say it once and confirm, with your boss, that your boss does not *oil the squeaky wheel* where

your peers who frequently complain about pay will get the bigger raises. Bosses often conveniently assume that if employees do not complain about their pay rates, they are satisfied with them.

14. Try to solve conflicts without going to your boss. No boss wants to have an employee who gets the boss into unnecessary conflicts.

15. If you have to put something in your boss's office, and your boss is not in there, do not bring anything else in there with you. You do not want someone telling your boss that you walked out of your boss's office with some papers or anything else.

16. If your boss walks into your office during working hours and you are working on personal stuff, do not cover it up or put it away. Covering it up or putting it away will result in a 100% chance that your boss will notice. In addition, your actions will indicate that you feel you should not have been doing personal work. Instead, leave the personal work right where it was. Your boss may not notice it; even if noticed, keep in mind that everyone has the right to take breaks during the workday. If your boss does notice, then for the next few weeks wait until your boss is not around before you take out any personal work during working hours.

17. Do not act as if you think you are a better employee than your boss is, even if you think you are. Do not needlessly demonstrate your work-related superiorities when you are around your boss and also be careful not to patronize your boss. Never put yourself down, to make your boss look better in comparison.

18. Suppose your boss reads a book, and wants you and others to read the book on your own time. At a minimum, you should scan the book and look for things to bring up in the event you get into a discussion about the book with your boss. Try to understand what it is your boss thinks everyone should learn. Keep an open mind; maybe your boss is on to something worth learning. Also, you do not want your boss to view you as someone who is *against learning new things* or *against change*.

    If you have serious reservations about following the book's recommendations, express them to your boss in private. Keep your criticism directed toward the book, not toward your boss. If your boss understands and rejects your criticism, do not bring them up again.

    Generally, if the company wants to make changes that affect you, such as implement a new management philosophy, use new computer software, or change how things are done, you want to *embrace change* and help with the change. Often change reduces the number of employees doing the work, which is usually the justification for the change, and those who fought the change are often the first to go.

19. If you have more than one boss, do not make the mistake of ignoring the one with whom you have the least amount of contact.

20. If your boss is replaced, do everything you can to get your new boss up to speed. Do not assume that your new boss will do things the way your old boss did them.

21. If a customer thanks you for an extra effort you made, mention how nice it would be if the customer could put the "thanks" in a letter to your boss.

22. Be aware of coworkers who complain to the boss about others with the goal of making themselves look good in comparison. When your boss comments to you about something negative that a person like this said about someone else, consider mentioning to your boss how this person seems to make others look bad in order to look good in comparison.

Chapter 28

Getting Promoted

When promotion opportunities exist, companies do not want to have to talk employees into being promoted. Promotions often go to those who (1) step up when a promotion opportunity exists by showing their eagerness and ability to move up and (2) have positioned themselves for promotion.

Stepping up When a Promotion Opportunity Exists

- When a promotion opportunity exists at work that you are interested in, make sure you are considered. Briefly tell the boss who supervises the position that you are both qualified and eager to show what a good job you can do. If the position is in a different department, let your current boss know you expressed interest. The first time you talk to your current boss about any promotion opportunity, be sure to explain your qualifications and offer to train your replacement.

- When a vacancy creates a promotion opportunity for you, look for ways to step up and take responsibility for the most important work that will be done by the person who ends up filling the position. If the work was done well, start by learning how it was done. If the work was not done well in the past, start by asking the recipients of the work what their needs are and what needs were not being met. Possibly, there is a better way to get the work done, or maybe some of the work done in the past was not needed. Do not make any major changes or deletions that cannot be easily corrected, without first checking with all applicable recipients of the work. For any work you drop, continue to keep all the source documents until you are sure the dropped work will not be needed in the future.

Proving yourself in a situation like this will require a lot of extra work, usually right away, because you will still have your current job, and new work always takes longer at first. Keep in mind that the results of your efforts on this new work may be heavily weighted in the decision concerning whether you can be counted on to complete the work properly in the future. Do not count on the decision makers taking into account the fact that you also have your current work responsibilities to fulfill. If you get into this type of situation where you have to prove yourself, read the Working Well with Your Boss chapter.

- If your boss starts talking like you may get a promotion or greater responsibility that you want, do the following:
  - Let your boss know that you are eager to take on the new challenges and will do a good job. Your boss does not want to have to talk you into it.
  - After telling your boss the above, explain that if the decision can be made now, you can start planning as soon as possible for your new responsibilities. You should try to get the commitment while your boss is leaning in favor of you.

Positioning Yourself for Promotion

- Act the way the company wants employees in higher positions than you to act. This usually involves a higher level of professionalism than is expected from someone in your current position, as listed below. Some of these things are repeats from earlier in the book, but they are worth repeating. You may not be able to do all these things, but the more the better.
  - Try to identify and inform top management about significant opportunities and risks for the company, before anyone else sees them coming.
  - Avoid *shooting from the hip*. If an idea is worth presenting, think it out in advance. Keep an open eye for new ideas. Sometimes changing circumstances make a previously discarded idea worth reconsidering.
  - Never criticize your company or anyone in upper management, even in jest.
  - Never challenge authority, especially in front of others. Disagree with people in authority over you in private only, unless your opinion is wanted, and always do it professionally. Never refuse to do your job.
  - Embrace diversity and never say anything negative about anyone or about any group of people.
  - Play by the rules. If you lose something you wanted, take it gracefully.
  - Do not bring personal problems to work. Bosses know what is going on, and they view time spent on personal problems as time they paid for and you wasted. The more personal problems a boss hears about an employee,

the more likely the boss may be to assume the employee spends too much company time on personal problems. Bosses are usually much more forgiving when the time is spent caring for a sick person versus a boyfriend/girlfriend type dispute, which is often more disruptive and consequently harder for employees to ignore while working. Bosses are least forgiving when employees use company time and resources on their own personal businesses.

  - Do not repeat gossip or even discuss it.
  - Do not overuse sick days if you are not sick.
  - Do not socialize with your direct reports, other than at work-related events.
  - Never let anyone from work see you consume more than one or two alcoholic drinks, even at a Christmas party.
  - Do not tell off-color jokes that could offend someone if repeated.
  - Never joke about drugs.
  - Never state an objection to random drug testing. If you are against it, you will probably be better off not saying anything.
  - Always have your temper under control.
  - Dress and act in a manner that would be considered appropriate for someone one level above you in the company.

- Be a valuable employee, as described in the Being a Valuable Employee chapter.

- Know the pronunciation of names, titles, and functions of the people above you in the company, including people in other locations. This seems to help with promotions because it makes you appear to be on friendly terms with those above you in the company. Take every opportunity to get on friendly terms with these people; be sure to present yourself professionally and make sure they know your name.

- Make sure those above you in the company are comfortable with how you manage the responsibilities you already have.

  Whatever you manage, you will need to discuss and report its status. Those above you in the company need to know that (1) you know what is going on and (2) you are making sufficient progress toward whatever goals have been set.

- Look at the business from top management's point of view. Identify the company's major problems and try to get involved in their corrections, as follows:
  - If costs are too high on a major product line, volunteer to put together or be on a team to lower costs. As an alternative, give top management information on competitors' costs that can be used by the cost reduction team for a benchmark.
  - If customers are having trouble dealing with a particular part of your company, identify exactly what the problem is so top management can set improvement goals.

- If customers for a particular product line are switching to a competitor's products, offer to get involved in analyzing the competitor's products.

For all teams involved in correcting the company's problems, try to be the person who presents the teams' progress to top management.

- When you complete a hard task, make sure your boss and others involved in the project, as warranted, know how hard it was in terms of time and effort. It is usually best not to mention any mistakes you made while completing the task. Mentioning these mistakes could raise questions concerning whether you have the decision-making abilities required for future promotion.

- Problems will arise for which you will be partially responsible; possibly, you should have caught your coworker's error. Keep in mind that it is best for you to be known as a problem solver rather than someone who goes around blaming others.

  Make sure your boss does not blame you for errors made by others. You are usually responsible for errors made by people working for you, unless they deliberately disregarded your directions.

- You want your boss's boss and others above you in the company to know that you make your boss look good, rather than bad. Someday these people may be considering you for a promotion into a position that reports to them and they will want someone who makes them look good, rather than bad.

- Management often puts employees in two categories:
  - Those who work and can be replaced
  - Those whom management wants to develop and keep for the long term, this is usually a much smaller group than the first group

    Make sure the company and your boss definitely classify you in this second category.

  Note: It should be noted that many employees in the first category above were originally in the second category but did not do a good enough job to stay there.

- Having gone back to school and earned an advanced degree will usually improve your odds when it comes to promotions. The advanced degree will also usually improve your prospects for finding a better job with a different employer.

- Often when a vacancy occurs within a company, the employees on the same level as the position to be filled are asked for their opinions of any internal candidates. Internal candidates who have already established good working relationships with these employees will usually have an advantage over lesser-known internal candidates, since actions speak louder than words.

- Maintain good working relationships with people in a position to criticize your work, especially if you are not in a position to observe their errors.

- When you are being considered for internal promotion, your working relationship with your current peers will most likely be examined. During this evaluation period, it is best that you have and maintain a good working relationship with your current peers. Mentioning that you are trying to be promoted can lead to unnecessary problems.

- In any work or team environment, *natural leaders* are noticed. Natural leaders are those who others are inclined to follow without being coerced. The two most common traits of natural leaders are (1) being respected for their accomplishments and (2) treating their team members in a manner that makes them feel good about being team members.

- When you are perceived as someone who could move up fast in a company, the envy of those you may pass up can turn to ostracism. This is another instance where being known as a helpful coworker will ease the situation.

  Never hold back on the quantity or quality of your work to avoid ostracism. People who are passed up often try to blame the people who passed them rather than blame themselves.

- In a small or medium size company, being involved in an office romance can block promotions and possibly lead to termination of employment. In large companies, especially those with multiple offices around the city, romances are not as problematic but they are still unadvisable. Companies will be reluctant to knowingly promote an employee to a position of authority over someone with whom the employee had been romantically involved. Business workers have it much stricter than government workers do when it comes to office romances.

  Dating someone who works for you, directly or indirectly, can easily lead to you being accused of sexual harassment. Companies are often quick to fire employees who are accused of sexual harassment because they do not want to be sued for maintaining an environment where sexual harassment occurs.

Chapter 29

Supervising and Managing Others

Employees are the most important resource a company has. Supervisors and managers need to make the most of this resource in the short term and in the long term. This chapter covers 26 things that concern supervising and managing employees.

1. It is very important that you develop the employees who work for you (your direct reports). Developing employees involves the following:
   - Teach them what they need to know in order to do their work. This involves explaining where to get needed resources (information and materials), what to do with the resources, and how to check their own work to make sure it is properly completed.
   - Improve their work skills with internal and external training, as needed.
   - Motivate them, which for most employees means making sure they have positive accomplishments that make them feel proud. You want them to feel good about the work they do. Pay them at least what other companies would pay them.

   As a supervisor and manager, you are judged based in part on the contributions to the company made by employees who work for you.

2. Before giving work to direct reports, you should organize and explain it thoroughly so it can be done as efficiently as possible. Ideally, have the employees organize the work with you. Start by explaining the desired end-result and then ask them to organize the work "so it can be done as efficiently

as possible." If they are stuck or off track, ask questions to give them hints. Involving employees in the planning and organizing of their work will improve their work skills and increase their sense of accomplishment.

3. When direct reports ask you a question, ask them what they think the answer is and why. If necessary, help them think out the answer, ideally by asking questions.

4. Do not be afraid to challenge direct reports with a complicated task. Most employees will try to complete the task. If they cannot complete the task, you will know their limit. Once you have identified their limit, you can help them go beyond it.

5. Use completion dates so direct reports can prioritize their work. Overuse of completion dates can lead to inefficiencies because meeting the completion dates can become more important than the quality of the work. The key is for you to move completion dates out when the scope of the work increases significantly or when you want other work done first.

6. Keep direct reports informed about how their work takes care of customers and how it fits in with the company's strategies that support the company's mission and vision.

7. Feedback to direct reports concerning their work, whether good or bad, should be provided as soon as there is enough time to adequately discuss the matter. The longer feedback is delayed, the less effective it is. Feedback is needed so employees will have a better idea of what to do and what not to do in the future. Without feedback, employees will tend to do things the same way in the future as in the past.

8. Above average work should be discussed with direct reports just as much as below average work. There are important lessons to be learned from each. The discussions should be structured to encourage above average work and to discourage below average work.

9. Tie pay raises to the completion of projects. Make sure direct reports know what needs to be done and when it needs to be done.

10. It is important that direct reports know you work at least as hard as they do. They also need to know that they are on the same team as you, where you support them and they support you. Make sure they always know that you will do the following:
    - Back them in a conflict, assuming they are right
    - Do whatever you can for them concerning raises, assuming they deserve a good raise
    - Never hold them back from a promotion
    - Not take credit for their work

11. The more you delegate to direct reports, the better backups they become for you; this is very important for you and the company. The more lower-level responsibilities you delegate, the more time you can spend on higher-level responsibilities.

12. If you get hired or promoted into a position where the direct reports are working inefficiently because of poor supervision or direction, avoid jumping right in and fixing whatever problems you see, for the following two reasons. First, you need to identify which problems are the highest priorities. Second, you need to fully involve the employees in determining the solutions to be implemented. The exceptions to this rule are problems whose solutions are obvious and critical to implement quickly, as well as problems your new boss says to fix as soon as possible.

    Start the improvement process by asking your boss and possibly your department's customers what they feel the major problems are. Be careful not to leave any of these people with unrealistic expectations about when problems will be corrected.

    Review each major problem with your applicable employees to determine the solution. Keep your ideas and possible solutions to yourself. Ask questions so the employees come up with the correct solutions on their own. Let them know that they will get credit for fixing the problem. After they get credit for fixing the problem, point out to whoever told you about the problem that it has been fixed.

13. If you are promoted or hired into a position where your predecessor had more direct reports than you will have, it may be hard for you to match your predecessor's departmental output. If the department's work requirements remain basically unchanged, do not let this reduction in staffing be forgotten. Consider asking your boss for advice on how to get any missing employees' work done. If you find yourself in this situation, consider the following:
    - Your department and your predecessor may have been working inefficiently.
    - Your boss may want you to upgrade one or more of the employees who work for you.

14. For direct reports doing routine detailed tasks, consider having them maintain detailed, up-to-date procedures. When they make an error, review the procedures with them. Either they failed to follow the procedures, or they need to revise the procedures. You should always have a copy of the latest version of the procedures, which will come in handy whenever training a new employee.

15. Before direct reports take planned time off, you should know how to get the necessary parts of their work completed while they are off. If they call in sick, ask them what needs to be done and, if necessary, how to get it done.

16. Be the kind of boss you would expect to work for if you were in the position of your direct reports in a well-run company. If you are not sure how to respond to a situation with an employee, imagine yourself as the employee and try to determine the appropriate response from the supervisor. Also, imagine yourself as an objective third party observing the situation and try to determine the advice you would give to the supervisor.

    The less you use your authority over your direct reports to make them do what needs to be done, the more cooperation you will usually get from them.

17. When you manage supervisors, you need to make sure they are properly supervising their direct reports.

18. The worst way to supervise and manage direct reports is to create an atmosphere where they are afraid to make mistakes. It could be argued that this method works adequately in the short term, but it definitely works much less than adequately in the long term.

    The best way to manage employees is to create an atmosphere where the employees want to live up to your expectations. Employees who are properly supervised and managed will be motivated to meet expectations they feel are reasonable. Involving employees in the determination of your expectations for them is a good way to make sure they feel that the expectations for them are reasonable.

19. When you manage a task, you take total responsibility for its proper completion. Whatever it takes, you need to assemble the needed resources and manage them. The direct reports you manage are your most important resource. Other resources include equipment, materials, supplies, computer programs, and services provided by people outside the company.

20. If one of your direct reports does not get enough work done, ask this employee to list what work is done in an average week or month, and how much time each thing takes. Have the employee email the list to you. Review the list and ask for details as needed. The list will make it clear that the productivity is unacceptable, assuming the list does not contain significantly more work than you thought was being done. Take the list, add everything else that should be done, and assign it all to the employee in an email so there is no question concerning what work needs to be done. Where applicable, the list should contain completion dates, and specifics about exactly what needs to be done. If the work on the list is not completed properly and on time, document the unsatisfactory performance. Work with the Human Resources Manager to make sure the following is done correctly:
    - Your documentation is adequate
    - The employee gets properly notified that failure to get everything on the list done on time will result in termination of employment

21. Do not be bullied by one of your direct reports. Suppose you have a direct report who (1) argues continuously with you when it comes to work that you want done, or (2) keeps disagreeing with you when it comes to being held accountable for things, or (3) talks to you in an insulating manner. The solution is to email all your requests for work, explanations, and changes in behavior. Emails should state that the direct report should respond with the work and explanations by a set date and that the replies be by reply email. If the direct report starts verbally discussing any of the matters, just say "put it in your reply email." If the direct report does not reply by the date you set, forward your email and request the reply. If the reply is inadequate, reply to it and request an adequate response. Write your emails in a manner that the Human Resource Manager would not object to in the event that the emails are used to discipline the direct report. Bullying that can be done verbally cannot be done in an email without documenting the unacceptable behavior.

    When you let a direct report bully you, you are empowering this direct report to bully others in your department, since it is usually less likely that you will stand up for others than stand up for yourself. If you are unable to use your position as a supervisor to stop bullying, you are not qualified to be a supervisor; work with the Human Resource Manager as needed.

22. If you have a direct report whose behavior causes unacceptable problems for you or for others in the office, keep in mind that the problems will most likely continue and probably get worse until you correct the situation. Give the employee a verbal warning, and explain that the next offense will result in a written warning that will go into the permanent personnel files.

    As soon as the next offense occurs, get this employee's side of the story, and write up the written warning, assuming it is still warranted. If the employee starts telling you about a personal problem, keep the following two things in mind. First, there are others with personal problems who do not take them out by causing problems in the office. Second, an employee like this is apt to exaggerate things you cannot verify, in order to gain your sympathy.

    Delaying your meeting with the employee, concerning the repeated offense, will provide time for a temporary change in the employee's behavior. This temporary change in behavior is irrelevant and it shows that the employee knows a written warning is warranted.

    A personnel problem can waste a great deal of time. Deal with it decisively and be done with it once and for all.

    If you are a forgiving person, you may find it difficult to discipline an employee who should be disciplined. Keep in mind that disciplining the employee is what the company needs done, and you, the supervisor, are the designated person to do it. In addition, if you are not willing or able to do this, the company may need to upgrade the person in your position.

23. Never say anything negative about one of your direct reports to anyone other than your boss or the Human Resources Manager.

24. Use positive reinforcement whenever possible to help get an unsatisfactorily performing direct report onto the right track. Positive reinforcement can start by acknowledging improvements in the employee's work. Then make sure the employee understands that continuous improvement will be rewarded. These rewards can involve things like work assignments, performance reviews, and compensation. Also, make sure the employee understands the following. First, if the employee's future performance is on the right track, the problems from the past will remain "in the past." Second, everyone in the company is on the same team, and you will make sure sustained good work by the employee will be noticed by others in the company.

25. If you have to fire someone, be sure to say, "the decision has been made and it cannot be changed."

26. Whenever direct reports quit or get fired, then before their last day, you need to get the following from them:
    - Update of all their work procedures
    - Documentation of the work they do
    - Location of all their computer and paper files

    Explain that the next time they change employers, you will probably be contacted for a reference. Tell them that if they do a good job wrapping things up now, you will only say good things when contacted for a reference.

Chapter 30

Hiring People

Since employees are the most important resource a company has, the hiring process must bring in the best employees for the money the company is willing to pay. Hiring the right person is very important because the better the new hire is to begin with, the better the new hire will most likely be after being developed by you. In addition, hiring, firing, and replacing the wrong person is costly and it delays the point in time when you have a trained person in the position you are trying to fill.

What to Look for in a New Hire

Before you offer someone employment, make sure you are comfortable that the answer is "yes" to each of these first three numbered questions and to the fourth, if applicable.

1. Is the candidate technically competent?

   Start by making sure everyone you interview has the education and experience you require. Where applicable, get confirmation of education and experience.

   Make a list of situations, responsibilities, and work your new hire will be doing. Then ask the candidate how each thing on the list has been dealt with in the past, and how each thing would be dealt with in the future if hired. Do not just write down the candidate's answers; ask for specifics and use hypothetical examples, if necessary, so you can make sure the candidate is technically competent.

2. Is the candidate truly eager to put forth the necessary effort after being hired?

   If the candidate seems eager to do a good job, ask for specifics concerning the major situations, responsibilities, and work requirements of the position. Write down the things the candidate says would be done, and ask if you can count on these things being done if the person is hired. The more unrealistic these things are, the less likely the candidate is being sincere, assuming the candidate fully understands what you are discussing.

   An indication of eagerness can be found in the follow-up letter you receive after the interview. There are two opposite types of follow-up letters you can receive. The generic follow-up letter does not contain any specifics about the position and is not a good sign of eagerness. The best follow-up letter you can receive is one that includes business related subjects discussed at the interview and provides new information and details concerning potential weaknesses you noticed during the interview. This second type of follow-up letter is a good sign of eagerness and an excellent sign of attentiveness and thoroughness, important traits many employees lack.

3. Will the candidate have a good working relationship with you and with others in the company?

   More specifically, ask yourself the following questions and make sure none of the answers are likely to be negative:

   - Is the candidate someone you could successfully work long hours with on a complicated problem? Will this person listen to your ideas or will you have to argue with the person concerning whose ideas should be pursued?
   - Will the candidate be conscientious enough to complete assignments from you on time or to tell you in advance when a due date may not be met?
   - Will the candidate be realistic when committing to getting work done?
   - Will the candidate's analysis and work be thorough?
   - Will the candidate be able to suggest solutions for problems that are encountered?
   - How will the candidate react to stress and necessary overtime?
   - Will the candidate be a team player where you both help each other? Will others in your department and the company consider this person to be a team player?
   - Is the candidate aggressive enough to get the job done?
   - Will others in the company consider this person to be a good addition to the company?

   Ask questions such as the following to candidates; ask for specifics and use hypothetical examples, as needed:

   - What significant work-related problems did you and your boss straighten out together and how did the process take place?

- What have you done in the past when circumstances made it very difficult to meet due dates for work from your boss?
- Have previous bosses ever asked for work that could not be realistically done by the due date? How did you handle the situations?
- How do you determine which things have to be done thoroughly and which things can be done by using approximations?
- When you tell your boss about a problem, who should start the discussion concerning possible solutions?
- What have been your most stressful work-related situations? How did they arise? How did you cope with them?
- Describe conflicts you have had with your boss, direct reports, and coworkers. How did they arise? How were they resolved? Be wary of anyone who "never gets into conflicts" or who blames others for conflicts.
- Do you have any objection to required overtime?
- What is the importance of teamwork with your boss, with those in your department, and with others in the company?

4. If applicable, is the candidate qualified for promotion in the future?

   Determine the attributes needed in someone who can be promoted in the future. Attributes such as education and experience are easy to check. Attributes such as being a team player and fitting in with the company's culture are harder to assess, but you should be able to at least get a good gut feel about the candidate's qualifications in these areas.

   Ask candidates where they see themselves professionally in ten years and in five years. Make sure the candidates are truly interested in staying at your company and being promoted.

Note: Remember that the most important resource a company has is its employees. When your employer gives you authority to hire someone, you should put the interests of the company ahead of your own interests. The worst hiring decision you can make is to hire poorly qualified workers in order to make it difficult for your employer to replace you.

Delayed Hiring

Do not delay either seeking approval to hire someone or the process of finding and hiring someone you need. Every week you delay is a lost week's worth of work done by your eventual new hire. This lost week's worth of work should be measured at the level of productivity the person will be at after being fully trained. It is a bad short-term decision to put off the approval and hiring process in order to do the work yourself that the new hire will eventually be doing. Work with your boss and the Human Resources Manager to determine what you need to do to keep the approval and hiring process moving.

Waiting for the Right Candidate

Hiring the wrong person is much worse than not hiring anyone, as the latter is much easier to fix. The hiring process must be thoroughly completed. Thoroughly identify what is needed in a new hire and thoroughly understand the qualifications of available candidates. If you do not find the right candidate in the first group of interviews, get a new group of candidates to interview. If you and the Human Resources Department do not have time to find qualified candidates to interview, get approval to use a recruiter. If the compensation you are authorized to offer is inadequate, explain to your boss why it is inadequate. If the work to be done by the new hire is not being done and cannot wait any longer, possibly get a temporary worker. If your boss gets impatient with the time it is taking to hire someone, explain that you are trying to make a good long-term decision; also offer to explain your efforts to hire the right person.

No Negative Surprises for a New Employee

Before you hire or promote someone, cover all the negative aspects of the job so the person will not feel misled. Also, for the same reason, do not over exaggerate the positive aspects of the job.

Planning for a New Employee's Success

Plan to build a new employee's confidence by starting the person off with work that can easily be done well. An employee will work hard to maintain a reputation for doing good work. On the other hand, an employee will be much less likely to work hard to overcome a reputation for not doing good work.

It is important that others in the company get a good first impression of your new hire's work. It is equally important for your new hire to know that others in the company have this good impression.

Often people form impressions of things based on the first bits of information they receive, and then disregard contradictory information received in the future.

Chapter 31

Changing Employers

If you ever consider changing employers, read the four thoughts in this chapter. You need to make sure changing employers is the right thing for you and if it is, you need to manage the process as smoothly as possible.

1. Sometimes changing employers is the best way to advance your career, as follows:
   - If you become ready for promotion, but there does not appear to be a higher-level position opening up for you in the company, finding a new employer may be the only way to advance your career.
   - Some companies are under so much pressure to make short-term profits that the top 25% of employees, based on job performance, get annual increases one to two percentage points higher than the bottom 25% of employees. If you are in this top 25%, you should consider working for a company that does more to retain its better workers.
   - You may have gotten into a bad rut with your supervisor or manager that you cannot correct. In this instance, a new employer may be the only way to get your career back on track. Make sure you understand how you got into the bad rut, so you can reduce the chance of it happening again.

   Before looking for a new employer, talk to your current boss/employer about any of the three problems above, or others, that are causing you to consider changing employers. Getting the problems fixed with your current employer is usually better than leaving the company. If your boss/employer asks if you are currently looking for a new employer, say "no."

When making the decision to leave the company, do not consider how much the company will appreciate your work after you quit. This appreciation will have no effect on your well-being and it may not be as great as you think.

2. Be careful not to get too comfortable in a job. Do not sacrifice your long-term goals because of short-term comfort. On the other hand, do not quit a good job for one that may be a little better.

3. Before you agree to visit a company for a job interview, ask some or all of the following questions so you can eliminate the companies you are not interested in working at:
   - What city would I be working in? Possibly, ask what area of the city.
   - What type of work would I be doing?
   - Is the salary range in line with my requirements?
   - What is the title of the position and what is the title of the person to whom this position reports?
   - What percent of the time would I be traveling?
   - Anything else that is important to you, such as "what are the annual sales?"

4. No one at your current employer should have any idea that you are thinking about leaving the company. People talk and you do not want your boss to start making plans to replace you, as the right replacement may come along before you find another job. If you are interviewing on a day you are going to work, do not wear your interview clothes to work unless they are what you normally wear. When you ask for time off to interview, just say it is for "personal reasons." The more you try to explain why you need to be off, the more it sounds like you are trying to conceal the real reason for being off.

Chapter 32

Exiting an Employer

There are two ways to terminate your employment. Either it is voluntary (you quit) or involuntary (you are fired). This chapter covers exiting an employer under both these scenarios.

Keeping the Door Open When You Quit

When you quit a job, do not *burn any bridges*. You may need to come back.

Arrange for your current boss/employer to be a good reference for you in the future. When you announce your resignation, get a commitment for a good reference in return for you organizing your work before leaving. Work with your boss to determine how it should be organized; for example, have copies of all reports, updated work procedures, and a list with the location of all files. Do not over commit to what you will accomplish.

Make sure your resignation letter leaves the door open as much as possible. Explain that you enjoyed (1) working at the company, (2) working with your boss, and (3) the work you did.

Possibly Getting Persuaded into Not Quitting

If an employer tries to talk you out of quitting by offering increased compensation or other benefits, you need to determine the motives. Are you someone the employer wants to keep long term, or just short term until a replacement can be hired? Possibly, ask your employer how you fit in with the long-term plans for the company, and listen carefully to the answer.

Being Fired

- Immediately start looking for a new job. Resumes sent out before your termination date can indicate that you are currently employed.
- Try to have your termination date pushed out into the future. Explain how long it will take to clean up loose ends, offer to train your successor or to at least leave good notes on how to do your job, and suggest projects you would be the logical person to complete. Possibly, you can work as a consultant, though continued employment is usually better. List the details for each thing that could extend your employment and prepare a written presentation that clearly defines the benefits to the company.
- Negotiate the best severance deal you can get. Do not send a letter of resignation. Do not sign anything until you bring it home and think about it. Consider contacting your local bar association to arrange an inexpensive 30 minute consultation with an attorney who specializes in employment law. Make sure the severance pay has everything included in the company's severance policy, such as two weeks pay in lieu of notice and one week of pay for every year of employment. Also, make sure your severance package includes unused earned vacation time. It may likely be that your employer will improve the severance package in order to get you to sign an agreement not to pursue legal action regarding the termination.
- Try to get a signed letter from your boss that says your termination was the result of things beyond your control, such as company downsizing, departmental consolidation, or lack of work. Often these are the reasons given for terminations, so ask for the signed letter as soon as possible. Draft the letter to make it easy for your boss to complete. If your boss is reluctant, possibly work it into your severance package negotiations. You will need to bring a copy of this signed letter with you to every job interview.
- Arrange with coworkers at your company to give good references. If you think a potential employer will be calling them, call them in advance so they will be prepared to emphasize certain aspects of your work.
- Apply for your state's unemployment compensation as soon as possible. Do not wait for your severance pay to end unless you agree to wait in the signed severance package.
- Do not lose confidence in yourself, even if you are somewhat at fault for the firing. Learn from your mistakes and be a better employee at your next employer. Whatever your trade/skills, there are companies looking to hire someone like you. Go out and find them, and let them know you will be a good addition to their company.

- Pursue the following to find a new employer:
    - Reply to advertisements on the internet and in newspapers.
    - Post your resume on the internet.
    - Contact employment agencies.
    - Send letters to companies that employ people with your skills.
    - See if your former school has placement services for alumni.
    - Contact professional organizations in your field for employment advertisements.
    - Check out trade magazines in your field for employment advertisements.
    - Contact business associates and friends. Do not keep your termination a secret to avoid embarrassment. Good business associates and friends will want to help.

- When you interview, maintain a positive attitude. You want your potential new employer to know that you are full of energy and ready to prove yourself in a new job. In addition, you want to make sure the interviewer does not feel that you are likely to keep looking for a better job after being hired.

  Never go into an interview with a negative attitude. Do not act as if you are so desperate that any job will do, or that you are looking for sympathy from the interviewer. Also, do not criticize your former employer or boss.

Book Two

Evaluating Opportunities To Start Or Buy A Business

Book Two explains how to evaluate opportunities to start or buy a business with an emphasis on the financial side of things. Also explained is how to manage an owned business or someone else's business with an emphasis on what it takes to be successful.

Chapter 1

Evaluating an Opportunity to Start a Business

Starting your own business can lead to the so-called real American dream (having your own successful business), but the road to success is not an easy one. This chapter is divided into the sections listed below.

The sections below that concern financial statements, expenses, investments, cash flow, and other financial decision-making matters are detailed further in the related sections of the last two chapters in this Book Two.

- Advantages of Working for Yourself versus Having an Employer
- Disadvantages of Working for Yourself versus Having an Employer
- Evaluating Your Motivation, Skills, and Willingness to Do Whatever It Takes to Succeed
- Evaluating Your Competitive Advantage
- Other Factors Concerning Working for Yourself versus Having an Employer
- Managing Expenses
- Managing Cash Flow
- Protecting Assets
- Pricing Your Products and Services
- Market Research
- Advertising
- Strategic Planning
- Sales Forecasting
- Cash Flow

- Business Plan Needed to Borrow Money
- Financing Your Business
- Financial Software
- Enterprise Resource Planning (ERP) Software
- Payroll
- Insurance
- Legal Matters
- Franchises

Be sure to read Book One before starting a new business, especially the Taking Care of and Selling to Customers and the Hiring People chapters.

Advantages of Working for Yourself versus Having an Employer

- You do not have any bosses, though you may find that customers and those who finance your business are just as bossy.
- Your chance of making a lot of money is greater, but so is your chance of losing a lot of money.
- You can do things your own way, though you may find that your flexibility is limited by things such as market forces, competition, governmental regulations, human nature of your employees, and other things that you cannot control.
- You can spend all of your time doing what you want to do to grow the business, assuming you can afford to pay others to do all the other things that need to be done.

Disadvantages of Working for Yourself versus Having an Employer

- You will work much longer hours, at least until your business is established. Do not forget that your time has value; you will be giving up the income you could have earned working for someone else as well as the leisure time you could have enjoyed.
- It will be much harder to go home at night and not think about problems at work.
- If things go bad or if you lose interest, it is much harder to get out of the situation.
- All of your investment funds will probably be invested in one business, at least until you pay off those who have financed your business.

Evaluating Your Motivation, Skills, and Willingness to Do Whatever It Takes to Succeed

- If you get personal satisfaction, such as feeling proud of yourself, from the reaction of others who hear that you are starting a business, stop and reconsider your motivation. The only reaction from others that should matter is how they react after you succeed or fail.

- Concerning skills, you will need to be able to do the following:
    - Get going without relying on anyone else.
    - Organize complex matters.
    - Explain things to others.
    - Convince others to believe what you believe.
    - Treat the following types of people in a manner that is best for your business: difficult customers, employees with no stake in your business, suppliers whose main interest is their own business, bankers and investors whose main interest is their money, and relatives and friends who want jobs that pay more than a regular employee would get.
    - Make decisions on the spot without all the facts and then be ready to adjust the decisions as facts become known.
    - Do whatever it takes to overcome obstacles and problems.

- If necessary, are you willing to work six or seven days a week at 12 to 15 hours a day? It is easy to do something you are good at, especially when you get a strong sense of accomplishment from it. Unfortunately, running a business involves many tedious administrative tasks.

Evaluating Your Competitive Advantage

- For non-franchise businesses, you need a competitive advantage. Without a competitive advantage you will be a "me too business" in an environment where (1) your competitors will probably be more efficient than you, as they will have learned from their experiences; and (2) your competitors will have higher volume than you to spread out their overhead expenses. In addition, if your competitors have a way to keep you from becoming a serious competitor for them, such as by lowering their prices and discouraging their suppliers from dealing with you, be prepared for their efforts to protect their businesses.

- Competitive advantages can come from the following:
    - Being well respected by your prospective customers can be a big competitive advantage. A renowned chef has a competitive advantage when it comes to opening a fancy restaurant. A new professional service firm made up of managers and partners from a similar type firm that is large and well respected has a competitive advantage over another small firm that is the

same except for having employees who are not from a large, well-respected firm. Well-known sport stars, local heroes, and other types of celebrities will probably have the advantage of being able to attract more customers as well as arrange better deals with investors and suppliers.

- Providing a service more efficiently than your competitors provide would be a competitive advantage, but it is not as easy as it seems unless you have a patented process that is significantly better than what your competitors have.
- Being able to produce and sell products more profitably than your competitors do will require a competitive advantage such as preferred access to inexpensive raw materials, cheap labor, inexpensive facilities, strong personal/business relations with big customers, and a patented process that is significantly better than what your competitors have.
- Being the first with a new service or product is a definite competitive advantage, but you will need to move quickly on a large-scale basis in order to capitalize on this advantage. You need to establish the need for your service or product and get it in front of your prospective customers before your competitors can react. Your competitors' reactions will probably include copying your idea as closely as possible, improving it if they can, and possibly selling it for a price less than yours. Be sure to ask yourself why your competitors have not already come up with your new service or product. If your idea is based on a new technology that your competitors are not aware of, you may have a good idea. If you think you know more about customer needs than your competitors, who know the customers' needs well, double check your assumptions before spending a lot of money.
- Having a good location can be a competitive advantage, such as having the first commercial location people come to after driving a few hours through an area.
- Having a good name or web address can be a competitive advantage, if it is closely associated with the service or product you are selling.
- Businesses make money by creating value, which is done by combining material, labor, and other resources that have a total cost lower than the value of the finished product, as determined by what customers will pay. Being able to create value better than your competitors can is a competitive advantage.

Other Factors Concerning Working for Yourself Versus Having an Employer

- Some business opportunities are nothing more than just frauds. Some legitimate businesses are ill conceived and have little chance of success. Never invest in a business opportunity until after you have had a trusted business advisor review it. You should also talk to others who have invested in the business opportunity.

- The best way to learn about a business and find out if you really enjoy it is to work for a company in the particular business. You will learn how the business operates as well as who the suppliers and customers are which will increase your chance of success in the eyes of the people you approach to get startup financing. Working as a real estate agent is a good way to (1) learn the local real estate market, (2) learn to sell, and (3) learn the legal aspects of selling. In the case of a professional service firm — the more promotions you have, the more credibility you will have when talking to prospective clients for your own firm.
- Be careful about starting a business to service one big customer. Once you have invested in equipment and facilities, your one big customer can and may likely lower your selling price to the point where you barely make a profit.
- When a successful entrepreneur explains the "simple" steps taken to success, keep in mind that 100 other people may have taken the same risks and failed.
- The U.S. Small Business Administration can provide a lot of good information on starting a business. They can put you in contact with retired executives who can answer your questions and provide advice, all without cost. They can be reached at www.sba.gov and (800) 827-5722.

Managing Expenses

- Do not manufacture anything you can get at a lower cost, by either buying it from someone or by having someone manufacture it for you. Your cost in this comparison is the incremental cost you incur by manufacturing the product. This incremental cost includes all variable costs and any fixed costs that will go down if you purchase the part, such as one less manufacturing supervisor. In addition, if not manufacturing the product will free up floor space or other assets that you will then use to generate profits, include the profits as an additional incremental cost. This additional incremental cost is called an "opportunity cost" and is not captured by regular financial statements. Find manufacturing companies that have the necessary equipment and also have excess capacity. Your agreement (contract) with the manufacturer should have the following four things. First, there should be penalties for not shipping minimum quantities on time. Second, there should be a provision where you can buy as much additional product as would be needed in the best of all circumstances, with a set lead-time and a set price. Per unit price should be lower for these additional units because overhead is spread over more units. Third, make sure you own all tooling that needs to be bought in order for the company to manufacture your product. Have the company buy all tooling and list it, with serial numbers where applicable, on the invoice to you. Fourth, there should be a restriction that keeps the manufacturer from becoming your competitor or selling to your competitors.

- Instead of hiring people based on expected need, you should wait for the need to arise and then hire the necessary people.
- Using personnel agencies (executive recruiters and headhunters) to find new employees can be expensive. Fees can be as high as 25%–35% of the new hire's annual salary. If you do use a personnel agency, make sure the invoices contain at least a 90-day guarantee. Guarantee should state that if employment terminates within 90 days, the agency would continue the search at no additional cost until you select a replacement.
- For temporary increases in production labor, it is usually better to rely on overtime and outside agency labor to get the work done, rather than hiring and then laying off people. The more layoffs you have, the higher your unemployment tax rate will usually be.
- Make sure the purchase of labor saving equipment is financially justified using incremental expenses and a reasonable projection of production quantity. If the savings are not large enough to make the investment an obvious good choice, read the Projecting the Financial Benefit of an Investment section of the Financial Decision Making chapter.
- Your office facility should be nothing more than a comfortable place for both your employees to work and for your customers to visit. When existing customers see an elaborate, expensive office facility, they may think that they have been overcharged to pay for it.
- Get competitive quotes, whenever possible, on everything significant you buy. There are sites on the internet where you can get prices from companies for most commodity type items you buy; be sure to qualify any of these companies before placing an order. Qualifying suppliers involves assessing their capabilities, primarily in the areas of quality and production. The goal of this is to identify suppliers whom you can count on to meet your needs.
- Before you pay for anything verify the following:
    - The price is what you agreed to pay.
    - You received the goods and services, in satisfactory condition.
    - Charges for freight are correct, usually goods are shipped "FOB Shipping Point," which means that the buyer pays for the freight. If you have a lot of stuff coming in on trucks, you can work out discounts with some carriers and request that your suppliers use your preferred carriers.
    - In some states, you do not pay sales tax on (1) items that will later be sold with sales tax charged or (2) equipment used to make products that will be sold with sales tax charged. Different states have different rules on when sales tax gets charged, so check with your business advisor. The important thing is only pay sales tax when it is actually due.

- For a retail business, see if any of your suppliers will pay for some of your advertising and promotion costs.
- Insist that your supplier gives you as low a price as they charge your competitors.
- If your suppliers offer a 2% discount for payment within 10 days, versus full payment in 30 days, try to pay within 10 days and take the discount. See the Working Capital Management section of the Financial Decision Making chapter for more on this.
- Before selling to customers on open account, get credit references from them and have them sign a statement that they will pay your collection costs in the event that they do not pay.
- Be sure to charge your customers for any freight between your business and theirs, unless their purchase order states "FOB Destination," which means you pay the freight and are responsible for the transit insurance. The decision on who pays the freight should be determined when the price of the product is determined.
- Sales commissions should only be earned and paid if and when the customer pays you. The commission should be a percentage of the profit on the sale, not a percentage of the sales amount. Keep the profit formula simple and make sure your salespeople understand it. If you do not have standard costs for your products, possibly calculate profit based on average profit per product line, adjusted for price reductions given to customers on each commissionable sale.
- If you maintain petty cash on hand, get approved receipts, with necessary details of expenses, for each disbursement.
- Other ways to manage expenses include the following:
  - Try to lower your property tax assessment. Use a lawyer who specializes in this field.
  - Respond immediately to all unjustified claims from former employees for unemployment compensation. Often the time to respond is short and failure to respond in time can result in your unemployment insurance rate being higher than it should be.
  - Look into buying electricity and gas from brokers. Your local utilities will still deliver the electricity and gas.
  - Work with expense auditors who are only paid a percentage of any refunds they generate by reviewing and finding errors in freight bills, sales tax payments, and the like.
  - Put all company cell phones under one master agreement.
  - Put all company cars under one master agreement.

Managing Cash Flow

- Minimize inventories by only buying materials you will most likely sell. Ideally, only buy materials when you have a purchase order from your customer for the finished product. Try to get a commitment from suppliers, before you place your order, to buy back inventory you cannot sell. Possibly, get your supplier to send inventory to you on consignment (where you only pay for what you use). For inventory you buy whenever your quantity on hand falls below a certain level, you will need a way to react quickly when sales are ending for the finished good that the inventory goes into. Sometimes customers want you to maintain your material inventories so that they can have quick delivery when they order. In this situation, ask customers to state in a purchase order or in a letter that they will buy a predetermined number of finished goods after they tell you that they plan to stop buying the finished goods from you. The predetermined number should be based on the maximum amount of raw material you could be holding for the finished good. As an alternative, the customers could agree to pay you for unused raw materials in the event that their last orders do not consume all of the applicable raw materials.

- If your invoices are "Net 30 days," call on the 31st day for all unpaid invoices. Get a commitment date for mailing the check. If the check has already been prepared, ask for the check number. Follow up if the customer does not send the check when promised. Your customer's accounts payable department should know that your company always calls when invoices get late. It is best that your salespeople do not get involved in the collection process. If your customer asks you to send another copy of the invoice, also send a proof of delivery.

  If you are the major supplier for a customer, be careful about letting the customer get in the habit of always paying you late. If the owner of this business always sees extra money in the cash account, it may be spent, which will make it harder for the company to start and continue paying you on time.

- Tell your suppliers that you pay invoices in 45 days. If some suppliers demand payment in 30 days, pay them in 30 days if you have to.

- Maintain an open line of credit with your bank for the maximum amount of money you could need to borrow.

Protecting Assets

- All incoming mail should be opened by a trusted employee who immediately stamps all checks — "For Deposit Only In (insert your bank name and account number)" and lists all the checks for comparison to bank deposits. Copy of the list should go to the General Manager.

- Minimize who can sign checks and keep the checkbook locked up. If there are two or more check signers, consider requiring two signatures on checks over a certain dollar amount.
- Reconcile the check register's cash balance to the bank statement.
- When materials are shipped to your business, the trucker will need a signature on the Bill of Lading indicating that they were received. Before signing, verify that everything listed on the Bill of Lading was received. Any damage to the boxes should be noted on the Bill of Lading.
- Inventory that could easily be resold should be secured with all receipts and issuances recorded, so that disappearances can be caught and investigated promptly.
- Limit the employees who can place purchase orders and approve invoices.
- Make sure that all outgoing shipments result in a sale and that the sale is recorded.
- Make sure you are paid for all scrap and recyclable materials that go out.
- Maintain your assets. Machinery may need oil and coolant changes. Buildings need repairs, such as repairing ceiling leaks before the water causes additional damage.
- Take pictures of machinery and other similar type assets that will be in use for more than one year. Keep the pictures with the asset's invoice and other related information.
- Cameras, real and phony, can cut down on theft by employees and non-employees.
- Do not feel obligated to pay for something you did not order. There are many frauds where people call your business and talk to someone about the type of things you buy and use, such as printers. Next, they send things like printer cartridges and say that the person at your company placed a verbal order. Sometimes they say that they are sending the final shipment on a previous order. Sometimes they tell people at your company that a gift will be sent to them in appreciation for past business. Office supplies seem to be an area where fraud operators try to dump a lot of junk at high prices. Twice I have heard from young women saying they are helping their fathers-in-law liquidate their business and they have a lot of office supplies. Another fraud starts with a call asking for information to go into a directory, which you will get a copy of, without any mention of cost. Next, you get an invoice for having your business listed in the directory, which you supposedly agreed to buy.

Pricing Your Products and Services

Selling prices are often dictated by competition, especially when you are a startup new business. Selling for less than your competition can be risky because your competitors probably have lower costs, due to higher volume and experience, and your customers may resist future price increases. Selling prices above your competitors' prices have to be justified in the customers' eyes based on something like better quality and/or better customer service.

The "average" product's selling price needs to cover (1) all its related variable costs, (2) a prorated share of fixed costs, and (3) a prorated share of desired profitability. Variable costs also include costs of the resources tied up in the business by the product, such as money to fund inventory and accounts receivable as well as floor space that would have otherwise been used for other products or rented out. This cost of resources is referred to as the opportunity cost and is the total profit that the resources could have generated in their next best use.

If fixed costs are forecasted to be twice the variable costs for the period, the average prorated share of fixed costs each sale should cover can be set at twice the amount of its variable cost. In reality, different customers and different products will cover different percents of both fixed costs and desired profitability. You need to make sure the average sale covers enough fixed costs because any shortfalls will come out of profits. Shortfalls can come from the fixed costs and desired profitability covered per sale being too low and from sales being too low on some product lines. In the real world, try to never sell for less than your variable costs, and charge as much as the market will bear. If product lines A & B are identical in every way except product line B requires a much higher level of inventory, then the selling price of product line B should theoretically be higher to cover the disproportionate amount of resource it ties up.

Desired before-tax profitability can be prorated based on sales, similarly to how fixed expenses are prorated. If you want before-tax profitability to be 10% of sales, divide the total cost by 90% (.9). This results in a selling price that is 90% cost and 10% profit. Different customers and different products will have different profit percents, as selling prices for some sales are limited by competition while others can be set as high as the market will bear. Your goal is to keep the average profit percentage of sales in line with your overall desired target. If sales are down and selling prices are not adjusted, profits will be down for two reasons. First, you will lose the profit on the lost sales. Second, you will have unabsorbed fixed costs on lost sales that will have to come out of profits. When you set the dollar amount of your desired before-tax profitability target, start with your desired after-tax profitability target and increase it for income taxes. Generally, 0.6 (decimal equivalent of 60%, which comes from 100% less 40% tax rate) is the least you would divide your after-tax profitability target by to get your before-tax profitability target. See your CPA firm for further details.

The following should always be considered when it comes to pricing your company's products and services:

- In the long term, you want to set your selling prices at as high a price as the market will bear. The key words in the preceding sentence are *in the long term* because you do not want to alienate your customers.
- Higher total sales do not necessarily mean higher profits. If your contribution margin (sales less variable expenses) on a product is $1.00, then a $.50 price reduction needs to more than double unit sales in order to increase profits. If you want to forecast the change in profits on a product caused by a change in its selling price, compare unit sales multiplied by contribution margin without the change in selling price to unit sales multiplied by contribution margin with the change in selling price. The more *elastic* a product is, the more its unit sales will change in response to a change in its selling price.
- Be careful about pricing a low volume product based on the price for a similar high volume product. Compared to low volume products, high volume products often have lower material costs, due to larger purchase quantities, and lower manufacturing costs, due to longer production runs. This difference can be widened significantly when the low volume product requires additional engineering design and when future sales of the product may not materialize.
- Selling products at reduced prices can sometimes be justified, such as when it gets customers to buy other products.

Market Research

Before you make any major commitments to start a business, such as buying or leasing a building, you need to identify your prospective market and assess the possibility that you can profitably sell products and services in the market. This section of the chapter is designed to help you get a rough estimate of potential sales. You can then use this sales estimate in the Cash Flow section of this chapter to assess projected cash flow, which can be adjusted to project profitability. If the projected cash flow looks decent, fine-tune your sales estimate by going through the Strategic Planning section of this chapter.

Start your market research by gathering as much information as possible, from the following as well as other sources:

- Scrutinize competitors' advertising, promotions, and catalogues. This can be an excellent source of information on existing products and new products being sold in the market along with their selling prices.
- For a retail competitor, visit the store and look at how products are displayed and their pricing.

- For publicly traded competitors, get their financial statements.
- Talk to prospective customers to find out what their needs are and what, including how much, they are currently buying. Surveys are a good way to get this type of customer information.
- Talk to suppliers for your competitors to get an estimate of how much and what kind of products your competitors are buying.

Use the information gathered about the market to estimate the total size of the market for the products you plan to sell. The segment of the total market you plan to go after is called your target market.

The last step is to estimate your share of the target market. Do not be overly optimistic. It usually takes a lot of time and money to get customers to switch from an existing business to a new startup business. The greater your projection of market share percentage, the more you should plan to spend on advertising, promotions, and other selling expenses.

Advertising

Even if you have the best product/service in the world, it does you no good with prospective customers who are unaware. Advertising, along with promotions and/or catalogs, is necessary to make your prospective customers aware of your products and services and to explain how to buy them. Advertising should also explain why the prospective customers should buy your products and services.

Do not do your own advertising. Contact an advertising agency that has active clients in the same business as yours. Find an agency with people who you are comfortable working with; trust their judgment when it comes to how an advertisement should appear in print or on the air.

Your advertising agency can make different recommended advertising campaigns for different proposed spending levels. When comparing the different advertising campaigns, you will need to compare the difference in their costs to the difference in profits before advertising expenses that they generate. There is a theoretical level of advertising where increases and decreases in advertising spending will both decrease overall profits.

You could spend years and a great deal of money to have the best quality, customer service, and value for the price, but be incorrectly perceived by your prospective customers as being not as good in these areas as a competitor who advertises better than you.

Your advertising agency can also help you with promotion planning, preparation of catalogues, and trade show display material.

Strategic Planning

Once competition sets in, only strong businesses prosper. A strong business is one that (1) makes the most of opportunities and (2) avoids/minimizes the effect of potential risks. Strategic planning will help identify the opportunities and risks as well as the changes your business will need to make in order to take advantage of the opportunities and to avoid/minimize the effect of potential risks. A strategic plan allows you to run your business more proactively as opposed to running your business reactively.

Strategic plans should be updated on a regular basis and updated whenever there is an unanticipated significant change in your business or in your business environment. Your business environment includes your customers, prospective customers, and your competitors.

Before you can plan changes for your business based on opportunities and risks, you need to determine where your business is relative to your business environment. You need to know your business's strengths and how you can make the most of them. You need to know your business's weaknesses and how you can correct them. The following is a list of areas where you could have potential strengths and weaknesses. Where possible, be sure to consider how your company compares against your competitors and remember that customer perceptions do not always match reality.

- Inside sales
- Outside sales/sales representatives/distributors
- Customer service (everything from sales inquiry through invoice payment)
- Effectiveness of advertising, promotions, public relations, and catalogs
- Location and aesthetics
- Quality/reliability/warranties
- Product selection and availability
- Price to customers
- Costs to provide goods and services
- Proper pricing relative to costs

  Note: If you and your competitor have equal costs but your selling prices versus competitor's prices are too high on some products and too low on others, you could end up selling more of the under-priced products and less of the over-priced products.

- Efficiency of operations

- Overhead costs
- Employee moral and cohesiveness

Note: See the Evaluating Your Competitive Advantage section of this chapter for other items that can be strengths or weaknesses. Be sure to consider everything that is important to customers.

Rate your strengths and weaknesses versus competitors based on how important each item is to customers. For some products, price is more important than lead-time. For other products, lead-time is more important than price. If you are not sure about what is important to your customers, ask them. A survey can be a good way to find out (1) what is important to your customers and (2) how your customers rate your business in each important area.

Generally, the first opportunities you want to take advantage of are the most important strengths you have over your competitors. If better quality is one of them, have your salespeople emphasize the benefits of your superior quality.

Generally, the first risks you want to avoid/minimize are those with your greatest weaknesses versus your competitors. If longer lead-times are one of them, lower your lead-times and make sure customers are aware.

Listed below are changes that can cause opportunities and risks for businesses as well as the changes that businesses can take in response. A missed opportunity is a risk if your competitor takes advantage of it. A risk is an opportunity if you and not your competitor can avoid it.

- Changes by your competition will primarily cause risks. If your competitor is trying to hire your salespeople, try to hire the competitor's best salespeople. If your competitor lowers prices, only match the lower prices when it is the only way to keep the business; explain to customers that your product is still a better deal at the higher price because of superior quality. If your competitor advertises superior delivery and service, make it known that your delivery and service is at least as good and make sure it really is.
- When your market share in an area reaches a point where growth is difficult because of competition, it may be time to focus your sales and marketing resources on areas with less competition. Make sure you hold on to market share in the aforementioned area.
- When your customers become comfortable with buying products from you, you have an opportunity to sell other products to them that they are buying from others.
- When the ethnicity around a retail store changes, the store is probably better off by making changes to the products being offered for sale and possibly making changes in its marketing efforts.

- When a new homogenous market emerges, the first serious marketer of a particular service or product can become well established. Hiring a Spanish speaking salesperson can be a good first step in penetrating a new Spanish speaking market like this.

- When customer preferences change away from the type of product you provide, provide the new type of product customers want. When people with families started to buy minivans instead of station wagons, the automobile companies shifted production to minivans. Other types of changing customer preferences include labor saving conveniences (household cleaners), having the latest technology (smallest wireless phone), and do-it-yourself products where in-store classes attract prospective customers.

- New technologies can be used to lower costs and improve quality.

- Price changes on alternative types of raw material can reduce costs, such as when glass bottles for soda were replaced by aluminum and plastic containers.

- Price changes on alternative products your customer can buy instead of buying your product can be a big risk, such as if you were a manufacturer of glass bottles in the last example. The ideal response would have been to recognize that you were in the business of providing soda containers and offering whatever products your customer needed.

- Changes in economic conditions can lead to many opportunities and risks. When the economy swings into a recession, consumer preferences for basic no frill products tend to increase. When interest rates go down, it is easier to sell products that require financing. When the inflation rate goes up, it is easier to sell investments that tend to go up in value with the inflation rate. When the U.S. dollar falls relative to foreign currencies, the price of imported materials, supplies, and components may go up relative to domestic suppliers; also the price of your overseas competitors' products may go up relative to your product, which gives you an opportunity to raise prices in the USA and export product to overseas markets.

- Changes in government regulations can cause opportunities and risks. Lower tariffs on U.S. imports can lower the cost of imported materials, supplies, and components relative to domestic suppliers. It can also lower the selling price of your competitors' imported finished goods. Lower tariffs in other countries can make it easier for you to compete in overseas markets. Environmental land use restrictions tend to increase the cost of similar land that is not subject to the restriction. Zoning land-use restrictions often allow exceptions for land use that was in use before the zoning restrictions were enacted; this could allow you to have the only business of your type in the zoned area.

- Changes in the earth's environment could lead to the sale of more sunglasses, sunscreen lotion, and skin treatment medications.

Your strategic plan should list all of the needed changes you come up with after examining your business's strengths and weaknesses as well as your business's opportunities and risks. Make sure the changes are made on a timely basis. Your strategic plan should have time-based goals that actual results can be measured against in order to make sure the needed changes are taking place on a timely basis. For example, if quality needs to improve, you can set a goal of reducing defects by 10% each month. For another example, if a new customer segment is targeted, you can set a percentage or dollar goal for increased sales to this customer segment each month.

Develop strategies to achieve your strategic plan's time-based goals. The strategies should have a follow-up procedure to make sure the needed changes take place on a timely basis. Without strategies, your strategic plan could end up being nothing more than an academic exercise.

Before making a radical change in your business, try to find out if it has been tried before and what the results were. If the idea has not been tried before, try to determine why. The ideal answer is that it is a new idea that would not have occurred to your competitors, rather than the idea would have occurred to most of your competitors but you know better than they do.

Strategic planning should start when you are planning how to set up your business, and include the following items, where applicable:

- Select a business name and an internet address that are easy to remember and are associated with the customer needs that you are fulfilling.
- Location of your business can be critical for a retail business and relatively important to a manufacturing company that wants to be close to workers and transportation facilities. Make sure there will be adequate parking for customers and employees. Be sure to consider potential changes in the neighborhood that could affect your business.

  Note: Before you buy or lease a building, make sure there are no zoning, fire, outdoor signs, or other regulations that could cause problems for you. Contact the zoning and planning department of the local government to find out about regulations and any licenses or permits you may need. Have an attorney (1) verify that you can do what you want to do with the building and (2) review the legal papers involved in the lease or purchase of the building. See the Choosing between Different Investments and Loans section in the Investing chapter, of Book Four, for information on how to compare leasing versus purchasing. Be sure to consider the effect of building appreciation in value.
- Try to determine why others have succeeded and failed at any new business you plan to enter.

- Try to determine the future for the business you plan to enter. The market is constantly changing. Getting in at the beginning of something new is generally better than getting in later when there are many established competitors. For example, starting a video rental business in the mid-1980s would have been easier than starting one today.
- Study how your competitors conduct business. Where applicable, visit their facilities, view their web sites, look at their advertisements, and talk to their suppliers and customers. The more successful they are, the more likely their business practices are on the right track. Put yourself in the customers' shoes and try to determine what it will take for customers to buy from you.
- Go to the library and study trade association magazines. Make sure you know whom your prospective customers are and what their needs are. Your business mission (purpose and direction of your business) is to serve these customers as profitably as possible.

If you need to put together a formal strategic plan for review by bankers or investors, it should include the following components:

- Strengths of your business and how you plan to make the most of them
- Weaknesses of your business and how you plan to correct them
- Opportunities for your business and how you plan to pursue them
- Risks facing your business and how you plan to avoid or reduce the effect of them
- List of everything that needs to be done based on the four components above, along with the accompanying time-based goals and specific strategies to achieve the goals
- Formal vision, mission, and strategies based on the five components above — See the Being a Valuable Employee chapter, of Book One, for the definition of business vision, mission, and strategies.

Note: Your goal is to convince the bankers and investors that you thoroughly understand (1) your business; (2) the market, including customer needs and competition; and (3) how to maximize the profit your business makes in the market. Your formal strategic plan should include any background information that furthers this goal.

Sales Forecasting

Sales are difficult to forecast. Often overly optimistic sales forecasts are estimated and treated as if they are more than just estimates. The most common method to forecast sales is to base it on past sales. This method requires that you identify the factors that affected past sales and determine how these factors, along with any new factors, will affect future sales. Sometimes you can base your products' forecasted sales on forecasted sales of other products that are easier to forecast. Forecasted new home sales can be the basis for the following two sales forecasts. A large increase in new home sales will usually result in a large increase in furniture sales; new homes and furniture are complementary products. A large increase in new home sales will usually have the opposite effect on the sale of new apartment buildings; new homes and new apartment buildings are substitute products.

Cash Flow

After you forecast sales, you should project cash flow from startup through the point in time when the business will have generated enough cash to repay your investment. Since there are many assumptions involved, there needs to be three separate projections, based on the Worst-Case scenario, the Most-Likely-Case scenario, and the Best-Case scenario. You need to make sure you will have the cash to both survive the Worst-Case scenario and profit the most from the Best-Case scenario.

Exhibit 1-1 has a worksheet for projecting cash flow as described in the preceding paragraph. After completing the worksheets for Worst-Case, Most-Likely-Case, and Best-Case scenarios, you will need to decide whether the projected cash flow before financing is adequate to justify starting the business.

Do not let any previous statement to others about starting a business cause you to start a business with an inadequate projected cash flow. Explain your decision not to start the business by saying you "ran the numbers and they were not as good as you had expected."

Business Plan Needed to Borrow Money

Before loaning money to you to start a business, the bank will want to see a formal business plan. Your goal in preparing a business plan is to convince the bank that there is a relatively low risk involved with loaning money to your business. A formal business plan should include the following:

- Cover page should have (1) your business's name, address, and phone number; (2) all the owners' names, addresses, and phone numbers; and (3) date prepared.
- Index should list all the components below for a formal business plan.
- Products/Services — Include a brief summary of your products/services and their market, with appropriate references to the accompanying strategic plan.

- Owners' Experience and Education — Include a brief summary of all owners' experiences and education as they (1) relate to the type of business and (2) involve starting and managing a business. Add a note stating that additional details are in the accompanying resumes.

  Resumes should include detail for the above, such as specific experience and education, years working in a similar business, number of people managed, specific involvement managing a business, and positive changes achieved for the business. Include references on the resume, and make sure the references listed are prepared in case they are contacted.

- Business Setup — Explain each of the following as detailed in other sections of this chapter:
  - Legal structure (sole proprietor, partnership, corporation, LLC, or other)
  - Location and why it is the best choice
  - Insurance coverage

- Business Process — Give an overview of your business from start to finish. Cover everything from how the sale is generated to how the product/service is delivered. Explain the process from the raw materials being purchased to the finished goods being sold. Be sure to describe your type of business, such as a retailer, wholesaler, manufacturer, distributor, or franchise. Be sure to cover whether there are any licenses or permits required and if there is any chance that they will not be granted.

- Pricing of Your Products/Services — Adapt the information in the Pricing Your Products and Services section of this chapter and include additional information as appropriate.

- Advertising — Adapt the information in the Advertising section of this chapter and include additional information as appropriate.

- Key Operating Guidelines — Have a section for each of the following three items, and get the basic information for each from the three sections of this chapter with the same names:
  - Managing expenses
  - Managing cash flow
  - Protecting assets

- Cash Flow — Include the three cash flow projections (Worst-Case, Most-Likely-Case, and Best-Case scenarios) from the Cash Flow section of this chapter. You may need to breakout the first year by months and the rest of the time by three-month periods until the business is projected to have generated enough cash to repay your investment. You should provide a detailed list of what makes up the expenditures for startup costs, land, building, equipment, and wages. Wages should be broken out by position with employee names for upper-level positions and an indication of who is an owner and who is a relative of the owner.

Exhibit 1-1 (part 1 of 2)

CASH FLOW PROJECTION (A)

(thousands of dollars)	Startup	1st 3 mths	2nd 3 mths (B)
Sales from Operations:			
Units sold		5,000	7,500
Average selling price		10	10
Gross sales (C)		50	75
Returns and allowances			(2)
Rebates and discounts			(1)
Bad debts			(1)
Net sales (D)		50	71
Change in accounts receivable (E)		(25)	(10)
Net cash flow from above		25	61
Operating Startup Expenses: (F)			
Signs	(5)		
Advertising	(4)	(16)	
Promotions	(10)	(10)	
Renovation/Remodeling	(15)		
Beginning inventory and supplies	(5)	(20)	
Utility hook up and deposits	(2)		
Insurance	(8)		
Professional fees	(5)		
Licenses and permits	(3)		
Other	(5)	(5)	
Net cash flow from above	(62)	(51)	
Operating Variable Expenses:			
Inventory purchases (G)		(30)	(40)
Change in accounts payable (H)		15	5
Payroll		(5)	(7)
Supplies		(2)	(2)
Repairs		(1)	(1)
Maintenance		(1)	(1)
Warranty		(1)	(1)
Commissions		(2)	(2)
Other selling expenses		(1)	(1)
Freight		(1)	(1)
Income tax		--	--
Other		--	--
Net cash flow from above		(29)	(51)
Operating Fixed Expenses			
Wages (I)		(20)	(20)
Rent		(5)	(5)
Utilities		(2)	(2)
Advertising		(5)	(5)
Insurance		--	(4)
Loan payments		(2)	(2)
Other taxes (J)		--	(2)
Outside agencies		--	--
Temporary services		--	--
Other		--	--
Net cash flow from above		(34)	(40)
Operating Cash Flow: (K)			
For the period, from all of the above	(62)	(89)	(30)
Investment in Business: (L)			
Land	(12)	(2)	(2)
Building	(26)	(6)	(6)
Equipment	(15)	(5)	--
Intangible assets	--	--	--
Net cash flow from above	(53)	(13)	(8)
Cash Flow before Financing (M)			
For the period, from all of the above	(115)	(102)	(38)
Total to date (N)	(115)	(217)	(255)
Financing:			
Money you invest	50		
Money others invest	50		
Loans (0)	80	50	50
Net cash flow from above	180	50	50
Total Cash Flow including Financing:			
For the period, from all of the above	65	(52)	12
Total to date (P)	65	13	25

Exhibit 1-1 (part 2 of 2)

Notes for the worksheet in part 1 of 2:

(A) Do three projections (Worst-Case, Most-Likely-Case, and Best-Case scenarios.)

(B) Use three-month periods for the first year and then six- or 12-month periods until at least the point in time when total to-date Cash Flow before Financing is positive.

(C) Gross sales are units sold multiplied by average selling price. This calculation will need to be done for each different type of product sold. If there are too many different types of products sold, try to use groups of products. It is important, for later in this worksheet, that you have at least a rough projection of the types and quantities of products your customers will buy.

(D) Net sales are gross sales less returns, allowances, rebates, discounts, and bad debts.

(E) Increases in accounts receivable offset sales in the cash flow calculation since accounts receivable are sales for which payment has not yet been received. In this example, the accounts receivable balance after the first six months is 35 (25 + 10).

(F) All purchases of land, buildings, and equipment are included in the Investment in Business section of the projection. Almost half of the startup costs, in this example, are after the startup period since the projection is based on when they are paid not when they are incurred. Be conservative when projecting the amount of credit that suppliers will give to a new business. The best time to discuss extended payment terms is when the vendors are trying to get your business.

(G) You will likely end up buying excess inventory due to minimum order quantities and misjudging expected demand. In addition, you will be buying inventory and holding/processing it for some period of time before selling it. Put the total amount of inventory purchased, regardless of when it is paid, on this line and adjust, in the following line, for when it is paid.

(H) Increase in accounts payable is a partial offset to the inventory purchases, since accounts payable are purchases for which payment has not yet been made. In this example, the accounts payable balance after the first six months is 20 (15 + 5).

(I) Add 10% to gross pay for taxes plus an additional 5% to 15% if you are providing health insurance. Make sure you include overtime pay as well as wages paid to yourself.

(J) Other taxes are all taxes other than income and payroll.

(K) Total of all the preceding in this worksheet

(L) Amounts in this section, for the purpose of simplicity, are based on when the payments are made.

(M) This is the amount of cash being consumed, and eventually generated by your business. The more time periods you add to the projection, the better your understanding of cash consumed and generated by your business.

(N) Total to date after the first six months is (255): (115) + (102) + (38).

(O) Exclude loans for land, building, and equipment that, for the purpose of simplicity, are accounted for in the Investment in Business section of this worksheet.

(P) The amounts on this line cannot ever be negative and should have a reserve for unexpected occurrences.

- Include a budget for the Most-Likely-Case scenario.
- Include a projected income statement and balance sheet for the first two or three years, based on the budget above.
- Accompanying Documents, such as the following, should usually be included at the end:
  - Strategic plan
  - Owners' resumes
  - All legal agreements in force or anticipated to be in force, including letters of intent and supplier commitments
  - Owners' personal financial statements
  - Licenses and Permits

Financing Your Business

Banks are in the business of loaning money to businesses that need to finance short-term investments and long-term investments, where the money loaned is relatively safe and there is a good chance that the investment will generate enough money to repay the loan on time with interest. An example of short-term financing is a loan to cover a seasonal build up of inventory and then the resulting receivables. An example of long-term financing is a loan to finance the expansion of sales into another country, which can involve hiring additional salespeople, setting up an office, and paying for an advertising campaign. From the bank's point of view, loans for a startup business are risky because the business does not have a record of success and the bank could lose part of its money in the event that the startup fails. The business plan in the preceding section of this chapter is the main thing bankers want to see when they are evaluating a startup business's loan request.

The other thing lenders are concerned about with a startup business is what collateral will be used to secure the loan, as follows:

- Land and buildings can be used as collateral up to the net amount the bank would get in the event of foreclosure and sale.
- Equipment can usually be leased or financed 100% from the seller, which is more than the bank will most likely finance.
- Inventory can be used as collateral up to the net amount the bank would receive in the event the bank took possession and sold it. When your suppliers give you open credit, they are in effect financing part of your investment in inventory.
- Accounts receivable can be used as collateral up to an amount the bank could collect if the bank took ownership.

- Investments to pay for both startup costs and the initial operating losses do not produce any assets that can be used as collateral. Banks will not usually finance these costs without a personal guarantee from someone, ideally the owner, who has the assets to cover the loan amount.

Bank loans often include covenants that put restrictions on things like how low your working capital can go and how much the owners can withdraw from the business. These covenants are usually negotiable; getting the restriction reduced is much easier before you sign the paperwork than after you sign.

There are sources of financing other than banks, as listed below. Ideally, you can get the financing you need without giving up any ownership in your business.

- Bring in another owner who will pay for a percentage ownership in your company.
- Borrow money from friends and relatives. Make sure they know how risky it is. If your business fails, bank loans will usually have to be repaid first.
- Get extended payment terms from suppliers that allow you to sell the finished goods and collect the money before paying the supplier. While this is unusual, it does not hurt to ask. Suppliers may be willing to do this if you give them a secured interest in their inventory and agree to always buy the inventory from them. Having a purchase order or similar commitment from your customer will help convince your suppliers that they will eventually be paid.
- Get customers to pay in advance. While this is unusual, it does not hurt to ask. Customers may be willing to do this in exchange for a reduced selling price.
- Venture capitalists and insurance companies will loan money for deals, but they often require a partial ownership in the company.

Financial Software

For invoicing customers, paying bills, keeping the financial records, and preparing monthly financial statements, you can buy some software such as Microsoft® Office Small Business Accounting or QuickBooks® and do it yourself. These software packages have companion software for payroll, income taxes, and basic enterprise resource planning.

Enterprise Resource Planning (ERP) Software

The more complex your business gets, the more likely you will need to get software to manage your operations. One of the names for this type of business software is Enterprise Resource Planning (ERP). ERP software links together the different parts of your business and covers the entire business process from the customer's original inquiry through payment of the invoice. With ERP software, automatically generated lead-time projections for customer orders will be close to the actual lead-times and purchase order requirements will be automatically generated based on incoming orders, available inventory on hand, lead-times, safety stock, and other relevant information. The simpler your products are, and the less variations that you sell, the easier it is to get by with a bare-bones low-cost ERP system. For example, inventoried parts you will continue to use and sell can be managed by just putting a card in the inventory location that says replenish stock when the number of parts falls below a predetermined level. You can learn about available software by reading articles and advertisements in trade magazines for your industry, talking to others who have businesses similar to yours, and attending trade shows for your industry. Buying a generic software package and hiring someone to customize it is expensive, and the expense usually ends up being ongoing. When your ERP software no longer meets your needs, replace it. Some software packages have links built in that can allow visitors to your web site to access information on inventory levels and on the status of orders they have placed. At a minimum, your software needs to provide the information and control necessary for you to be sure of the following:

- Make sure you are paid the correct price for everything that goes to customers, unless you specifically say it is "no charge." Amounts not paid for at delivery must go into the accounts receivable listing. All supporting documents for the accounts receivable, such as signed Bill of Lading and customer purchase order, must be readily available. Accounts receivable listing needs to be organized, so invoices not paid by the due date can be easily identified. Bad debts should be aggressively pursued. As a last resort, use a collection agency that is only paid a percentage of the amount collected. Typically, collection agencies get 25%–40% of the amount collected.

- Make sure your invoices look professional, as they have an impact on what your customers think about your business.

- Make sure you charge sales tax whenever applicable, as you could be stuck paying the tax out of your own pocket.

- Make sure you pay no more than the correct amount for all expenses. Amounts not paid for at delivery should go into the accounts payable listing along with due date. Accounts payable listing needs to be easily sorted by due date.

- Make sure the change in total cash and marketable securities on your books for any period equals everything you were paid for less everything you paid for, plus any changes in financing for and investments in your business. When you withdraw cash without recording it as an expense, consider it a change in the amount you have invested in your business. Monthly, the total cash on your books should be reconciled to the bank statement account balances. Cash is very important to monitor because (1) it is by far the most frequently stolen significant business asset and (2) cash problems are often the first sign of profitability problems.

- Make sure incoming orders are input and processed properly so you can accurately project shipment dates, meet customer expectations, and issue invoices without any problems.
- Make sure inventory records are maintained in such a manner that at anytime you can physically count some or the entire inventory and have a book balance that your count should equal.

Payroll

Payroll can be very complicated and small errors can cause major problems. I recommend always using a payroll service. Based on my experience, I would start by talking to ADP (Automated Data Processing Inc.). ADP can be an expensive alternative if your company is very small. Your payroll service needs to be able to do the following, at a minimum:

- Prepare and be responsible for all payroll related forms and other information that are submitted to governmental agencies
- Prepare paychecks and handle direct deposits
- Withhold all taxes and submit them to applicable government agencies
- Calculate and pay all employer's payroll taxes such as unemployment compensation, social security, and Medicare
- Break down labor by department and by job
- Take care of garnishments totally, where all you do is give the payroll service all paperwork you receive
- Prepare year-end W-2s
- Help you set up all necessary accounts at government agencies
- Administer section 125 Cafeteria Plans
- Explain miscellaneous payroll subjects such as the following:
    - When overtime and double pay are required
    - How to respond to claims for unemployment compensation
    - Other government rules and regulations that apply to payroll and fringe benefits

Depending upon how big your company is, you may want a payroll service that can also do the following:

- Make all the payroll disbursements from its own bank account, deduct the total amount directly from your bank account, and prepare the month-end payroll journal entry that should be transmitted to you. This will make reconciling your payroll bank account much easier and will help ensure that payroll expenses are recorded correctly.
- Calculate, and show on the paychecks, how much unused vacation and sick pay each employee has
- Interface with the time keeping system, so the time-clock information can be automatically downloaded into the payroll system and the time-clock punches can be printed on the check stubs
- Manage your 401(k) plan, including year-end discrimination testing, which would simplify the administration of this employee benefit
- Interface with your human resource software
- Handle unemployment compensation claims
- Arrange training in the following areas:
    - Sexual harassment
    - Equal employment opportunity
    - Family and medical leave
    - Employee personnel files
    - Disciplinary Policy
    - Nepotism and fraternization

Insurance

For insurance, contact at least two separate insurance agencies and have them bid on all the insurance you will need. Tell them that the insurance companies need to be "A" or "A+" rated. In addition, the liability and workers compensation insurance companies need to provide free loss prevention consulting to show you how to minimize risks. Every year you should have at least two insurance agencies submit bids for your business. Make sure you request information on losses from your current agent in plenty of time, possibly three or four months before renewal, so the loss information will be available for other agencies that are bidding for your business. Ask the other agencies what information they need and the maximum time your current insurance company can take to provide the information.

The different types of insurance you need to discuss with your agent are listed below. Higher deductible levels, where applicable, can keep small claims from getting into your loss information that insurance companies use in the future to set the rates in their bids.

- Property — Mortgage holders will require this. Make sure the insurance pays *replacement value* in case of a loss.
- Business Interruption — This will reimburse you for lost profits if certain events keep you from doing business.
- Automobile — Businesses should normally have higher coverage limits than individuals.
- Workers Compensation — The law requires this coverage if you have any employees. This insurance pays for any harm that comes to your employees because of employment by you.
- Health Insurance — You may be required by law to provide this for your employees.
- Product Liability — This protects you in case someone is injured by one of your products or services.
- General Liability — This protects you if your business injures someone.
- Fidelity and Surety — This coverage is for employees who handle cash, marketable securities, and similar assets. It protects against theft and negligence by employees.
- Life insurance on key employees — This can cover the negative effect on your business if a key employee dies.
- Life insurance on your life — This insurance should be owned by those who would inherit your business in the event you die. They would then have the option to invest the money in the business or sell the business and keep the money.

Legal Matters

For legal matters, contact acquaintances who have businesses and ask for the names of good business attorneys. Possibly, contact the local bar association to get the names of a few attorneys who (1) specialize in starting up a business and (2) will talk with you for 30 minutes at a minimal cost. Ask each attorney for the price to register your company name and trademarks or service marks as well as to set up and register your business as required by federal, state, and local governments. Ask if there is anything else you need to do from a legal point of view, and get the price to do it. Read the following concerning legal structures for businesses, and discuss your tentative choice with each attorney.

- Sole Proprietorship is a business owned by one person. This form of business has the least governmental restrictions, which makes it the easiest to set up and operate. Profits are just passed to the owner and taxed on the owner's personal tax return. A big disadvantage is that the owner is personally liable for business debts including judgments that result from a lawsuit. The other big disadvantages are that (1) banks are less likely to loan money to a sole proprietorship and (2) investors cannot buy a piece of the business.

- Partnerships are similar to a sole proprietorship except they have more than one owner. Partnerships need to have a partnership agreement that specifies each partner's required investment, compensation, percentage share of profits and losses, and authority. The agreement should specify how to handle disputes and provide a procedure for changing and dissolving the partnership. Limited partners, as opposed to general partners, can have their liability limited to the amount of their investment as long as they are not involved in running the business.
- "C" Corporations are subject to double taxation; the corporation pays income tax and investors pay income tax on any dividends. In addition, they need to be approved by a state government and registered with the federal government. Corporations have many government regulations that make them expensive to set up and to operate. A big advantage of this type of business is that the owners (stockholders) are not liable for the debts of the corporation; the most they can lose is their investment in the corporation's stock. Another advantage is that banks are more likely to loan money and investors can easily buy and sell shares of stock. It should be noted that officers of the corporation could be held liable to stockholders and to the government for misconduct.
- Subchapter "S" Corporations are similar to "C" Corporations except that they are not subject to double taxation, are limited in size, and have some restrictions on their type of activity. Income is passed to owners, similar to a partnership.
- Limited Liability Company (LLC) and Limited Liability Partnership (LLP) are business structures that provide some protection for the owners.

Your attorney should read all legal agreements before you sign them or within the time period the agreement allows you to void the agreement without penalty.

An example of a legal agreement your attorney should read is your lease. Your attorney can explain how your share of property taxes, repairs, maintenance, and insurance will be calculated. In addition, your attorney may suggest that the lease contain the following provisions:

- No Disturbance Clause — This will protect you from having to move or sign a new lease if the property is sold.
- Exclusivity Provision — This will keep any competitors of yours from renting other units in the facility.

- Right of First Refusal — This allows you to rent any vacant space in the building before it is offered to the general public. Your lease terms and costs for the space should be the same as for the general public.
- Sublet Provision — This will allow you to sublease your unit to others, without permission from the property owner. This can be an important provision if the lease is for a long time and you may want to move.

Franchises

With a franchise, you (the franchisee) pay for the land, building, equipment, inventory, supplies, and other expenses. The franchiser directs where the money goes, takes care of all the details, and provides you with instructions and training on how to operate the business. The franchiser then usually gets a share of your profits but none of your losses. Big name franchises have a high success rate because they have a proven business system.

Before investing in a franchise, you should consider the following list. The more money you are investing, the more important it is to thoroughly consider all of the following:

- Is there anything in the Disclosure Document that you or your franchise attorney sees as a possible risk? You should be able to determine (1) if the franchiser is strong financially, (2) the startup and operating costs, and (3) if there are any lawsuits against the franchiser. Contact some of the franchisees, not necessarily the ones the franchiser says to contact, and ask them if they have any regrets, if the franchiser followed through on all promises, and for advice you should follow.
- Are the products and services right for you?
- Is there a proven market in your area?
- What kind of competition is in your area?
- What is the size of your exclusive territory?
- Does the franchiser make more money from you being a successful franchisee or from you buying the franchise?

Chapter 2

Evaluating an Opportunity to Buy a Business

Buying a business can be a quicker way to the so-called real American dream (having your own successful business) than starting a business, but it is not necessarily an easier road to follow. This chapter is divided into the sections listed below.

- Pitfalls of Buying a Business
- Finding a Business to Buy
- Evaluating a Business (Due Diligence)
- Determining the Value of a Business
- Different Ways to Purchase a Business
- Making an Offer
- Closing the Sale
- Financing the Purchase

Be sure to read Book One and the preceding chapter before buying a business.

Pitfalls of Buying a Business

There are many potential pitfalls when buying a business. These pitfalls include the following:

- The owner of the business may know things about the future of the business that you may not find out about before buying the business. Possibly, major customers have started to shift some of their purchases to competitors and the products of the business for sale will not be able to compete in the long term. Possibly, the business for sale pursued long-term marketing and manufacturing strategies that were radically different from competitors, and the competitors' strategies have just started a long-term shift in the market away from the business for sale. Possibly, there are favorable (1) agreements with suppliers and customers or (2) leases that will not be renewed with such favorable terms. Possibly, a planned widening of the street will create a center island that automobiles on the other side of the street cannot cross.

- The owner of the business may have cut expenses during the last year or two for things that will negatively affect profit after the business is sold. Examples of these types of expenses include advertising, catalogs, maintenance, and non-direct-labor personnel costs. Cuts in non-direct-labor personnel costs could include vacant positions not filled as well as cuts in compensation and benefits. As the buyer of the business, you will get the negative effect of these cuts. In addition, any resumption of these expenditures will result in expenses you did not anticipate.

- For retail business there may be negative goodwill in the neighborhood or changes in the neighborhood, such as increased crime or loss of parking spaces that will reduce the number of shoppers. In addition, the building lease may not be renewed or a major competitor may be moving in across the street.

- Key employees such as a sales manager, who the customers will follow, or an engineering manager, who has a good relationship with customers, may have left the business to work for a competitor.

- The business may have grown as large as it can with the abilities of its employees and the capability of its business software. Upgrading employees and implementing new business software are two difficult and costly things to accomplish. If either of these two things is not accomplished properly, it could be a disaster for the business.

- Union organizing may have just begun and there may be a high level of animosity between the current business owner and the employees.

- Maybe there is a pending EPA (Environmental Protection Agency) or OSHA (Occupational Safety & Health Administration) issue that will likely result in an expensive clean up and an expensive change in operations.

- Maybe the most expensive piece of manufacturing equipment is too worn to be able to hold the tolerances that customers demand.

Finding a Business to Buy

Finding a business to buy can be very time consuming. After you determine your general criteria (the types, sizes, and conditions of the businesses you would consider buying), pursue some or all of the following sources to find prospective candidates to purchase:

- Sunday newspapers in large cities and The Wall Street Journal have businesses for sale. Libraries have other publications that list businesses for sale. Trade publications also list businesses for sale.
- Accountants and attorneys who have clients in the type of business you are looking for may know about some suitable businesses for sale. Make sure the accountants and attorneys know that you have an adequate net worth, understand what is involved with buying a business, and will likely use their services when you buy a business.
- Business brokers generally sell small businesses. These brokers work for and are paid a commission by the seller. Commission is around 10% of the selling price.
- Merger and acquisition specialists can help you find businesses with sales over $100 million. These specialists work for you and are paid a fee by you. Fee is around 5% of the selling price. In addition, these specialists are usually capable of and willing to help with both the purchase process and financing. You may have to pay a search fee if you do not end up buying one of the businesses the merger and acquisition specialist finds for you.

Note: Every business you look at should provide basic information you can use to determine if the business appears to meet your general criteria for purchasing.

Evaluating a Business (Due Diligence)

Evaluating a business (due diligence) is the first thing you want to pursue after identifying a potential business that appears to meet your general criteria for purchasing. Due diligence involves the following:

- Get a detailed overview of the business in each of the following areas:
  - History
  - Legal structure
  - Owners
  - Strategic plan, or whatever information is available concerning information that goes into a strategic plan — See the Strategic Planning section of the Evaluating an Opportunity to Start a Business chapter.
  - Facilities and equipment, with information concerning what is owned and what is leased — Get a copy of all financing agreements and leases. For owned assets, determine if any remaining mortgages or other financing payments extend past the business's need for the asset. If any payments go beyond the business's need, try to determine if the asset could be sold when it is no longer needed, for an amount that would cover the remaining

payments. For leased assets, determine if any leases go beyond the business's need; if any do go beyond, try to determine if you could then sublease them to someone else. Also, make sure the lease payment amounts are reasonable. Possibly, the building is being leased from the owner of the business at an excessively high payment amount for a long period of time. The selling price of the business needs to be adjusted down for financing and lease payments that go beyond the business's need and also for the excessive portion of any lease payment amounts.
- Personnel, including organizational chart with job descriptions, pay rate, and length of time in the position — For the top positions in the organizational chart, try to find out about everyone who left the business recently. Ask why they left, how long they were with the business, and if they went to a competitor. Find out about non-direct-labor positions that were usually filled during the last three years but are currently vacant. Find out about cuts in pay and benefits, as well as any delayed pay increases. Find out about trade union activity.
- Total expenses in each of the last three years for maintenance activities as well as for advertising, catalogs, and other marketing activities
- Measurement system for quality and efficiency that show trends during the last few years
- Business software and how well it works
- Sales credits as a percentage of sales and how it has changed during the last three years
- Pending legal matters, including EPA & OSHA issues

- Review the balance sheet, as follows:
  - Accounts Receivable — Get an explanation for unpaid invoices that are 60 days or more past their due date. Find out how credit is granted. Determine if the reserve for bad debts is adequate. Review the business's procedure for properly invoicing everything that should be invoiced as well as the procedure for pursuing past due accounts. Unpaid invoices that are 90 days or more past their due date are excessively past due and should be considered uncollectible.
  - Inventory — For every part in inventory, project forecasted usage for the next 12 months, as follows. Get the usage during the last 12 months and adjust it for differences between sales during the last 12 months and forecasted sales for the next 12 months. There is no easy way to do this; you will just have to do the best you can with the available information. As an alternative, get the BOM (Bill of Materials) for all items that are in the sales forecast and multiply the quantities in each BOM by the sales forecast quantity for the next 12 months. Inventory for any part in excess of 12 months' future usage should be considered as excess/obsolete and paid for as follows. Tell the seller of the business that you will pay for the excess/obsolete inventory if and when you use it. Possibly, put some money

in an escrow account to pay for any of the excess/obsolete inventory you use. If future usage is too hard to get, offer to pay for all inventory used during the next 18 months. Pay for part of the inventory when you buy the business and use an escrow account to pay the difference between what you use during the first 18 months and what you originally paid. To audit the inventory, select some of the parts with a high dollar value and some with high usage. For all items selected, verify the quantity on hand, usage, and the price per each. Identifying the products that the parts go into and checking sales of the product can verify the usage. The price per each can be verified against the latest purchase price plus inbound freight. For items with a high dollar value, make sure the actual physical parts (1) match the description in the inventory list and (2) are new and unused. Determine if the inventory on hand is adequate to competitively meet customer needs; if not, you may have to increase inventory levels.

- Property, Plant, and Equipment — Is it everything you will need in the foreseeable future? Will you need to spend money to get these assets ready for your use? If applicable, are all mortgages assumable and leases transferable? Determine how the book value (purchase price less depreciation) of owned assets compares to their market value.
- Intangible Assets (patents, trademarks, and goodwill) — Determine how their book value (purchase price less amortization) compares to the value that the intangible assets will be to you.
- Current Liabilities — Get an explanation for anything that is 45 or more days past the due date. Make sure accrued expenses, such as payroll and income taxes, are included. Check the accrued wages by looking at the dollar amount and pay period of the first payroll paid after the balance sheet date. Ask for a list of potential liabilities not included, such as items in dispute and contingent liabilities such as possible pending legal action.
- Long-Term Liabilities — Determine the interest rates, whether there are any prepayment penalties, and when the principal amounts are due. If a debt is not assumable or is accelerated upon sale of the business, the whole amount may be due upon sale of the business. Also, determine if the pension plan is over or under funded.

- Review the income statements, as follows:
  - Sales — Make sure sales only include the sale of items normally sold by the business. Other sales and income should be excluded from the operations section of the income statement.
  - Expenses — Make sure expenses are included in the same period as the sales they were incurred to generate.
  - Other Income and Expenses — Make sure operating expenses are not included in other income and expenses, which would overstate income from operations.

- Review the cash flow statements to see if operations generate positive or negative cash flow. Net cash from operations is at the top of the statement and excludes net cash from investments and net cash from financing.

Notes concerning your financial statement review of the balance sheet, income statement, and cash flow statement are listed below:

- Look at the last three or more years' financial statements.

- Financial statements with an unqualified opinion, signed by a licensed CPA are ideal for you to review with your CPA. Be sure to read all notes that go with the financial statements and understand the basis upon which the financial statements were prepared, which (unless specified otherwise in the opinion) is usually Generally Accepted Accounting Principals (GAAP), consistently applied. If the opinion is qualified, adverse, or there is a disclaimer, show it to your CPA and ask for an explanation. Sometimes CPAs review and compile financial statements, which means that the CPA has not checked the financial statements and is not expressing an opinion. If the financial statements do not have an unqualified opinion signed by a licensed CPA, ask for a copy of the federal income tax returns that your CPA can reconcile to the financial statements.

  Note: Companies in compliance with the Sarbanes-Oxley Act of 2002 (SOX), will have two other opinions from their auditors. SOX Section 404 requires the auditor's opinion on management's assessment of the effectiveness of the company's internal controls over financial reporting. SOX Section 103 requires the auditor's opinion on the effectiveness of the internal controls over financial reporting. Problems with internal controls over financial reporting of a company you are analyzing should be discussed with your CPA.

- Analyze the financial statements and look for negative and positive trends. Try to project how these trends will affect income and cash flow in the future.

Note: In order to get access to the confidential business information necessary to do due diligence, you will need to sign a confidentiality agreement and show a personal financial statement. In the confidentiality agreement, you agree not to reveal confidential information to others. The personal financial statement is to show that you have the wealth necessary to buy the business.

Determining the Value of a Business

The dollar value for you of a business is based on your projected income and cash flow that results from buying the business. This value to you should be the maximum you should be willing to pay. Be careful about increasing this value (the maximum price you are willing to pay) based upon how good you will feel when you own your own business. Use projected financial information to determine the value of the business to you, as follows:

- Set up three worksheets, one for each of the following: income statement, balance sheet, and cash flow statement.

- Start with three columns on each worksheet that contain the last three years' actual financial statements, with the most recent year on the right. The information in these three columns needs to be the most reliable information available, which is why you should thoroughly go through the due diligence process before determining the business's value.

- Add ten columns to the right side of each worksheet, one for each of the first ten years that follow the most recent actual year on the worksheet.

- Make three copies of each worksheet. Label one set of financial statements Worst-Case scenario, label one set Most-Likely-Case scenario, and label the last set Best-Case scenario.

- Fill out the three sets of projected financial statements excluding the purchase price you will pay and any other money you may have to put into the business, see Notes concerning the ten-year financial projections later in this section of the chapter.

- If you want cash generated by the business during the first ten years to pay for the purchase of the business, see how much of a loan you could get assuming all and only the cash flows in the ten-year Worst-Case scenario get used to repay the loan. Calculate the projected loan amount by discounting the future cash flows (projected loan repayments) to their present value using a discount rate equal to the prime rate + 2%. For example, if the discount rate is 6% and the future cash flow is five years in the future, divide the future cash flow by 1.06 five times. This projected loan amount would then be the amount you should be willing to pay. Your actual loan amount would be this projected loan amount less your down payment. Your down payment would be the money you have available to invest in the business less at least one month's projected operating expenses. As soon as the loan(s) to buy the business is paid off, the positive cash flows will all go to you and to any other owners. You can use the Most-Likely-Case scenario cash flow instead of Worst-Case scenario, but it will be more risky.

- If the ten-year projected cash flow in the Best-Case scenario requires more cash at the beginning than the other two scenarios, possibly caused by cash needed for expansion, make sure the funds will be available.

- Notes concerning the ten-year financial projections are as follows:
  - See the Cash Flow section of the Evaluating an Opportunity to Start a Business chapter for information on projecting cash flows.
  - The more you know about both the business and the industry it is in, the better your projected financial statements should be. In this regard, being an employee, supplier, or customer of the business would be beneficial. You

can get information about the industry the business is in from trade magazines, suppliers to the industry, and customers of the industry. With a little research, you should be able to compare the business's operations to operations in general for the industry. The comparison should cover sales growth, product innovations, marketing strategies, and anything else of interest you can find.

- Worst-Case scenario should be reasonable, such as sales growth at one-half of the last three years' actual growth rate, assuming no major changes in the market.
- Most-Likely-Case scenario should be reasonable, with an equal chance of actual results being favorable or unfavorable.
- Best-Case scenario should also be reasonable. If your sales projections are very high, be sure to include all supporting expenditures such as an expanded facility, more office employees, and higher marketing expenses.
- Debt the seller will pay for from proceeds of the sale should be moved from the liabilities and added to the equity in the three years' actual sections of the worksheets. This is done to exclude the applicable principal and interest payments from the ten-year cash flow projection.
- Any long-term debts other than mortgages, such as bank loans or bonds, that will not be paid off in ten years should have an adjusted payment schedule in the ten-year financial projection so that the debt would be paid off in ten years. For mortgages that will not be paid off in ten years, increase the payment amount during the ten-year projection period so that the projected net market value of the mortgaged asset in ten years will at least equal the mortgage's payoff amount.
- Accounts receivable, accounts payable, and inventory in the ten-year projections should usually be the same percentage of sales as in the three years of actual financial statements. Inventories are the most likely exception to this relationship. The actual inventory levels may have been inadequate to meet customer needs, and you may plan to drop some products and add others.
- If additional facilities and equipment will be needed during the ten years, include their cost with financing periods that do not exceed their projected useful lives. Also, include the cost of getting existing facilities and equipment ready for your use.
- Make sure non-operating income in the actual financial statements is included in the other income and expense section of the income statement.
- The actual wages and benefits including entertainment, automobile, and health insurance of the owner should not necessarily be used in the ten-year financial projection. If you plan to run the business, use the wages and benefits you could have earned elsewhere. If you plan to hire someone to run the business, use the wages and benefits you will most likely have to pay.
- Be sure to consider expenses that were inappropriately cut in the last year or two. In addition to resuming these expenses, you may need to spend more

to catch up for the period of time when the expenses were cut. Examples of these types of expenses include maintenance, advertising, catalogs, other marketing expenses, and personnel. Personnel costs may have been cut by not filling vacancies, limiting pay levels, and cutting benefits.

- Possibly, you will have to upgrade current personnel in order to grow the business.
- Possibly, you will have to replace the business software in order to grow the business.
- Possibly, there will be additional expenses to do things like improve product quality and penetrate new markets.
- There could be significant expenses to upgrade facilities and equipment so they comply with OSHA, EPA, or other government regulations.
- There could be increased costs due to union activity.
- Do not forget about income taxes. Be sure that your tax-deductible expenses include an estimate of interest expense on the loan you take out to buy the business. If you will be set up as a sole proprietor, a partnership, an LLC, or an "S" corporation, the business's income and expenses will flow to you and be taxable as personal income. If you will be set up as a regular "C" corporation, have your accountant figure your projected income taxes. For information on the five types of businesses mentioned above, see the Legal Matters section of the Evaluating an Opportunity to Start a Business chapter.

Have a business appraiser give you a valuation of the business. Make sure the appraiser is aware of all the negative information you discovered during due diligence. Reconcile the appraiser's valuation to your projected purchase price that is based on a ten-year cash flow. Never reveal the higher of these two valuation amounts in your negotiations with the seller.

If you are buying a franchise business at a price that is similar to what other similar franchises have been and are projected to sell for, your risk is somewhat reduced.

If you are buying a business for a price equal to the fair market value of the assets less their selling costs and all liabilities, your risk is somewhat reduced. It should be noted that inventory, especially non-commodity parts that are not ready for sale, could be difficult to sell at the cost used for balance sheet valuation; the same holds true for equipment. In addition, accounts receivable may not all be collectible, especially accounts that are past due. On the other hand, the market value of real estate may exceed its balance sheet book value.

The value of the business to the seller/owner is the higher of what others will pay and the financial benefit to the owner of keeping the business. This value is the starting point in determining how low of a selling price the seller will accept.

Theoretically, the selling price of a business should end up being higher than the seller's value of the business and lower than the buyer's value of the business. As discussed later in this chapter, tax and other legal consequences affect how the sale of a business gets set up and the selling price. Sometimes sellers want out quickly and will sell for a low price. Sometimes sellers pretend that they want out quickly, so potential buyers will think the asking price is low.

Different Ways to Purchase a Business

You can purchase a business's non-cash assets or purchase its outstanding common stock. In addition, you can set up the purchase so the purchase price is somewhat dependent upon the business's earnings after the sale.

When you purchase a business's non-cash assets, the seller pays the liabilities using proceeds from the sale. As the buyer, it is usually best for you to modify this arrangement by paying less and taking responsibility for paying the accounts payable. This modification eliminates the possibility of supplier problems caused by the seller not fully paying all the accounts payable. The buyer's main advantage of purchasing a business's assets, versus buying its common stock, is that the buyer is not taking responsibility for undisclosed and unknown liabilities of the business.

Tax laws, which are always changing, have a big effect on how the purchase of a business's assets should be arranged. Sellers usually want as much of their gain to be capital gains, which have a lower tax rate, rather than ordinary income. For ordinary income, they may want to spread it out, using consulting or covenant not-to-compete agreements, into the future when their tax rate is lower. Buyers usually want to minimize the amount of the purchase price that is not tax deductible, such as land, and quickly expense the rest of the amount paid. The portion of the purchase price attributed to depreciable assets is expensed, as depreciation expense, over the tax life of the assets. Assets with shorter lives, such as most equipment, result in a quicker tax deduction than assets with longer lives, such as buildings and leasehold improvements. The portion of the purchase price paid to the seller under consulting and covenant not-to-compete agreements will be expensed over the term of the agreements. The IRS has complicated restrictions on how the purchase price can be split up, so consult with a tax attorney who specializes in business sales and purchases.

When you purchase a business's common stock, you own the whole business and there is a minimal effect on the business's operations. For the most part, customers and suppliers do not care and usually there is no need to renegotiate legal agreements, like leases, or to re-register with the government to do business. As the buyer, you can protect yourself from undisclosed and unknown liabilities by using an escrow account or by having an indemnification agreement.

Earn-Out purchases lower the risk and lower the upside potential for a buyer of a business. Typically, the buyer pays part of the purchase price up front and then the rest is paid as a percentage of net income for a predetermined number of years. A minimum and maximum can be set up for the amount that is paid as a percentage of net income; this will protect the seller and buyer, respectively. Earn-Outs are a good way to get the former owner to help ensure that the business makes a smooth transition to new ownership.

Making an Offer

Before making an offer, you will need to lower the seller's expectation of the selling price as much as possible. Adjust the business valuation that supports the seller's expected selling price for both the following. First, replace overly optimistic assumptions. Second, factor in everything negative discovered during due diligence. Make sure the seller sees how your adjustments affect the selling price. Keep the negotiations professional. Confrontational negotiations can easily lead to a breakdown in rational decision making.

Hire an attorney who specializes in business sales and purchases to prepare your offer letter and to prepare and review everything else you sign concerning a purchase of a business.

Your offer should be contingent upon you being able to arrange financing, and should contain the following:

- The offer price for the business
- The amount and terms of any financing you want the seller to provide
- A list of assets and liabilities to be purchased, excluding obsolete inventory and excessively past due accounts receivable, both of which are defined in the Evaluating a Business (Due Diligence) section of this chapter
- A breakdown of the offer price to specific assets, which affect the tax consequences of the sale and purchase
- The closing date
- Any conditions of the purchase, such as the following:
    - All legal agreements, such as mortgages and leases, will transfer to buyer, or that buyer can make acceptable alternative arrangements
    - An option to renew any leases be obtained, at acceptable terms
    - All business licenses and registrations will transfer to buyer or that buyer can get the licenses and registrations
    - The business complies with all government regulations, such as zoning — Specifically that there are no governmental actions going on, such as by OSHA or the EPA, that could result in expense to the business.

  - The business facilities pass all required government inspections for sale and required inspections by your lender
  - The bulk transfer requirements of the uniform commercial code will be met, for the sale of business assets as opposed to the sale of common stock
  - The seller has clear and marketable title to all assets being sold
  - Arrangements are in place so all assets are insured before and after the sale
  - Inventory gets counted and valued at the time of the sale
  - All equipment is in good working condition at the time of sale
  - Business will be run until it is sold in a manner that will not hurt its value
  - All legal agreements that will transfer with the sale have been listed, and that no others will be entered into before the sale
  - Information that could not be verified prior to making the offer, such as financial statements, will be verified prior to sale
  - Seller will give buyer all deposits and other unearned income that customers will expect credit for in the future
  - Buyer will pay seller for all prepaid expenses at the time of sale

- Items to be reserved for in an escrow account, such as the following:
  - Liabilities that are undisclosed/unknown
  - Warranty expenses on products produced before the business was sold
  - Taxes due for periods prior to the business's sale
  - Undisclosed defects in business assets, such as governmental actions
  - Excess/Obsolete Inventory
  - Accounts receivable not collected, in excess of the reserve for bad debts

Note: Your offer, as described above, should leave room for negotiations, especially in the offer price.

Closing the Sale

After you and the seller agree to the terms and conditions in your offer letter, the following necessary legal paperwork can be prepared for signature:

- Settlement Statement, similar to when a home is sold, that says who pays what and how the proceeds will be distributed

- Bill of Sale that lists the assets and liabilities that are being transferred

- If the seller is financing part of the sale, the seller will most likely want the following:
  - Promissory Note that has the amount and terms of the financing
  - Security Agreement for the assets being sold, which is like the mortgage on a home
  - Financing Statement so the seller's security in the assets gets recorded with the government, similar to how a mortgage on a home gets recorded

- Escrow Agreement whereby the seller puts funds in an account for a set period of time that will get paid to buyer in the event certain things occur

Financing the Purchase

Financing the purchase of a business can be as simple as the seller financing the portion of the purchase price that the buyer does not have. For other financing arrangements, see the Financing Your Business section of the Evaluating an Opportunity to Start a Business chapter.

Chapter 3

Understanding and Analyzing Financial Statements

This chapter has an example of the three basic financial statements (balance sheet, income statement, and cash flow statement). Each of these financial statements is explained and then analyzed. An example at the end of this chapter shows (1) how some basic financial transactions get reflected in financial statements, (2) how the income statement gets closed out to the balance sheet, and (3) how the cash flow statement is based on transactions posted to the balance sheet and the income statement.

It should be noted that there is no required standardized format for financial statements. Financial statements just need to clearly present all relevant information. It should also be noted that the three basic financial statements were designed to meet the needs of bankers, investors, and tax authorities, not the needs of those who manage businesses. IFRS (International Financial Reporting Standards), as explained at the end of this chapter, is going to change how financial statements are prepared in the U.S., starting with the largest publicly held companies.

Balance Sheet Description — Exhibit 3-1

The balance sheet calculates the equity (book value of investment) by subtracting total liabilities from total assets. The most frequently used account groupings are described and listed below in sections that correspond to the sections of the balance sheet where they are included.

Assets are items that will likely contribute to future economic benefits

- Current assets have a likely contribution to future economic benefits within a year and include the following:
  - Cash includes cash in the bank, in transit to the bank, on hand, and in petty cash.
  - Marketable securities are short-term investments that can easily be converted into cash.
  - Accounts receivable represent the amount that is expected to be received for sales that have not been paid for.
  - Inventory is purchased materials, possibly with labor added, that is expected to be sold to customers.
  - Prepaid expenses are expenses for future periods that have already been paid.

- Long-term investments include money loaned to or invested in other companies in order to influence their operations.

- Property, plant, and equipment include all tangible non-current assets used in the business, which for the most part is comprised of land, buildings, and equipment.

- Intangible assets are usually comprised of goodwill, patents, and trademarks. Goodwill can contribute to future economic benefits when there is a loyal customer base. Patents and trademarks contribute to future economic benefits by providing exclusive rights.

- Other non-current assets include prepayments and deferrals for matters involving operations more than a year in the future.

Liabilities are items that will likely consume some future economic benefits

- Current liabilities have a likely sacrifice of future economic benefits within a year and include the following:
  - Accounts payable are the unpaid balances for materials and supplies already received.
  - Accrued expenses are expenses, like salaries and commissions that have been incurred but not paid.
  - Unearned revenue and deposits are amounts received from vendors for goods and services that have not yet been provided.
  - The current portion of long-term debt is the portion that matures in the current period.
  - Income tax payable is for income tax that has been incurred and will be paid in the current period.

- Long-term liabilities have a likely sacrifice of future economic benefits that will not occur within a year and include bank loans, bonds, and mortgages.

- Deferred income taxes result from timing differences, where the income to be taxed has been included in the financial statement income but has not yet been taxed.

Equity is the net book value of the owners' investment

- Common Stock issued at par value is the total shares issued multiplied by their par value. Par value of the stock is the price that was set when the company authorized issuance of the stock.

- Additional paid-in capital is any amount paid by investors that exceeded the par value.

- Retained earnings are earnings of the company that have not been distributed to the owners. Distributions of earnings to owners are made in the form of dividends.

Income Statement Description — Exhibit 3-2

The income statement calculates the net profit earned in the period. This is the amount that (1) is added to the equity at the end of the period; (2) the banker uses, along with cash flow, to judge the company's ability to repay loans; and (3) is basically used to calculate income taxes. The two most important rules concerning income statements are as follows. First, make sure all expenses are recorded in the same accounting period as the sales to which they relate. Second, remember that you cannot have a reliable income statement until you have a reliable balance sheet. The income statement starts with income and expenses from operations followed by other income and expenses and then income taxes.

- Income is generally not recognized until (1) ownership of the item being sold has passed or service has been rendered and (2) the seller has done everything needed to have a valid accounts receivable for the sale. Returns, allowances, discounts, rebates, and bad debt expenses usually are subtracted from gross sales to get net sales.

- Expenses directly related to a sale such as inventory, manufacturing labor, and sales commissions should be included in the same period as the sale. Expenses related to a particular period such as the president's salary, insurance, and rent should be included in the period they were incurred. Expenses are recorded based on dollar cost of the expense, and include the following:
    - Inventory sold to customers. Inventory cost should include inbound freight. If the customer does not pay outbound freight, it should be included in allowances that are subtracted from gross sales to get net sales.
    - Warranty expense should include a reserve (additional expense) to cover future warranty expense on products already sold.

- Wages should be split between manufacturing and overhead based on whether or not the person works in manufacturing. Manufacturing includes everyone who manufactures products as well as inventory control, manufacturing management, industrial engineering, purchasing, quality, and maintenance.
- Depreciation should be charged to the department using the asset being depreciated. In the case of building depreciation, it can be split up to departments based on square footage that each department takes up. Depreciation expense is the cost of tangible assets spread out over their useful lives.
- Amortization expense is the cost of intangible assets spread out over their useful lives.

- Other income and expenses are incidental gains and losses, which are not part of operations and kept separate so that the income statement can identify income from operations. Incidental gains and losses include gains and losses on the sales of assets not normally sold by the company as well as costs from discontinuing some of the company's operations.

  Other income and expenses on the income statement should be used for all and only non-operating income and expense. Too many publicly traded companies misuse this section to overstate income from operations.

- Income tax expense is the last expense listed on the income statement, so the income statement can identify net income before income taxes.

Cash Flow Statement Description — Exhibit 3-3

The cash flow statement breaks the change in cash into the three following sections:

- Net cash from operations equals net income plus non-cash expenses (depreciation, amortization, and the like) minus the increase in non-cash current assets and plus the increase in current liabilities.

- Net cash from investments in the business is the change in net cash tied up in land, buildings, and equipment. When the purchase of these assets is financed with long-term debt, the purchase and the financing are treated as separate transactions. The full cost of the asset goes in this section and the long-term amount financed goes in the following section.

- Net cash from financing is the increase in long-term debt plus additional investments by owners minus dividends paid out.

Note: References to "cash" above refer to cash and marketable securities.

Balance Sheet Financial Analysis — Exhibit 3-1

- Current ratio is current assets divided by current liabilities. The 1.86 current ratio in this exhibit (206,000 divided by 111,000) is between 1.5 (minimum ratio for a company like this) and 2.0 (ideal ratio for a company like this). Current assets less current liabilities equal working capital.

- Quick ratio is the same as the current ratio, except non-liquid assets such as inventory and prepaid expenses are excluded. The 1.26 quick ratio in this exhibit (40,000 + 10,000 + 90,000 all divided by 111,000) is greater than the 1.0 minimum ratio for a company like this.

- Days' Sales Outstanding (DSO) in accounts receivable is a measurement, using averages, of how many days' sales are unpaid. It is calculated by dividing accounts receivable by average daily sales (total annual sales divided by 365 days). If your invoice terms are "net due in 30 days," a DSO of 40 is good and a DSO of 60 is not good. The DSO at Dec. 31, 2009 in this exhibit is 55 (90,000 accounts receivable divided by 1,644 average daily sales).

- Inventory turnover is a measurement, using averages, of how long inventory is held before being sold. It is calculated by dividing cost of goods sold for the year by average inventory. Many factors affect this measurement such as lead-times from your suppliers, length of time to convert the purchased inventory into finished goods, and the requirements of your customers for quick delivery. The 7.5 inventory turnover in this exhibit (451,000 cost of goods sold divided by an assumed average inventory of 60,000) is usually considered good. An inventory turnover of 6 means that you are holding enough inventory for an average 2 months' sales (12 months divided by the 6), which is about the most you want to be holding. If the finished goods in inventory exclude any of the items in cost of goods sold, these excluded items should be subtracted out of the 451,000 in this calculation. Inventory turnover on raw material inventory is average raw material inventory divided by 366,000 (the raw material portion of the 451,000). Inventory turnover should theoretically be based on future goods sold in the time period the inventory will be consumed.

Income Statement Financial Analysis — Exhibit 3-2

- Contribution margin percentage of gross sales is 26.3% (158,000 contribution margin divided by 600,000 gross sales, converted to a percent). Contribution margin is gross sales less variable expenses (returns, allowances, discounts, rebates, bad debts, inventory consumed, warranty expenses, manufacturing direct-labor wages, and sales commissions). All expenses are either variable, which means they go up or down as sales go up or down, respectively, or they are fixed, which means they remain unchanged while sales fluctuate within the expected range. Variable and fixed expenses are explained in the Variable and

Fixed Costs section of the Financial Decision Making chapter. Contribution margin percentage of sales is important because it shows the effect on income of changes in sales, as follows. A 20% increase in gross sales (120,000 increase) will more than double income from operations. The 120,000 multiplied by 26.3% results in a 31,560 increase in income from operations.

- Breakeven point is the sales level where income equals expenses. The breakeven point can be calculated by dividing the 128,000 of fixed costs by the 26.3% contribution margin percent, which results in breakeven point sales of just less than 487,000.
- Income from operations excludes non-operating income and expenses; therefore, it is a better measurement of the business operations' profitability than net income before income tax.
- Income from operations as a percentage of sales varies significantly among different types of businesses and is best used for comparing to prior years and to averages within your type of business. The 5% (30,000 divided by 600,000) income from operations as a percentage of sales is at the bottom of the 5% to 10% range that could be typical for a business like this.
- Return on equity is net income after tax as a percentage of equity and is a measurement of what the owners earned on their investment. The 17% (24,000 divided by 142,000) return on equity is in line with what most investors are looking for, when you consider the risk involved. Differences between the market value and net book value of land and buildings are not in net income and consequently not in the return on equity calculation.

Cash Flow Statement Financial Analysis — Exhibit 3-3

- Total net cash from operations is the most important number on this statement. If net income, with non-cash expenses added back in, does not significantly exceed the increase in non-cash working capital, then there is a potential big problem that needs to be analyzed.
- The total net cash from financing in excess of total net cash from investments in the business of 7,000 (14,000 less 7,000) is nothing more than cash from borrowing or issuing common stock in excess of the cash needed for investments in the business. The more that cash invested in land, buildings, and equipment comes from operations rather than financing, the better.

Note: The Cash Flow section of the Evaluating an Opportunity to Start a Business chapter has an example of how to project cash flow for a startup business.

Note: References to "cash" above refer to cash and marketable securities.

Exhibit 3-1

XYZ INC
BALANCE SHEET
Year Ended Dec. 31, 2009

Assets

Current Assets:			
Cash		40,000	
Marketable Securities		10,000	
Total Accounts Receivable	91,000		
Provision for Bad Debts	(1,000)		
Accounts Receivable		90,000	
Finished Goods	55,000		
Raw Materials	3,000		
Work In Process	2,000		
Inventory		60,000	
Prepaid Insurance	2,000		
Prepaid Rent	4,000		
Prepaid Expense		6,000	
Total Current Assets			206,000
Property, Plant, and Equipment:			
Land (Cost)		40,000	
Building (Cost)	90,000		
Building Accumulated Depreciation	(10,000)		
Building		80,000	
Equipment (Cost)	30,000		
Equipment Accumulated Depreciation	(10,000)		
Equipment		20,000	
Total Property, Plant, and Equipment			140,000
Intangible Assets:			
Goodwill		3,000	
Patents		7,000	
Trademarks		10,000	
Total Intangible Assets			20,000
Total Assets			366,000

Liabilities

Current Liabilities:		
Accounts Payable	60,000	
Accrued Expenses	25,000	
Unearned Revenue and Deposits	13,000	
Current Portion of Long-Term Debt	5,000	
Income Tax Payable	8,000	
Total Current Liabilities		111,000
Long-term Liabilities:		
Bank Loan	60,000	
Mortgage	50,000	
Total Long-Term Debt		110,000
Deferred Income Taxes		3,000
Total Liabilities		224,000

Equity

Common Stock Issued at Par Value	120,000
Additional Paid In Capital	10,000
Retained Earnings	12,000
Total Equity	142,000
Total Liabilities and Equity	366,000

Exhibit 3-2

XYZ INC
INCOME STATEMENT
Year Ended Dec. 31, 2009

Gross Sales			600,000
Returns and Allowances		6,000	
Discounts and Rebates		5,000	
Bad Debts		4,000	
Total Deductions			15,000
Net Sales			585,000
Cost of Goods Sold:			
Beginning Raw Material Inventory	55,000		
Ending Raw Material Inventory	(60,000)		
Inventory Purchases	369,000		
Inbound Freight	2,000		
Inventory Consumed		366,000	
Warranty Expense		5,000	
Manufacturing Direct-Labor Wages		50,000	
Manufacturing Depreciation		6,000	
Other Fixed Manufacturing Expenses		24,000	
Total Costs of Goods Sold			451,000
Gross Margin			134,000
Overhead (non-manufacturing):			
Overhead Wages		60,000	
Overhead Depreciation		3,000	
Interest Expense		2,000	
Intangible Amortization		1,000	
Sales Commission		6,000	
Insurance		8,000	
Other Overhead		24,000	
Total Overhead Expense			104,000
Income from Operations			30,000
Other Income and Expenses:			
Gain on Sale of Building		6,000	
Discontinued Operations		(6,000)	
Total Other Income and Expense			0
Net Income Before Income Tax			30,000
Income Tax Expense			(6,000)
Net Income			24,000
Earnings Per Share (10,000 shares outstanding)			$2.40

Exhibit 3-3

XYZ INC
CASH FLOW STATEMENT
(RECONCILIATION OF NET INCOME TO THE CHANGE IN COMBINED CASH AND MARKETABLE SECURITIES)
Year Ended Dec. 31, 2009

Net Cash from Operations:		
Net Income	24,000	
Depreciation	9,000	
Amortization	1,000	
Increase in Accounts Receivable	(8,000)	
Increase in Inventory	(5,000)	
Increases in Other Non-Cash Current Assets	(2,000)	
Increases in Accounts Payable	6,000	
Increase in Accrued Expenses	2,000	
Increases in Other Current Liabilities	1,000	
Increases in Other Non-Long-Term Debt	0	
Total Net Cash from Operations		28,000
Net Cash from Investments in Business:		
Net Purchases of Property, Plant & Equipment	(7,000)	
Total Net Cash from Investments in Business		(7,000)
Net Cash from Financing:		
Proceeds — Bank Loan	20,000	
Proceeds — Issuance of Common Stock	11,000	
Principal Payment on Mortgage	(5,000)	
Payment of Dividends	(12,000)	
Total Net Cash from Financing		14,000
Total Net Cash from the Above		35,000
Cash:		
Balance at 12/31/08	15,000	
Balance at 12/31/09	50,000	
Change During the Year		35,000

Note: References above to "cash" refer to cash and marketable securities.

Exhibit 3-4 (part 1 of 2)

	See explanation below for each column — (dollars in thousands)									
Balance Sheet:	Beg. Bal.	A	B	C	D	E	F	G	H	I
Cash & Mrkt. Securities	50	12	20	(25)	(5)	(1)		(45)	(6)	
Accounts Receivable	90									80
Inventory	60						50			(45)
Prepaid Expenses	6									
Land	40			10						
Building (Net)	80			30						
Equipment (Net)	20				5					
Intangible Assets	20									
Accounts Payable	(60)						(50)	45		
Accrued Expenses	(25)									
Other Current Liabilities	(26)									
Bank Loan	(60)		(20)							
Mortgage	(50)			(15)						
Deferred Inc. Tax	(3)									
Common Stock	(120)	(10)								
Additional Paid In Cap	(10)	(2)								
Retained Earnings	(12)									
Total Balance Sheet	0									
Income Statement:										
Net Sales										(80)
Inventory Consumed										45
Manufacturing Wages									4	
Manufacturing Depreciation										
Other Fixed Mfgr. Expenses										
Overhead Wages									2	
Overhead Depreciation										
Insurance										
Other Overhead						1				
Other Income & Exp										
Income Tax										
Total Income Statement										
Total of Accounts Above	0	0	0	0	0	0	0	0	0	0
Cash Flow Statement:										
From Operations						(1)		(45)	(6)	
Investment in Business				(40)	(5)					
From Financing		12	20	15						
Change in Cash/Mrkt. Sec		12	20	(25)	(5)	(1)	0	(45)	(6)	0

Beg Balance — Prior period ending balance
A — Sell stock with $10 par value for $12
B — Borrow $20 from bank, long term
C — Buy land and building for $40 ($15 long-term mortgage)
D — Buy equipment for $5
E — Buy office supplies for $1
F — Buy $50 of inventory on account
G — Pay $45 for inventory previously purchased on account
H — Pay wages of $6
I — Sell $45 of inventory for $80, on account

Exhibit 3-4 (part 2 of 2)

	See explanation below for each column — (dollars in thousands)									
Balance Sheet:	J	K	L	M	N	O	P	Q	R	End Bal.
Cash & Mrkt. Securities	70	(2)	(6)			(1)	61		(3)	58
Accounts Receivable	(70)						100			100
Inventory							65			65
Prepaid Expenses			3				9			9
Land							50			50
Building (Net)					(4)		106			106
Equipment (Net)					(4)		21			21
Intangible Assets							20			20
Accounts Payable							(65)			(65)
Accrued Expenses				(3)		(3)	(31)			(31)
Other Current Liabilities							(26)			(26)
Bank Loan							(80)			(80)
Mortgage							(65)			(65)
Deferred Inc. Tax						(2)	(5)			(5)
Common Stock							(130)			(130)
Additional Paid In Cap							(12)			(12)
Retained Earnings							(12)	(6)	3	(15)
Total Balance Sheet										0
Income Statement:										
Net Sales							(80)	80		
Inventory Consumed							45	(45)		
Manufacturing Wages				2			6	(6)		
Manufacturing Depreciation					6		6	(6)		
Other Fixed Mfgr. Expense										
Overhead Wages				1			3	(3)		
Overhead Depreciation					2		2	(2)		
Insurance			3				3	(3)		
Other Overhead							1	(1)		
Other Income & Exp		2					2	(2)		
Income Tax						6	6	(6)		
Total Income Statement							(6)	6		
Total of Accounts Above	0	0	0	0	0	0	0	0	0	0
Cash Flow Statement:										
From Operations	70	(2)	(6)			(1)	9			9
Investment in Business							(45)			(45)
From Financing							47		(3)	44
Change in Cash/Mrkt. Sec	70	(2)	(6)	0	0	(1)	11	0	(3)	8

J — Get paid $70 for inventory previously sold on account
K — Pay interest expense of $2, that was not previously accrued for
L — Pay $6 for current period's and next period's insurance
M — Accrue for earned wages not yet paid of $3
N — Take depreciation expenses for the period of $8
O — Calculate $6 of income taxes. Defer $2, pay $1 owe $3
P — Subtotal trial balance for the period before closing entries. The total of all balance sheet plus income statement accounts should equal $0, as each entry totaled $0. The income statement in this column gets used for the final income statement.
Q — Closing entries to clear income and expense accounts and move the $6 net income to retained earnings.
R — Distribute $3 of retained earnings to owners
End Balance — This final balance for the period gets used for the final balance sheet. Positive balances above for assets show up as positive numbers in the balance sheet. Negative balances above for liabilities and equity also show up as positive numbers in the balance sheet. This is why assets equal liabilities plus equity in the balance sheet while they all add up to zero in the general ledger as shown above.

Financial Statement Transaction Examples — Exhibit 3-4

Exhibit 3-4 shows how 18 basic financial transactions affect the balance sheet, income statement, and the cash flow statement. The following items concern the information presented in this exhibit:

- There is an account set up in the general ledger for everything that goes into the balance sheet and the income statement. All financial transactions that affect the balance sheet and the income statement are posted to the applicable general ledger accounts. Balance sheet accounts include all the different asset accounts such as accounts receivable, liability accounts such as accounts payable, and equity accounts such as retained earnings. Income statement accounts include all the different income accounts such as sales and all the expense accounts such as wages. Preparing the balance sheet and income statement basically involves nothing more than putting in the account balances from the general ledger.
- All financial transactions are posted to at least two accounts in the general ledger, with debits (positive numbers) and offsetting credits (negative numbers). The debits always equal the credits for each transaction, so in total all the account balances add up to zero, which is referred to as having the "books in balance." In the general ledger for balance sheet accounts, asset accounts are debits while liabilities and equity accounts are credits. In the general ledger for income statement accounts, expense accounts are debits while income accounts are credits. Debits and credits are just a way to keep the books in balance, and are not designed to indicate what is good and bad. Asset and expense accounts are debits, while liability and income accounts are credits.
- Financial statements do not show liabilities, equity, and income account balances as credits (negative amounts), which they are in the general ledger. The financial statements' general ledger accounts in Exhibit 3-4 keep liabilities, equity, and income all as credits, in order to show that debits and credits add up to zero.
- The cash flow statement is based on transactions that are posted to the balance sheet and the income statement.

IFRS (International Financial Reporting Standards)

U.S. GAAP (United States - Generally Accepted Accounting Principles) is going to be eventually replaced by IFRS. IFRS will be the "world standard," which U.S. companies will need to adopt in order to attract international investors. Most countries modify IFRS to suit their needs, so there will never really be one "world standard"; the U.S. will probably also modify IFRS for the same reason. Financial statements prepared using U.S. GAAP will, in all likelihood, be more detailed and more reliable than financial statements prepared using whatever version of IFRS the U.S. officially adopts.

Chapter 4

Financial Decision Making

As stated at the beginning of the Understanding and Analyzing Financial Statements chapter, financial statements were designed to meet the needs of bankers, investors, and tax authorities, not the needs of those who manage businesses. For example, financial statements include fixed costs in inventory, which results in profits being overstated when unit production exceeds unit sales. The units produced in excess of units sold will end up in inventory. The fixed costs allocated to these additional units in inventory will come out of the fixed costs that get included in the income statement.

Financial decision making is concerned with improving true profitability, which requires that only the actual change in income and expenses be considered when making a financial decision. Financial statements do not reflect all actual changes in income and expenses such as with opportunity costs, described in the first section below, and property appreciation. This chapter is divided into the sections listed below.

- Variable and Fixed Costs
- Deciding Which Products to Produce and Sell
- Working Capital Management
- Short-Term Financing
- Projecting the Financial Benefit of an Investment
- Long-Term Financing
- Cost Measurement Systems
- Costing Methods

Variable and Fixed Costs

The costs for all financial decisions are either variable, which means they go up or down as sales go up or down, respectively, or they are fixed, which means they remain unchanged while sales change. It should be noted that these costs are only variable or fixed within the relevant activity range being considered in the financial decision. Variable costs include the following:

- Material consumed making products that go to the customer, including the cost of inbound freight and scrap
- Labor and supervision, including fringe benefits, to process purchased inventory and get it ready for sale to customers — If workers are paid whether or not there is work, then this cost is not variable.
- Tools, equipment wear, repairs, and supplies consumed getting products ready for customers
- Sales commissions
- Outbound freight if not paid by the customer
- Bad debt percentage on credit sales
- Variable inventory ordering, handling, storing, shrink, and obsolescence costs
- Variable quality costs for prevention (to avoid defects), appraisal (inspection), internal defects (defects found before shipping), and external defects (defects found after shipping)
- Opportunity cost, which is the profit that the assets being used would have generated if they were used in their next best use — Floor space being used could generate profits by being leased to someone else or by being used for a different product. Money used to finance equipment, inventory, and receivables could have earned interest if invested elsewhere.

Contribution margin, as explained in the Understanding and Analyzing Financial Statements chapter, is gross sales less variable expenses. A 25% contribution margin percentage of sales means that a $1,000 increase in sales will increase the contribution margin and net income by $250 (25% of $1,000). A $5.00 contribution margin per unit means that a 1,000-unit increase in sales will increase the contribution margin and net income by $5,000 (1,000 multiplied by $5.00). Buying labor saving equipment to lower direct-labor costs will lower variable costs and raise fixed costs. This cost shift will increase both the contribution margin percentage of sales and the per unit contribution margin, which is good if sales exceed the level that justified purchasing the equipment and is bad if sales are below the level that justified purchasing the equipment.

The breakeven level in sales dollars, as explained in the Understanding and Analyzing Financial Statements chapter, is the level of sales where net income is zero. This breakeven level is calculated by dividing fixed expenses by the contribution margin percentage of sales. If fixed costs are $400,000 and the contribution margin percentage of sales is 25%, then sales of $1,600,000 ($400,000 divided by 25%) are needed to break even. The contribution margin on the sales will be $400,000 ($1,600,000 multiplied by 25%), which equals the fixed costs. In order to determine the sales level for a $100,000 profit, just add $100,000 to the $400,000 in this calculation and then divide by the 25%.

The breakeven level in unit sales is very useful for new product planning. This breakeven level is calculated by dividing fixed costs by the contribution margin per unit. If fixed costs are $400,000 and the contribution margin per unit is $5.00, then sales of 80,000 units ($400,000 divided by $5.00) are needed to breakeven. The contribution margin on the sales will be $400,000 (80,000 multiplied by $5.00), which equals the fixed costs. In order to determine the sales level that results in $1.00 profit per unit, just subtract $1.00 from the $5.00 in this calculation before dividing it into the $400,000.

When deciding whether to manufacture or purchase a part, compare the variable manufacturing costs to the purchase price including inbound freight. If purchasing a part, rather than manufacturing it, will reduce fixed costs such as one less manufacturing supervisor, then this fixed cost is actually a variable cost within the applicable activity range. Opportunity costs should also be considered. Purchasing parts, instead of manufacturing them, may (1) reduce flexibility when it comes to getting parts quickly and (2) reduce in-house expertise

Joint products are two or more products produced together. Splitting the total cost between the products can be difficult, especially if one or more of them require additional processing before being sold. Any decision you make concerning production or the selling price of these products should be evaluated based on the resulting change in total sales and change in total expenses; fixed expenses that do not change, do not need to be considered.

Deciding Which Products to Produce and Sell

Product rationalization is the process of deciding whether you should be selling a particular product. When rationalizing a potential new product or an existing product, you need to determine the following. How does the change in contribution margin (sales less variable expenses, which include opportunity costs) compare to the change in fixed expenses. If the products being rationalized will increase or decrease other products' sales, then the increase or decrease in contribution margin and fixed costs for these other products needs to be included in the comparison. It all comes down to the change in total sales and the change in total expenses; fixed expenses that do not change, do not need to be considered.

If a customer wants you to produce a one-time order that will not use up your unused production capacity, then your minimum selling price only has to cover variable costs. If you do not have enough unused production capacity, then your minimum selling price has to also cover the lost contribution margin on the products you will not be able to produce.

Suppose you have two or more versions of a product to sell but you do not have the production capacity to produce as many as you can sell of them all. First thing you should do is identify the applicable constraining factor in your manufacturing operation, such as total hours available on a specialized piece of equipment. The version of the product with the highest contribution margin per machine hour on the specialized piece of equipment should be produced in quantities equal to the total quantity that can be sold without lowering the selling price. Remaining machine hours on the specialized piece of equipment should then be used first for production of the version with the next highest contribution margin per machine hour.

Suppose you have an opportunity to produce or purchase a quantity of a perishable product and then take it to an event where you will sell it. Suppose further that when you are at the event (1) you will not be able to get more of the product to sell, and (2) you will have to throw out any unsold product. First thing you need to do is develop a sales forecast with percentage probabilities for different potential sales levels. If your contribution margin percentage of sales is 50%, then the cost of one lost unit sale equals the cost of throwing out one unit; in which case, you should bring enough units to equal the weighted average sales forecast, which is the total of your different potential sales levels multiplied by their percentage probability expressed as a decimal. If your contribution margin percentage of sales is 25%, then the cost of one lost unit sale is one-third of the cost of throwing out one unit; in which case, you should bring just enough units to equal a sales forecast that is low enough so that it has a 75% (100% minus the 25%) chance of at least occurring. If your contribution margin percentage of sales is 75%, then the cost of one lost unit sale is three times greater than the cost of throwing out one unit; in which case, you should bring just enough units to equal a sales forecast that is high enough so that there is only a 25% (100% minus the 75%) chance of at least occurring. If you can adjust your selling price based on how sales are going at the event, it may be advantageous for you to bring additional product. Lower the price too much and you may sell less at full price during the next event.

Working Capital Management

It costs money to fund working capital (current assets less current liabilities). Calculations may be needed to determine how to manage working capital.

If a vendor offers you a 1% discount for payment in 10 days instead of the 50 days you normally take, you can approximately earn 9% annually on the early payments [1% multiplied by 360 divided by 40 (50 less 10) equals 9% annually]. The 1% for 40 (50 less 10) days is like 9% on an annual basis because 40 days is one-ninth of a 360-day year. The 1% for 40 days, divided by one-ninth (or multiplied by 360/40) equals 9% for 360 days.

If a bank lock box costs $100 a month and gets your receipts, which average $10,000 a day, in your bank account two days earlier, then it is the same as borrowing $20,000 from the bank at a 6% annual interest rate [($100 multiplied by 12) divided by ($10,000 multiplied by 2) equals 6%]. You will be paying $1,200 to get $20,000 for a year.

If hiring a $40,000, including fringe benefits, person can lower your average inventory by $1,000,000, it is the same as borrowing $1,000,000 from the bank at a 4% annual interest rate ($40,000 divided by $1,000,000 equals 4%). You will be paying $40,000 to get $1,000,000 for a year.

Inventory safety stock has a cost (interest and other carrying costs to fund the additional inventory) and a savings (reduced stock-out costs). The optimal safety stock level is where the cost to fund the safety stock equals the weighted average cost of stock outs. The weighted average cost of stock outs is the total cost of the different potential stock out possibilities after being multiplied by their percentage chance, expressed as decimal, of occurring.

Short-Term Financing

The five most common sources for a business to get short-term financing are described below. In the example for each, you need $100,000 for a year.

Easiest loan to calculate cost for is a loan where all you pay is interest and it is due when the loan is repaid. A $100,000 loan like this at 10% interest means that you pay $110,000 in a year. You will be paying $10,000 to borrow $100,000 for a year.

Some bank loans are on a discounted basis, which means you only get part of the loan amount but repay the full amount, without a separate interest charge. If the bank discount rate is 10%, you would have to borrow $111,111 ($100,000 divided by 90%) to get $100,000. At the end of the year, you will pay the bank $111,111. You will be paying $11,111 to borrow $100,000 for a year.

Some bank loans require a compensating balance, which means that part of the loan amount stays at the bank, without earning interest, while you pay interest on the full amount. A 12% compensating balance means that you would have to borrow $113,636 ($100,000 divided by 88%) to get $100,000. If the stated interest rate is 9%, you will be paying $10,227 ($113,636 multiplied by 9%) to borrow $100,000 for a year.

Issuing commercial paper is an option only available to larger companies with excellent credit ratings and is usually for periods less than a year. You could issue $104,000 of commercial paper to net $100,000 for six months. Doing this twice would result in paying $8,000 to borrow $100,000 for a year.

Factoring is an expensive way to borrow money and should usually be only used when no one else will loan money to your business. A factor basically (1) buys some or all of your accounts receivable; (2) holds a reserve for bad debt; (3) charges a commission; and (4) loans the remaining amount to you with an interest charge. The commission charge and interest expense in the following example are deducted in advance. If the factor holds a 10% reserve, charges 1% commission, and charges 1.5% monthly interest, you will have to pay $31,962 to borrow $100,000 for a year, assuming your accounts receivables are due in 30 days. The $31,962 is made up of $18,274 interest at 1.5% per month in advance [(($100,000 divided by 98.5% (100% less 1.5%)) less $100,000) multiplied by 12 months] and $13,688 for the 1% commission on $1,368,847 of accounts receivable sold to the factor. The $1,368,847 is calculated by dividing the $100,000 by 98.5% (100% less 1.5% interest), then dividing the result by 89% (100% less 10% reserve and less 1% commission), then multiplying by 12 (number of months that accounts receivable will be sold to the factor). Each month on average, $114,071 ($1,368,847 divided by 12) of accounts receivable will have to be sold to the factor. The factor will (1) hold a reserve of 10% — $11,407, (2) deduct commission of 1% — $1,141, and (3) deduct interest expense of 1.5% of amount loaned — $1,523. The remaining $100,000 goes to you. It should be noted that the $31,962 would be partially offset by lower collection costs on your part. Factoring may cause your customers to question how long your business may be in operation. It looks bad when the factor's name and address for remittances are on your invoices.

Projecting the Financial Benefit of an Investment

This section of the chapter describes different tools for projecting the financial benefit of an investment. For the most part, these tools are designed to create a valid comparison of an investment's future after-tax cash flow to its current after-tax cash flow. These tools can be used for, among other things, evaluating labor saving equipment, deciding whether to lease or buy, and deciding whether to refinance. In order to use the tools, you will need to determine the following:

- Determine the investment's projected effect on before-tax cash flow by year. This is usually both the most difficult and the most important thing to do. For labor saving equipment, only include incremental savings and expenses. If a production worker will just be standing around while a potential labor saving piece of equipment does a task that the production worker currently does, then the cost savings for this production worker's time has to be based on the shortened time to complete the task not the current time it takes for the production worker to complete the task. For a building lease versus buy comparison, be sure to consider building appreciation. Your financial projection for the purchase can have the building being sold when the lease would have ended. For a refinance comparison, be sure to consider how long you may own the property. The shorter the time period, the less likely that the costs to refinance will be offset. If your cash flow projections are based on something with a high level of uncertainty like a new product sales forecast, you may also want to put together Worst-Case and Best-Case projections.

- Determine which of the before-tax cash flow items in the preceding bullet are taxable or tax deductible. For assets with a life over one year, consult with your tax advisor to get the amount of tax-deductible depreciation expense for each year. This information can be found in a U.S. tax guide.

- Determine your marginal (incremental) tax rate, which is the percentage of additional taxable income and expense that your income taxes will go up or down, respectively. A 40% marginal tax rate means that a $1,000 increase or decrease in taxable income will increase or decrease, respectively, income tax by $400. Your tax advisor can provide this rate. For a profitable company, the rate is around 40%. For an individual, the rate is around 35%. The 40% and 35% can be fine-tuned by finding the projected taxable income in the IRS tables and looking at what the percentage change is for a $1,000 change in taxable income; state income tax should also be included in the calculation. Marginal tax rate may not be the same each year.

- Determine, using the information described in the three preceding bullets, the after-tax cash flow for each year.

- Determine your cost of capital, which can be thought of as the interest rate you will pay to fund the investment's after-tax cash outflows and the interest rate you will earn on the investment's after-tax cash inflows. This cost of capital needs to be stated on an after-tax basis, using your marginal tax rate. If the interest is taxable or tax deductible and your marginal tax rate is 40%, then 10% before tax equals 6% after tax [10% multiplied by (100% minus 40%)]. Cost of capital for a company is detailed in the Long-Term Financing section of this chapter. Cost of capital may vary by year. Sometimes the cost of capital is called the "hurdle rate." Sometimes the hurdle rate is higher than the cost of capital, to adjust for investment risk.

Financial tools below use after-tax cash flows and cost of capital

- Net present value tool discounts, using cost of capital, the future cash flows back to the current (present) time period. These discounted future cash flows are added to the current cash flows to get the total net present value. If the total is positive, then this positive balance represents your projected earnings on the investment. If the total is negative, then this negative balance represents your projected loss on the investment.

- Profitability index tool ranks projects that have a positive net present value, and uses the two amounts that add up to the net present value. In the profitability index, the discounted future cash inflows are divided by the current cash outflows, stated as a positive number. This index would rank a $10,000 investment with a $5,000 net present value higher than a $25,000 investment with a $10,000 net present value.

- Internal rate of return tool finds the discount rate, not the cost of capital, that discounts the future cash inflows to an amount equal to the current cash outflows (initial investment). This discount rate is called the internal rate of return. If the internal rate of return exceeds the cost of capital, the investment is profitable since you earn more on the money than you pay to use the money. If the internal rate of return is less than the cost of capital, the investment is not profitable since you earn less on the money than you pay to use the money.

- Modified internal rate of return tool starts by identifying the end date when the cash inflows from the investment end. An ending total value for all the cash inflows is determined by assuming they earn an interest rate, equal to the cost of capital, from when they are received until the end date. The modified internal rate of return is the rate at which the current cash outflow (initial investment) would have to grow in order to equal the value of the cash inflows as of the end date. If there are additional cash outflows after the initial cash outflow, then these future cash outflows would be discounted at the cost of capital and added to the initial cash outflow for use in this calculation. If the modified internal rate of return is greater than the cost of capital, the investment is profitable since you earn more on the money than you pay to use the money. If the modified internal rate of return is less than the cost of capital, the investment is not profitable since you earn less on the money than you pay to use the money.

- Payback tool calculates the time period from the initial cash outflow (initial investment) to when the undiscounted accumulated cash inflows equals the cash outflows. This calculation is easy to do and easy to understand. Disadvantages of this calculation are that cash inflows are not discounted and those occurring after the payback period are not considered.

- Bailout payback tool is the same as the payback tool except the bailout payback tool considers potential early salvage value less costs to terminate the investment. Salvage value is the net amount for which the investment's assets could be sold. The bailout payback period would be shorter than the regular payback period, assuming the salvage value of the investment is greater than the costs to terminate the investment. This method is useful when the investment has a high resale value and continuation of future cash inflows is risky.

- Breakeven time tool is the same as the payback tool except for two things. Breakeven time tool uses discounted cash flows, at the cost of capital, and the breakeven time period begins when the project begins, not when the initial cash outflow is made.

- Accounting rate of return tool should never be used, in my opinion. This tool divides the undiscounted average annual net income, including depreciation expense, by the initial investment or sometimes by the average investment.

Notes concerning the preceding tools

- If you do not have a business calculator, discount future cash flows as follows. To discount a $10,000 cash flow occurring in three years into current dollars using an 8% cost of capital, just divide the $10,000 by 1.08 three times. The $10,000 in three years is worth $7,938 today based on an 8% cost of capital.

- If you are comparing two investment options where you plan to do one or the other but not both, the following short cut should be looked at. Subtract the cash flows, by year, for the option with the smaller current cash outflow (initial investment) from the option with the larger current cash outflow. If the choice between the two options is not obvious based on the differences in each year's cash flows, continue as follows. Use net present value or internal rate of return tools to determine if the higher initial cash outflow is worth the higher future cash inflows. In addition, when comparing two options like this, you can exclude cash flows that are the same in each.

Long-Term Financing

Cost of capital is the weighted average after-tax current cost for the following three or four sources of capital financing. These costs need to be expressed as a percentage calculated by dividing the cost to get funds by the funds received.

- Debt includes bonds, notes, and other loans. The following information on bond costs can be used to determine the cost of notes and other loans. Cost of bonds being issued is annual interest paid divided by proceeds received. Proceeds received equal the face amount of the debt plus or minus any premium or discount, respectively, and minus any flotation costs. If bonds are not currently being issued, then base the cost on what they could be issued for, such as 125 basis points over the U.S. Treasury bonds rate. This total cost would be calculated by adding 1.25 percentage points to the U.S. Treasury bond rate. Since interest on debt is tax deductible, multiply the before-tax cost by 100% less your marginal tax rate percentage to get the after-tax cost.

- Preferred stock cost is the required annual dividend per share divided by the net price per share of a new issuance, which is after deducting issuance costs per share. Ask the company's stockbroker for the likely net price per share for a new issuance or base it on the current price per share if it can be reasonably expected to be the same for a new issuance. Stock dividends are not tax deductible.

- Common stock cost is the annual dividend per share divided by the net price per share of a new issuance, which is after deducting issuance costs per share. This calculated cost of common stock financing has to be increased for future increases in the amount of dividends paid per share. An accepted method to do this is to add the projected annual percentage increase in dividends per share to the calculated cost of common stock financing, expressed as a percent. The company's stockbroker may be able to give you the likely net price per share for a new issuance or you can base it on the current price per share if it can be reasonably expected to be the same for a new issuance. As a third alternative, you can use the capital asset pricing model. This model uses (1) the U.S. Treasury bond rate; (2) the average equity market-segment rate of return, which is the weighted average annual dividend divided by the weighted average common stock price per share for companies in the segment of the market that the company is in; and (3) the company's beta. Beta represents the expected percentage change in the company's stock price relative to a percentage change in the total market segment that includes the company. A beta of 1.5 means that a 6% swing in the average share price in the market segment will theoretically be accompanied by a 9% (6% multiplied by 1.5 beta) swing in the company's stock price. The capital asset pricing model starts by calculating the equity market-segment risk premium, which is the average equity market-segment rate of return less the risk-free return (U.S. Treasury bond rate). Then multiply this equity market-segment risk premium by the company's beta to get the company's risk premium. Then add the company's risk premium to the risk-free rate (U.S. Treasury bond rate) to get the rate of return that the market will require from the company. This rate is the cost of common stock, and should be increased slightly for stock issuance costs. Stock dividends are not tax deductible.

- Retained earnings used to finance investments often has its cost calculated similarly to how common stock cost is determined, even though the company does not have to pay anything to use retained earnings. I think that retained earnings should not be included in the weighted average cost of capital calculation because the cost of retained earnings theoretically equals the weighted average cost of capital for debt, preferred stock, and common stock, as follows. Retained earnings used for investments is net income the owners left in the company to finance investments. The owners presumably left the retained earnings in the company because the best return they can get on the retained earnings used to finance investments is the cost of the outside financing (debt, preferred stock, and common stock) that the company will not have to incur because of using retained earnings. It should be noted that the cost of retained earnings could be slightly lower than the cost of capital that will not have to be raised, due to using retained earnings, because generally the more capital you raise, the higher the perceived risk and the higher the cost of capital.

The weighted average of the above capital sources is based on the proportion that each source is of the company's current total capital mix (structure). It could be argued that the weighted average should be based on the optimal mix, rather than the current mix of capital sources, since the optimal mix is more in line with current capital financing used for current investments. Optimal mix of capital sources is the mix that results in the lowest total cost of capital. If capital needs are always met by using the lowest cost source of capital, then a company will be lowering the overall total average cost of capital and moving closer to the optimal capital mix. Debt usually has a lower cost than common stock. It could be argued that adding debt does not lower the average cost of capital as much as expected because higher debt increases perceived risk, which increases the cost of future common stock financing. It could also be argued that selling more common stock will not increase the average cost of capital as much as expected because additional equity, in place of debt, will lower the cost of future debt.

"Hurdle rate" is often used in place of "cost of capital," when investments are being considered. Sometimes the hurdle rate exceeds the cost of capital because the company is trying to adjust for investment risk. If hurdle rate includes an adjustment for risk, then each investment being considered should theoretically have its own hurdle rate that is based on its level of risk.

A small privately held company could determine cost of capital based on cost of debt and cost of equity. Cost of equity would be what the owners could earn on funds that could be invested or withdrawn from the company.

Cost Measurement Systems

Everything you pay for has a cost and an expected benefit. The cost should be expensed as the benefit is consumed. Every manufacturing cost should eventually get charged to a final cost object such as a job or a product. Costs may first go to a cost pool such as a general department where all labor is charged and then possibly to an intermediate cost object such as a specific department associated with a job, product, or process. Cost drivers are underlying measurable activities such as units produced that drive costs. Direct costs such as direct labor and direct material can usually be charged directly to final cost objects using cost drivers. Other costs (indirect costs) can be charged to final cost objects, using cost drivers with the highest correlation. Cost measurement systems should break all costs out into what is variable and what is fixed, as defined earlier in this chapter.

Manufacturing service department costs need to be charged to production departments in order for the costs to end up in a final cost object. Service department costs can be charged, using the direct method, to production departments based on the percents of the service department's labor and material that are spent on each production department. If there is more than one service department and at least one of them does a significant amount of work for one or more of the others, then you have to decide whether the direct method above is good enough. If you want to allocate service department costs to other service departments, you have two choices. The step down method can be best explained by using an example with three service departments (A, B, & C), where A does the most work for the other service departments and B does more work for C than C does for B. Start by allocating department A costs, on the percentage basis used in the direct method above, to departments B, C, and all the production departments. Then allocate department B total costs to departments C and the production departments. Then allocate department C total costs to the production departments. The reciprocal method of allocating costs among service departments is the most accurate method but its use of simultaneous equations makes it too complicated for this book.

You need to select the cost measurement system that is best for your business. You also need to understand the system well enough to use it. The most important consideration is to select a system that best generates the information you need to make decisions that involve manufacturing costs. The four basic cost measurement systems are described below:

- Standard cost system is the most widely used cost measurement system. Companies generally develop standard costs each year for the parts they plan to sell, as well as for the purchased parts and subassemblies that go into the parts they plan to sell. The standard cost for a purchased part includes the purchase price, inbound freight, and ideally, all costs associated with ordering, receiving, handling, and storing the part. The standard cost for a manufactured part is usually broken out into direct material, direct labor, variable overhead, fixed overhead, and outside processing. These five pieces of a manufactured part's standard cost are typically developed as follows. Direct material is the total standard cost of the parts that get used; these parts and their standard quantities used are in the Bill of Materials for the manufactured part. Direct labor is the standard hours to build the part, which is in the part's router, multiplied by the standard labor rate for the work center where the part is built. Variable overhead is the standard direct-labor hours in the part's router multiplied by the variable overhead rate. The variable overhead rate is the total budgeted variable overhead for the year divided by the standard direct-labor hours budgeted for all parts to be produced during the year. Fixed overhead is typically developed the same as variable overhead. Outside processing has a standard cost that is often put in the part's router.

- Process cost system is best suited for continuous operations, such as breweries, that consume resources as they convert (process) products for eventual sale. Resources (direct materials and conversion costs) consumed are assigned to products produced, as follows. For any given period such as a month, the cost of direct materials consumed is totaled and the conversion costs incurred are totaled. Next and EUP (Equivalent Units of Production) is developed for both direct materials consumed and conversion costs. EUP can be best explained by the following example of EUP calculated on the FIFO basis. If beginning WIP (Work In Process) had 100 units 25% complete, 150 units were completed during the period, and ending WIP has 50 units 75% complete, then the EUP for the period is 162.50 units [150 (completed) plus 50 (ending WIP) multiplied by 75% minus 100 (beginning WIP) multiplied by 25%]. The total cost of direct materials consumed is divided by the EUP for direct materials to get the direct material cost to be charged to each completed unit. The total conversion cost is divided by the EUP for conversion costs to get the conversion cost to be charged to each completed unit. The weighted average method of assigning direct materials consumed and conversion costs to completed units does two things differently than the FIFO method described above, as follows. The weighted average method (1) does not subtract anything from EUP for beginning WIP inventory, and (2) adds the cost of beginning WIP inventory to the direct materials consumed and conversion costs incurred during the period. The cost of beginning WIP is equal to the preceding period's ending WIP, which was calculated based on total cost divided by EUP.

- Job order cost system is best suited for a company that (1) does each job separate from other jobs and (2) can economically keep track of costs by job. This system is often used by consultants and other service firms. Job cost sheets can be used for each job to track costs. The payroll department will need to know hours spent on each job. Materials and supplies will need to be assigned to a job when they are dispensed. Overhead costs will need to be allocated based on something like hours charged to each job.

- Operation cost system is a combination of the process cost system and the job order cost system; this combination cost system can be used in each of the following two situations. A company that converts raw rubber into sheets that it uses to make trampoline surfaces and wet suits could use process costing for the cost of making sheets and job costing for the costs to make trampoline surfaces and wet suits. A company that makes wood trim that has two separate product lines that are identical, except that one is made with inexpensive wood and inexpensive finishes while the other is made of expensive wood and expensive finishes, could use operations costing. Process costing could be used for the conversion costs and job order costing could be used for the material cost.

Costing Methods

- Activity based costing ties costs to the activities that drive them. It breaks the activities into value-added activities, which create value for customers, and non-value-added activities that should be eliminated/reduced. Activity based cost drivers are concerned with getting costs charged to jobs and products, which is explained in the first paragraph of the Cost Measurement Systems section of this chapter.

- Variable costing only charges variable manufacturing costs to products. Fixed manufacturing costs are expensed when they are incurred. This is a good way to charge manufacturing costs, primarily because it avoids the massive confusion caused by allocating fixed costs.
- Actual costing uses actual costs for direct and indirect costs.
- Normal costing uses actual costs for direct costs and budgeted rates for indirect costs.
- Life cycle costing starts by projecting all costs over a product's life, including research and development as well as new product market introduction costs. Once all the costs have been projected, you can project the selling price required to justify pursuing the product. You then need to determine if the required minimum selling price is reasonable considering alternatives your prospective customers may have.
- Lean accounting is a costing method for lean manufacturing and lean thinking. Lean accounting has been presented as being better than full absorption standard costing for costing decisions, despite the fact that full absorption standard costing is not used in any accepted/preferred methods for making costing decisions. Variable costing, described above, is better than lean accounting for costing decisions because lean accounting uses value-stream costs, which include fixed costs. Activity based costing's value-added activities, described above, are more accurate and detailed than lean accounting's value-stream activities when it comes to information for breaking out products' variable costs. Lean accounting is more appropriate for performance indicators than for financial decision making.

Book Three

Building A Solid Foundation For A Successful Career

Book Three covers matters that people need to understand and consider when setting and pursuing goals. These matters involve how people can take necessary control of their lives and their environments, so they can make the right things happen for themselves.

Chapter 1

Accomplishing Things

People who consistently get things done well are usually motivated by a strong sense of accomplishment from their work. The nine thoughts in this chapter concern accomplishing things.

1. The first person to accomplish something will usually get more credit than others who later accomplish the same thing. The possible exception is when someone does it significantly better.

2. Do not rest on your laurels. The more recent an accomplishment, the heavier it is weighted in other people's opinion of your work.

3. To stay motivated, think about how good you will feel when you accomplish a particular goal. Avoid imagining that you have already accomplished the goal because the resulting false feeling of satisfaction will diminish your drive to get the real feeling of satisfaction. Similarly, avoid imagining that a bad result you are trying to prevent has occurred. Once you imagine that the bad result has occurred, you may start thinking about how to cope with it, which will diminish your drive to prevent it.

4. Do not celebrate an accomplishment too soon. Wait until you are certain it has been, or will be, accomplished.

5. Be persistent. Persistence is required to accomplish your goals. Before you start to pursue a goal, identify what you need to learn and the steps you need to take in order to accomplish the goal. If you still feel that the goal is worth

pursuing, be persistent in learning what you need to know and in taking the steps needed to accomplish your goal.

6. Aim at accomplishing your goal. Your goal is successful completion. Your goal is not to be able to say, "I tried." The difference between *successful completion* and a *failed attempt* is often just a little more effort in planning, thoroughness, and/or following through.

7. Avoid tunnel vision while you pursue your goals. Keep an open mind concerning both of the following as you pursue your goals:
   - Your initial projection of the work involved to accomplish the goal may have been significantly under- or overestimated.
   - Changing circumstances in your life may modify the goal you should be pursuing.

   Note: Do not let short-term thinking cause you to change long-term goals. If in doubt, ask yourself the following two questions:
   - Is the remaining work worth the benefit of accomplishing the goal?
   - In the future, will you regret not accomplishing the goal?

8. Do not set a goal to accomplish something just to accomplish it. Make sure your planned accomplishments fit in with your goals and are worth the required effort.

9. Rarely do people get the acknowledgement they deserve for their accomplishments. The less experience a person has, the more important acknowledgement becomes. When someone does a good job, acknowledge it.

Chapter 2

Understanding Things

The better you understand things, the better you can deal with them. For simple things where all relevant facts are known, your understanding can be as simple as knowing that cold water in a household sink is usually to your right and hot is usually to your left. For complicated things where relevant facts are not all known, your understanding may just be an assumption (not based on proof), a speculation (based on incomplete information), an opinion (based on your judgment), or a belief (accepted as fact but not based on fact). The 20 thoughts in this chapter concern improving your understanding of things.

1. The goal of thinking about something is to form an accurate mental picture. The first step in analyzing something is to identify its components: parts, processes, and synergies. Then, you need to understand the components and their relationships to each other. Next, you need to distinguish between what is known to be true (the facts) and what is likely true (inferences based on available information and evidence). The last step in forming the mental picture is to put the components together in your mind, based on (a) your understanding of them, (b) their relationship to each other, and (c) your purpose for analyzing the matter, as follows:
   - To fix something, determine what is broken and how to fix it.
   - To improve something, make a list of possible improvements and decide which ones to implement.
   - To understand how something works, create a flow chart with all the components.
   - To learn how to do something, make a list of the steps necessary to do it.

- To determine how something affects you and what you can do about it, make a list of the effects and determine what you can do to alter and deal with them.
- To see how something will affect things in the future, determine when it will occur and the effect of the occurrence.

2. The mental picture you form only has to be as comprehensive as needed for the thing you are trying to understand. Always keep your goal in mind when you analyze something. If you are fixing something, start by identifying the most likely components to be broken. If you are helping someone, start by identifying the likely help that is needed.
3. When you encounter information that is contrary to what you understand, you should analyze the difference and, if applicable, modify what you already understand. Being "close-minded" is the simplest way to deal with contradictory information, but it denies you the opportunity to improve your understanding of things.

   Facts based solely on your own observations are the best. Facts based on information from others need to be analyzed, as follows:
   - Has the source been reliable in the past? For a variety of reasons, people sometimes misrepresent things they say as being facts.
   - Is the source objective? An example of a source that is not objective is salespeople who say their competitors' products are not as good as their products.
   - How does the information compare to other available information?

   Do not slant facts in order to avoid admitting to yourself that you have made an error. Erroneously shifting blame in your own mind to other people or things will corrupt your understanding of the other people or things. Erroneous information accepted as fact can be difficult to correct, especially after assumptions have been based on it.
4. When information from one source appears to confirm what you learned from another source, make sure the two sources are independent from each other.
5. Your understanding of things will evolve for many reasons, including the following:
   - People change; the younger they are, the more they usually change.
   - You will learn new things.
   - You will discover new relationships among things.
   - The priorities and importance of things in your life will change.
6. The more you analyze things, the quicker you will be able to analyze similar things.

7. If someone is explaining to you the rooms and contents of a building you have not seen, a floor plan of the building would usually be helpful in forming your mental picture. Also, if you talk to someone on the phone a lot, it is usually helpful if you have a mental picture of the person's face and physique to associate with the voice.

8. Almost every observation you make will have an influence on your understanding of things.

9. Advertisements are designed specifically to alter your understanding of things. An advertisement with happy people using a product is designed to get you to associate being happy with using the product.

10. When you read or listen to the news, keep in mind that any discussion or analysis of political matters is often not objective; look to see if it is slanted toward the liberal or conservative point of view.

    Once you know the news source's point of view, you can correct for it. When the source supports one side in a dispute and says the "facts are hard to sort out," most likely the facts go against the side supported by the source. Similarly, if the source says that many people support the side that the source supports, most likely less than 50% support it.

    Pictures can be very misleading, such as enlarging the image of one presidential candidate relative to the image of the other candidate.

    Sometimes a news source will quote the opinion of someone. You cannot evaluate this quoted opinion unless you know how the person being quoted stands on other related issues. Also, keep in mind that it is easy to misquote someone by only publishing part of what was said or by not explaining the context in which it was said.

    It is easy for a news source to make it look like almost everyone supports one side in a dispute. All that is needed is to just show interviews of people who support the side. Another trick is to select and show the interview of a disreputable looking/sounding person who supports the other side.

    Surveys can be very misleading. It is easy to manipulate people's answers by (1) how a question is worded, (2) giving people information before asking a question, and (3) asking a preceding question that gets people thinking about something that will affect their answer for the important question.

    Only consider facts from the news. Reputable news sources will not knowingly publish wrong facts, unless they have a major ax to grind. Keep in mind that you may only be getting the facts that support one side of the story. Sometimes the other side of the story will be presented, so the news source can claim to be objective, in a manner that is unclear. Two ways to make something unclear are to use awkward sentences and to use words the average person does not understand.

I once saw a bumper sticker slogan asking something to the effect: "What did you think before you let the news do your thinking for you?" The author of this slogan is raising a good question that many people need to consider.

11. Just because something cannot be disproved, does not mean it is true.
12. Trust your judgment. If you hear or see something that seems untrue, check it out for yourself.
13. The more that new information agrees with preconceived ideas, the less it will be questioned. This is why you should keep an open mind and not put too much faith in first impressions.
14. When you are pursuing an explanation, do not discard information that is contrary to any tentative explanation you already have. Your goal is to find the facts, not to back up your tentative explanation.
15. Do not blindly accept other people's explanations about things as your own explanations. Check things out for yourself.
16. People who are insecure about their own beliefs often try to get others to join in their beliefs.
17. The biggest difference between how a human and a computer think is that the computer does not worry about its existence. The human brain is constantly analyzing input, from the senses and from conscious thoughts, to understand how the person will be affected by events. This analysis causes much stress.
18. In order to advance knowledge in a particular field of study, you usually need to be on the cutting edge, where you understand all there is to know about the field of study. When analyzing information, keep in mind how it fits into the overview of the subject. Also, keep in mind that the overview of the subject will change as new facts and theories are discovered. Furthermore, keep in mind that the currently accepted overview may have been modified many times to incorporate new facts and theories without adequately considering how the new facts and theories affected the whole overview. New facts and theories in related fields of study can also affect the overview of your particular field of study.
19. Genius is not about what you know. Genius is about analyzing what you know and seeing relationships and patterns that others are rarely capable of seeing. Theories are usually based on relationships and patterns.
20. Goals are created to facilitate changes in things. An inadequate understanding of a particular thing can lead to suboptimal goals and suboptimal pursuit of goals.

Chapter 3

Making Decisions

Most successes and failures in life can be primarily attributed to good and bad decision making. This chapter contains 18 things to consider about making decisions.

1. The more important a decision is, the more important it is to consider the effect on your long- and short-term goals. Before making an important decision, test it for reasonableness by asking yourself the following three questions:
   - In the future, when you look back at the situation, which choice will you feel was the right one?
   - Which choice would you feel the most comfortable with when explaining your rationale to people whose opinions you trust concerning the matter?
   - If you were an objective-third-party observer, which choice would you recommend?

2. A good understanding of a matter being considered is the foundation for good decision making; see the Understanding Things chapter. The more important a decision is, the more important it is to understand the matter being considered.

3. Consider advice you receive from others. Everyone can at least occasionally benefit from advice provided by others.

4. When people give you advice concerning decisions you are considering, take into consideration their possible motives, especially when the advice was unsolicited.

5. If a person is pushing you for a quick decision, ask yourself the following questions:
   - Is the person trying to minimize how much time you have to consider the choices?
   - Why you were not asked earlier?
   - What does the person stand to gain and is it at your expense?
   - If you were in the other person's position, how would you have handled the situation and what response would you have reasonably expected?

   Note: Do not hesitate to say you need more time.

6. Do not make significant decisions based primarily on information received from a source that you do not know to be reliable.

7. Risk is involved with every decision where the outcome of the decision is uncertain. When making a decision, the best choice is the one where the weighted average of potential results is the greatest in terms of meeting your goals. Make sure you adequately define your goals, as in the following decision. If you were ready to retire and had enough money to meet your future needs, would you risk all your money in an investment with a 50% chance of losing everything and a 50% chance of at least tripling your investment? In this instance, money is just the means to the end.

   You can improve the weighted average of potential results by minimizing the effect of the Worst-Case scenario and maximizing the effect of the Best-Case scenario. Suppose you are going to start selling a new product where the potential sales could be very low or very high. In this instance, do not commit to purchasing more than enough of the product to meet your lowest sales forecast and get commitments from suppliers so, if necessary, you will be able to purchase enough of the product, on a timely and cost-effective basis, to meet your highest sales forecast.

   Your goal in life should not be to minimize risks; a pursuit of this goal will minimize your chance of accomplishing anything worthwhile. Your goal should be to minimize the risk involved with pursuing your goals.

8. Do not let short-term joy or excitement cause you to make decisions that are in conflict with your long-term goals.

   Avoid making spur-of-the-moment decisions that could have long-term negative consequences for you. Usually, a quick analysis of how the decision could affect attainment of your goals will either identify ways to minimize the possible negative consequences or determine if the decision should be at least postponed.

The more your decisions are based on long-term goals, the straighter and shorter the path to attainment of your long-term goals.

9. Involve your unconscious mind in decisions about matters that affect how you feel. For these types of matters, start by analyzing the facts and determining the advantages and disadvantages of each alternative. After your conscious mind is done with this analysis, let your unconscious mind think about it. Your unconscious mind may need only a day when it comes to the color of a new car and may need much longer when it comes to deciding where to live. Eventually, your conscious and unconscious minds will come together concerning the decision and you will know which alternative to choose. Unfortunately, time constraints often do not allow enough time for this process to occur.

10. If your analysis of the facts and advice favors a particular choice, but something does not seem right, then if possible, hold off committing yourself until you figure out what does not seem right. Possibly, your unconscious mind has an uneasy feeling about the decision, but cannot quickly quantify the reason in a manner your conscious mind will understand. If you have not figured out why something does not seem right, and you have to make a decision, then at least review again the Best-Case and Worst-Case scenarios about the choice you are about to make.

    Make sure your feeling of something not seeming right is not really just a matter of having *cold feet*. Best way to determine this is to recall how you felt before making other decisions that were similar in terms of significance.

11. Your decisions based on gut feelings have a greater chance of success when you are very familiar with the matter at hand and when you have previously made similar decisions. For example, the more people you have hired for a particular type of position, the more reliable your gut feelings should be regarding a prospective new hire.

    Before making a gut-feeling decision, you should ask yourself the following two questions and make sure you are comfortable with the answers:
    - Should I get more facts to base the decision on? In the example above, you can contact references for a prospective new hire.
    - Should I postpone the decision until I have more facts? In the example above, you can hire a person on a temporary basis before deciding whether to offer full-time employment.

12. If you cannot decide whether to say something, consider the following. Assuming a delay in saying something will not cause a problem, consider waiting because it is much easier to say it later than to retract it later.

13. You may want to postpone making a decision even though you have all the necessary information. The question you have to ask yourself is whether there

is a benefit of keeping your options open. Just be sure your choices will remain open and you are not needlessly causing problems for others. For example, if two salespeople are trying to sell you the same item that you do not need yet, consider postponing your decision in order to get a better deal, assuming the salespeople's offers will remain open.

14. Avoid making decisions you do not have to make. For example, two of your friends have a dispute and they ask you who is right.

15. A decision concerning two options does not necessarily mean one or the other. If you have to make a choice that may be reversed in the future, look for ways to keep your second choice open while you work with your first choice. For example, college students who have to declare a major may want to take courses that are required in both their primary and secondary choices for a major.

16. Deciding when to act is often important. Just like it is best to wait for fruit to ripen and then eat it before it spoils, many situations have a best time to act. For instance, new computer software usually gets released for sale when it is developed to the level of being "good enough," which is usually months before all the problems are fixed.

17. If you decide to do something, do it. It is a waste of time to determine what you should do and not do it.

18. Sometimes you will have to "rewrite the rules" in order to achieve your goals. Make sure you adequately consider the possible consequences of your changes.

Chapter 4

Learning In General

Learning from the discoveries and experiences of others is usually much easier than learning on your own. The ten items in this chapter concern learning in general.

1. When you learn a new motor (physical activity) skill or mental skill, it takes one or two nights sleep for the skill to sink into your mind. Motor skills seem to sink in faster. As soon as the skill has sunk in, it is very important to use it at least once as thoroughly as possible to reinforce what was learned. Ideally, if you have two similar skills to learn, delay learning the second skill until the first skill has sunk in and then been used thoroughly at least once.

2. Before you can become proficient at something, you need to thoroughly understand and apply the fundamentals, which include all the applicable rules, procedures, and methods. You will not become proficient until you have consciously applied all the fundamentals enough times for your unconscious mind to take over and properly apply all the fundamentals without you consciously thinking about it. The unconscious mind has the ability to instantaneously recall similar experiences from the past and take actions based on what was learned from the experiences.

3. Being proficient does not necessarily make someone a good instructor. The reason for this is that the proficient person no longer consciously thinks about the fundamentals and how they apply. For example, a person with a proficient golf swing is generally not as good an instructor as the person was right after

learning to properly apply the fundamentals concerning how to swing a golf club.

An ideal instructor is someone who thoroughly understands the fundamentals and has enough experience using them to fully understand and explain/demonstrate how they apply.

4. Learn from your experiences. When you succeed, figure out what you did that caused the success so you can apply it to other situations. When you make a mistake, figure out what you should have done instead so you can avoid making the mistake again. Whenever you recall the mistake, review what you should have done instead.

   Learn the right lessons from your experiences, as in the following. Receiving poor assistance should not necessarily lead you to being more self-reliant. Perhaps, the correct lesson is to do a better job of sourcing, using, and/or understanding the limits of assistance.

   If you make a mistake that is offset by good luck, do not think that the mistake was not a mistake. Conversely, if a good decision was offset by bad luck, do not think that the good decision was a mistake. Luck refers to things beyond your control that you could not have foreseen.

5. When you learn something new, make sure you fit it in with other things you know about the same subject. Reconciling differences is necessary in order to have a clear and concise understanding of the subject. If you are having trouble reconciling some thoughts, see how they fit into your applicable overview of the subject. Keep in mind that there are different ways to look at things. In psychology, there are the biological, behavioral, humanistic, Freudian, and other approaches. In physics, there are the wave and the particle theories that each explains a portion of light's known behavior.

   Learning new information as described above may take longer in the short term to get started, but it will usually take less time in the long term to fully understand the new information.

6. When learning something new, do not wait too long before you start putting the pieces together. It is often better to make a wrong assumption and learn from it than to keep missing an obvious connection. To learn from a wrong assumption, you should consciously think of the wrong assumption and correct it so that the corrected version will replace the wrong assumption in your mind. Make sure you minimize any significant risk involved with taking actions based on assumptions. Getting others to review your plans of action can often minimize this risk.

7. Do not spend so much time learning how to control your environment, such as your social life, that you do not put enough time into learning what you need to know for your chosen occupation in life.

8. Be a perceptive listener and observer; sometimes it is what the other person does not say or do that is important. If your boss does not respond to an idea you present, probably your boss is hoping you drop the idea on your own. If people cross their arms after you start presenting your argument, consider backing off and trying a different approach before they can outright reject your argument.

9. Often when you cannot remember something or figure out a problem, the answer occurs to you later as soon as you think about the subject again. Somehow, your unconscious mind collects and organizes everything relevant, including things you were not consciously considering. Then, the next time you think about the subject, everything you have to consider is in place for you to answer the question or at least be closer to the solution.

   The following should facilitate your unconscious mind's effort to collect and organize relevant information:

   - Clearly define the problem in your mind.
   - Review and organize what you have already figured out. If applicable, relate it to an overview and see how it all fits together.
   - Make one last effort to solve the problem with what you have already figured out and identify what does not fit or is missing. Review your assumptions for reasonableness.

10. Your unconscious mind stores experiences, such as when you lose your footing on ice, that it can instantaneously recall in order to base actions on when the same or similar experiences occur again. The next best thing to these stored experiences is to rehearse how you would act in a given situation.

Chapter 5

Having the Right Attitude

Attitude is a state of mind that directly influences how you are affected by your experiences. With the right attitude, you can make the most of your experiences. The seven thoughts in this chapter concern having the right attitude.

1. Life is full of great opportunities. If you wait for opportunity to knock on your door, you will not get your fair share. Look for opportunities that will help you achieve your goals.

2. Go into every situation prepared for good and bad breaks; they may not always be apparent. Take advantage of good breaks. Do whatever is necessary to overcome bad breaks. It should be noted that losers use bad breaks as an excuse for failure.

   Be proactive so you can see potential good and bad breaks before they occur. This will often give you a chance to change the outcome. You can often position yourself to get more from good breaks and to suffer less from bad breaks.

3. Whenever you are involved in something with other people, expect things to go your way. Events often occur along the lines people expect, similar to how things work out with a self-fulfilling prophecy.

4. Do not settle for being mediocre in anything that is important to you. Life's rewards disproportionately go to those who excel.

5. Imagine you and your peers walking through life in a group. Anyone willing to do a little work can keep up with the group. Work harder than your peers and you will move nearer the front where it is more pleasant. If you fall on your face (lose a job or suffer a significant financial loss), remember the following. The longer it takes you to get back on your feet, the farther back you will be. Also, do not count on others to help you, though you should use whatever assistance is offered or is otherwise available. You need to get back on your feet as soon as possible and work extra hard to get back to where you were.
6. Do not feel unworthy of success as a result of being more able or having received more breaks than others. This feeling may unconsciously cause you to partially sabotage your successes. Most likely, there are many people with more ability and more breaks than you who are putting 100% of their effort into getting ahead.
7. Believe in yourself and tell yourself that you deserve to be successful. Most likely, there are many people less deserving than you who are more successful than you, so do not hold yourself back in your pursuit of success.

Chapter 6

Developing Self-Confidence

Self-confidence, as explained in this chapter's four items, seems to be rooted in the unconscious mind and it has a major impact on people's successes in life.

1. Often when people fail or do poorly the first time they do something, their reaction is to think, "I am no good at this." Their confidence concerning the matter is set very low based on just one experience. Conversely, when people are successful the first time they do something, their confidence is set high based on just one experience. These reactions are likely caused by people putting too much faith in the first impressions that are processed by their unconscious mind.

   Sometimes when people think they are "no good at something," they make matters worse by telling themselves that they do not care about being good at it.

2. Confidence affects you at the unconscious level. If you think you can do something, you have a better chance of doing it. If you think you cannot do something, you have a worse chance of doing it.

3. Fear of failure caused by lack of self-confidence is probably the biggest reason many people in the United States today do not come close to reaching their potential; the other major reason is lack of persistence when the going gets tough. Sometimes people will not try their hardest to overcome a difficult challenge because it is more difficult to accept defeat after trying their hardest than to accept defeat when they did not try their hardest.

When you are faced with a difficult challenge that has to be overcome, consider the following reasons to try your hardest:

- You may be successful on your first try.
- In the future, you will most likely wish you had tried your hardest.
- If you try your hardest and fail, you will have a good idea of what you need to do before attempting it again. Many successes follow failures, most people just talk about their successes.

4. Develop confidence in your own judgment about things. Rather than accept other people's judgments, you should start by basing your judgments on your own experiences and knowledge. Reconcile your judgments to the judgments of others and determine if there are some additional facts you should consider. It is a big mistake to just follow other people's judgments, by acting and feeling the way they do. If you cannot make judgments for yourself, you cannot effectively think for yourself and your chance for success in life will be diminished.

Chapter 7

Self-Improvement

Self-improvement should be a continuous endeavor for everyone. This chapter is divided into the following sections.

- Personal Betterment
- Taking Care of Yourself
- Taking Control of Your Situations/Environments
- Dealing with Problems
- Other People's Opinions of You
- Being Happy

Personal Betterment

- If you want to be one of the best in your chosen field, start by identifying someone who is one of the best in your field. Determine what makes this person one of the best, such as level of knowledge, application of knowledge, innovation, record of accomplishment, good collaborative abilities, good listening skills, and willingness to instruct others. Then, improve your skills and abilities and do whatever is necessary so you have these attributes as well.

  It should be noted that the person you use as a model will probably not do everything right and possibly have some faults. You may identify things you should do better, such as being more up to date on knowledge, and things you may not want to do at all, such as being somewhat arrogant.

- Do not accept and learn to live with your faults. Correct your faults. Correcting them will take much less effort in the long term than living with them. Often, people who continue to make the same mistakes are people who do not fully acknowledge the negative effects of the mistakes on their lives.
- Do not waste time blaming others for your current situation. Take charge of your life and start making improvements.
- Automobiles often have governors that limit the top speed. Do not put a governor on your imagination, creativity, persistence, or ambition. It is okay to limit these four items when you have other things to do; just do not limit these four items in order to keep from getting too far ahead of your peers.
- Your mental capability can continue to grow throughout most of your life. From birth through early/middle twenties, the links between neurons (electrically excitable nerve cells) in your brain keep improving at a rapid but diminishing rate. After that, the lessons learned in life can increase your mental capabilities. The key here is that using your brain makes it more capable.
- Your conscious mind and unconscious mind need to work together as efficiently as possible. The unconscious mind can make excellent quick decisions based on gut feelings when it comes to simple matters but it cannot plan ahead very well, which is possibly why conscious thought evolved. The unconscious mind has to sort through conscious thoughts, so it would seem helpful for the conscious mind to summarize thoughts in a manner that would help the unconscious mind. This may be why it seems to be a good idea to write down and regularly review your goals and the strategies to achieve them. Goals and strategies should always be reviewed whenever a possible change comes to mind.

Taking Care of Yourself

- The decision on whether you should be self-sufficient concerning a need usually comes down to whether self-sufficiency simplifies or complicates your life in the long term. It usually is not worth being self-sufficient in matters such as growing and raising your own food as well as building your own home. It usually is worth being self-sufficient in matters such as getting to work every day and paying your own bills.
- In life, the situations you are in will change. Your primary situations involve where you live, where you work, and your relationships with others. Your goal is to keep improving your situations. Do not let spite or anger cause you to worsen your situation.

- Sometimes things work out better than expected and sometimes things work out worse than expected.

  Be more aggressive when things are going better than expected. Be sure to determine why things are going better than expected, so you can learn what can be done to make things go better in the future.

  Be less aggressive when things are going worse than expected. Determine why things are going worse than expected, so you can correct the situation and keep it from happening again.

  An example that can be used for both scenarios above is a salesperson making cold calls (contacting prospective customers for the first time). If the success rate of the cold calls is greater than expected, the salesperson should make additional calls using the same process. If the success rate is less than expected, the salesperson should make fewer calls and reassess the process.

Taking Control of Your Situations/Environments

- The more you know about what you are doing, the less you have to worry about making a mistake. An experienced house painter does not overly worry about spills; the painter is just extra careful when the chance of a bad spill is high and is always prepared to clean up spills.
- The more you understand your environment, the more you can see things coming. This allows you to be proactive rather than just react to life. Your environment includes everything you function within, such as your work, family, friends, neighbors, and the like.

Dealing with Problems

- Life's inconveniences are inevitable though they can be mitigated by proper planning, such as by allowing extra time and having backup plans. When you encounter one of these inconveniences, deal with it and put it behind you. If applicable, learn from it so you can avoid or mitigate similar problems in the future. Do not waste time thinking about inconveniences that have been dealt with and learned from, if applicable.
- At the end of each day, take a few minutes to reflect back on how the day went. Think about what did not go as it should have and why. Also, think about what went well and why. Determine if these experiences should change how you act in the future. Let go of any anger toward an inconsiderate driver or a rude stranger you may have encountered; it is irrelevant to your life.

Other People's Opinions of You

- Maintain higher standards for your own actions than the standards others would expect from someone in your situation. Civilization is based on people keeping their actions at or above commonly accepted minimum standards of behavior.
- Make sure others perceive your good work as being good work. If not, it will not be considered when people form opinions of you and your work.
- At times, you will need to portray yourself differently from how you really feel, such as not showing fear and acting confidently. Others will judge you based on what you say and do, not on your concealed inner thoughts and feelings. You need to consistently maintain the image you portray, especially when the going gets tough. Avoid saying how you would act in a given situation that could arise where you would not want to act as you had said.
- When you do something for the first time, such as making a presentation or winning an award, act as if it is not the first time.
- Protect your reputation. If a few members of a group do something that is disreputable, the disreputable act could stain everyone in the group.
- Your reputation is based on what others perceive that you have done. Make sure your reputation is not tarnished by any misperceptions.
- If you do something embarrassing and nobody knows or needs to know about it, keep it a secret.
- If you are a "jack-of-all-trades," keep it to yourself.
- Praising or criticizing yourself in front of others will usually lower the opinion of you held by others. Praising yourself will make all your accomplishments look suspect. Criticizing yourself could make your mistakes look worse than they really are.
- It is better to do what you should do on your own rather than to wait for someone else to tell or make you do it.
- Maintain your dignity. Try not to do anything that could lower the opinion of you that is held by people whose judgment you care about and respect.
- Do not commit to something you do not want to do. If you later decide not to follow through, your credibility will be compromised. Remember, a vow is like a rope in that the tighter it binds you the more likely it will be broken.
- When evaluating other people's judgment of your work, you should put yourself in their position so you can try to determine if they are being objective. If you feel that they are not being objective, adjust the judgment for their subjectivity.

- No matter what you do, bad or good, you can always find someone who will condemn or praise it. Only concern yourself with the opinions of people who are important to you, such as family, friends, and coworkers.

- Your self-esteem may be heavily influenced by how you fit in with your peers. Do not let a negative first impression, such as one that is based on how you fit in with schoolmates in grade and high school, go unchallenged and become a self-fulfilling prophecy.

Being Happy

- Feelings such as happiness are rooted in the unconscious mind and the conscious mind can only speculate about what causes them. An incorrect speculation can cause you to look for happiness in the wrong places. I believe the key to happiness, based on my speculation, is a combination of the following four items:
    - First, appreciate and be part of the amazing joy and wonder of life in the world. The more you do to improve life in the world, the more you will appreciate and be a part of it. Do not expect others to do more for you than you do for them. Do not harm others. If you accidentally harm someone, make up for it. Find and enhance what is good in yourself and others; discourage what is not good in yourself and others. The older you get, the greater the positive impact you will want your existence to have had on life in the world.
    - Second, be part of a community of family and friends where others are looking out for your well-being and you are looking out for their well-being. If no one besides yourself is concerned about your well-being, it is hard to ever slow down and relax. Even if you never need help from others, you will feel good when you help others who are in need. Be willing to stand up and defend what is right, even if it puts you in danger. Accept the responsibilities that go with your position in life, such as when you are a parent.
    - Third, be proud of your accomplishments, no matter what advantages you have had in life. No one discounts the accomplishments of an Olympic runner who was born with genetically strong legs and had good coaching from an early age. Accomplishments are the reason human life is better today than in the Stone Age and will continue to get better in the future. Positive accomplishments are a good measure of a person's self-worth relative to other people.
    - Fourth, have fun as long as no one is getting hurt.

- Unhappiness caused by events in the past needs to be dealt with as described in this paragraph. Blocking this pain is a short-term solution that is not good in the long term. You need to recall the painful memories and put them in a new perspective. The new perspective will become a revised version of the memory and will replace the old version of the memory in your mind. Putting things in perspective can involve (1) not blaming yourself for things beyond your control, (2) understanding that mistakes you made are similar to those that others in your position have made, and (3) accepting the randomness of life. When you have to deal with grief, be aware that there are four stages of grieving which are (1) denial, (2) guilt, (3) anger, and (4) acceptance. These stages do not always occur in the order above.

Chapter 8

Interacting with Others

Civilization is based on how people interact with each other. The following sections of this chapter concern your interaction with others.

- Helping Others
- Treatment of Others
- Being Helped by Others
- Dealing with Others
- Not Being Taken Advantage Of
- Conflicts
- People to Avoid
- Judging Others Based on Their Actions
- Being Judged by Others, Based on Your Actions
- Human Nature

Helping Others

- If you want to help someone, consider what the person needs. Do not assume that others need and want the same things you need and want.

- Helping people by giving them knowledge and advice is usually better than taking on their burdens. For example, if someone is carrying a heavy load, it would most likely be better to provide advice concerning use of a cart with wheels rather than for you to carry the load yourself. The more you confine your help to knowledge and advice, the more time you will have to help others. You can probably teach a dozen people how to fish in the time it would take you to catch enough fish to feed one person's family for a day.

- Do not exaggerate the help you are giving to someone, especially in front of others whose opinions are important to the person you are helping.
- Most advice and all constructive criticism should ideally be given in private.
- If you do too much for people, they may want to sever their relationships with you for two reasons. First, they may not want to feel too indebted to you. Second, they may feel insulted that you are acting as if they cannot take care of themselves.
- When people are upset and acting irrationally, it is often best to let them regain control by themselves. Two exceptions to this general rule are (1) when the people might hurt themselves or others and (2) when the people stay in the irrational state too long.

Treatment of Others

- If a friend is complaining about someone you will probably never meet, avoid questioning your friend's version of the story.
- Treat people with courtesy and they will most likely return the courtesy.
- Always leave before you wear out your welcome.
- In life, you will need to deal with many different people in many different types of situations; the key is treating everyone appropriately. For example, with family and friends be more forgiving and less competitive. Also, in general, do not subject your coworkers to your views on religion and politics.
- Know the people whom you are dependent upon, and treat them accordingly.

Being Helped by Others

- Do not ask people for something when they are more likely to say "no", such as when they are mad, sad, or they just told someone else "no" to a request that was the same or similar to yours.
- Sometimes you have to follow the pack quietly in order to get the pack to follow you in the future. Criticizing the collective judgment of the pack is usually not as effective as waiting for the right opportunity and presenting a better course of action. Disassociate yourself from the pack when you do not want to be associated with its collective judgment. Oppose the pack when it is doing something that violates your moral principals. You will be a Moral Coward, as defined by Mark Twain, if you avoid ostracism by being part of a pack that does things in violation of your moral principals.

- Whenever others see you do something new, you will get more attention than normal. During this period of extra attention, you will have a greater chance of having your ideas heard and accepted.
- It is much better to praise actions of others that deserve praise than to criticize actions that are wrong. People are more likely to do more of the things for which they are praised than less of the things for which they are criticized.
- Most people will be inclined to help you if they feel that you would have helped them in a similar situation.
- If you have a reputation for trustworthiness, others will be more likely to deal with you and they should be more likely to give you a better deal.

Dealing with Others

- Before you share your good fortune with other people, consider whether the other people would share with you if the situation were reversed. For example, suppose you ask someone to drive you to the store. At the store, you buy a lottery ticket and win a million dollars. The person who drove you to the store then feels entitled to some of the winnings. Ask yourself, if the situation were reversed, how much of the winnings would the person share with you.
- If someone does something to you accidentally and you do not know how to react, reverse the situation in your mind and determine how you would expect the other person to react. For example, suppose someone opens a car door into the side of your car resulting in a scratch on your car. The other person then tells you that your car has been "dinged" before in other spots and that it happens frequently.
- Conversation is an art; you need to simultaneously consider your opinion, the other person's opinion, and the similarities and differences between them. Unfortunately, most people just look at their own opinion and try to get the other person to accept it. If your goal is to persuade someone to accept your opinion, which is not the same as having a conversation, start by understanding the basis for the person's opinion. Then get the person to modify their opinion, based on shortcomings you point out, so it is the same as your opinion.
- When people confide in you, never use the information against them or tell it to anyone else.
- Do not tell anything to a friend that you would not want the friend to know if your friendship ended.
- Serious matters should be treated seriously. Others do not necessarily need to know what you consider to be a serious matter.

Not Being Taken Advantage Of

- Start dealing with all strangers on an arm's-length basis. Be careful about getting closer based totally on unsubstantiated information from the stranger. Do not assume that people are whom they first appear to be. First impressions of untrustworthiness are generally more accurate than first impressions of trustworthiness.
- As an honest person, you will have an initial tendency to assume that others are honest. This can make you vulnerable to a dishonest person who acts honestly.
- Do not be tricked into revealing a secret, by being misled into thinking it does not matter anymore or that others already know.
- Do not be tricked into agreeing that you did something that you did or did not do, by someone who implies that it was a clever thing to have done or that it does not matter anymore.
- When rational people make an offer where it seems like they will get less in return than they contribute to a deal, look to see if they have a hidden agenda.
- If people compliment you for something that does not really merit a compliment, ask yourself the following questions:
    - Are they looking for a compliment in return?
    - Is this how they get along with people?
    - Do they not understand what you did?
    - Are they trying to mention in front of others that you did something?
- In an ideal world, people are willing to give at least as much as they receive. Unfortunately, in the real world, there are people who want more than they are willing to give.

Conflicts

- Minor conflicts need to be resolved before they become major conflicts.
- If there is a possibility that someone may start a conflict with you, be prepared. Anticipate the person's possible first moves and have your responses ready. Possibly, block the first moves by fixing or having an explanation ready for whatever could be criticized.
- If a conflict is unavoidable, it may be better to proactively initiate it rather than to reactively wait for the other person to make the first move.
- People have things they enjoy more than most other people do and have things they dislike more than most other people do. Be careful to whom you reveal your likes and dislikes.

People to Avoid

- Avoid associating too closely with annoying people such as those in the following examples:
    - Avoid people who needlessly put their associates on the spot with ill-timed questions and acts. This offense is even worse when done in front of others whose opinions are important to the person being put on the spot.
    - Avoid people who point out inconsistencies in what their associates say or do, unless it is done in private with the intention of being helpful.
    - Avoid people who disagree just to disagree. It should be noted that people like this might not be taken seriously in the future when they have a legitimate disagreement.
    - Avoid people who are hypocrites. It should be noted that hypocrites' inconsistencies usually lower the credibility of all their opinions.
    - Avoid people who criticize others who are held in high esteem by their associates. It should be noted that the more someone criticizes others, the less credibility the criticisms have.
    - Avoid people who needlessly do or say things to make themselves look better than their associates.
    - Avoid people who do things that embarrass both themselves and others who are associated with them.

- It is one thing to lose fairly, but quite another to lose because of being cheated. Minimize your dealings with anyone who has a reputation for being a cheater. If you have to deal with such a person, always assume the worst. Protect your own reputation, by correcting misunderstandings whenever anyone feels you may have tricked them.

Judging Others Based on Their Actions

- The more a person inquires about other people's faults, the more faults the person probably has.

- People who change their mind easily may not have well-thought-out opinions in the first place or they may lack confidence in their own opinions. On the other hand, people who rarely change their minds may be "close-minded."

- In order to judge a person based on the person's actions, you need to consider the circumstances that were in effect when the actions were taken.

- As Albert Einstein said, "Anyone who doesn't take truth seriously in small matters cannot be trusted in large ones either."

Being Judged by Others, Based on Your Actions

- Do not let misconceptions about your actions strain relationships with people who are important to you.
- The greater the difference between how you view yourself versus how others view you, the greater the chance for misconceptions concerning your actions.
- Avoid exaggerating. The more you exaggerate, the more that people will assume you always exaggerate which will diminish your credibility.
- If you joke around too much, others may have trouble knowing when you are serious.
- The less you call attention to yourself for your accomplishments, the more recognition you will usually get in the long term. If people think you take too much credit, they may assume credit for future accomplishments is overstated.
- When people treat you with respect and honor for things you have done, accept their praise. Do not insult people who give you respect and praise by being unduly modest.

Human Nature

- The more that people take responsibility for their actions, the more careful they will be concerning how their actions affect others.
- The more that people are involved with determining how they should do something, the greater their incentive to overcome unanticipated problems.
- People have a tendency to act in a manner consistent with the type of person they feel others think they are. A wise and successful entrepreneur once told me the following, which he learned from his mother: "Treat everyone like you trust them, but do not trust anyone."

  People's actions can range from good to bad. If you are good to people and treat them like they are good people, their actions will most likely be on the good side of their range.

- People have a tendency to see other people as they see themselves.

  Do not assume others do things for the same reasons you do things. For example, some people think things out before acting, while others act impulsively.

  Do not assume that what makes you happy is what makes other people happy. Too often people give presents based upon what they themselves would like to receive rather than what the recipient likes.

Chapter 9

Perceiving Reality

Reality includes everything, including you. Every decision you make is based, in whole or in part, on your perception of reality. Except for basic things, there is usually a difference between your perception of reality and reality as it exists. For example, a fence could be a source of privacy to a person, an eye sore to another person, an object blocking sunlight on a garden to another person, and an impediment to someone whose path is blocked by the fence. The real reality of the fence, if it can even be defined, is irrelevant to these four people. People's immediate perception of reality is based on how they think they are directly and indirectly affected.

This chapter covers two ways to view reality, lists things that can distort your perception of reality, and has information on how you can challenge your perception of reality.

It is very important that you have a good perception of reality that is based on both of the following two ways to view reality:

- How you are affected, directly and indirectly — A situation where you are interacting with three peers in a group would be viewed as you in relation to three peers.
- An objective third party's point of view — The situation where you are interacting with three peers in a group would be viewed as four peers interacting in a group.

Viewing Things Based on How You Are Affected, Directly and Indirectly

- You categorize things for storage and generalizations based on their effect rather than what they really are. Generalizations are needed to simplify the thinking process but can cause problems when they are not based on a representative sample of occurrences.
- When it comes to planning how to accomplish goals, this view helps identify what you need to do to accomplish your goals.
- You can identify opportunities where working with others is more productive than working alone.

Viewing Things from an Objective Third Party's Point of View

- You can see how you fit in with a group (club, work place, society, and the like), so you can determine (1) how you want to fit in and (2) what you have to do to fit in the way you want to fit in.
- You can evaluate groups based on what they do and decide which groups you may want to join.
- You can form relationships with others based on "consideration" and "kindness" that go beyond relationships based on "you do this for me and I will do that for you."

  Relationships based on consideration and kindness bond people together in societies. The more of this bonding, the friendlier greetings and less rudeness that members of the society will theoretically experience.
- You can see and understand the value of making sacrifices for the greater good, where the cost of your sacrifice is less than its benefit to others.

  Societies, from small local societies to a country's society, break down when the percentage of people making sacrifices for the greater good falls too low. This fall can be caused by these people feeling that their sacrifices are being taken advantage of too much by others.
- You can see the importance of having a lifetime goal for your life to have had a significantly positive effect on others.
- You can understand what it means to be proud of yourself and why you have to start doing more of the things that make you feel proud and less of the things that do not make you feel proud.

Things That Can Distort Your Perception of Reality

- First impressions — If your first attempt to do something results in failure, you may then believe that you are not good at whatever you were attempting. If your first attempt results in success, you may then believe that you are good at whatever you were attempting.

  Once you think that you are good or not good at something, the following can be a guide to your future success doing it. If you think you can do something, you probably can. If you think you cannot do something, you probably cannot.

- First experiences — The first time you meet someone from another country, you may assume that others from the country are the same as the one person you met. This assumption simplifies the thinking process when it comes to evaluating other people from the country.

- Associations — The more caring and helpful a child's teachers are, the more caring and helpful the child will believe future teachers will be.

  Neurons in your brain, such as those involved with the perception of a teacher and those involved with the feeling of being cared for and helped, that are active at the same time will link together. These neurons will eventually unlink after they stop being active at the same time.

- Assumptions adopted from others — Prejudices are often picked up from people who are making assumptions that may not be based on fact.

  Sometimes you may easily end up adopting the assumptions of a group that you join.

- Assumptions made to explain occurrences — Your mind needs to draw conclusions concerning situations you encounter. There is not enough time to adequately analyze every situation, so your mind will often assume the situation is the most likely thing to have occurred based on your perception of reality. These assumptions then become part of your perception of reality.

  The above is why we sometimes have trouble seeing what we think is impossible.

- Beliefs — People who believe that success always eludes them will be less likely to do everything that can be done to succeed. People who believe that they are normally successful will be more likely to do everything that can be done to succeed.

  Beliefs, correct and incorrect, have a tendency to become self-fulfilling prophecies, as people tend to pursue results that are the same as they have previously experienced in similar situations. These results cause emotional states, such as the feeling of success and the feeling of failure, which need to be repeated. These emotional states, whether good or bad, become addictive where the more you experience them, the more you need to keep experiencing them. You can replace these incorrect beliefs with the correct beliefs, as follows. Whenever thoughts about a matter cause you to experience the negative emotional state associated with an incorrect belief, tell yourself that the correct belief is the reality of the matter and keep doing so until you experience the positive emotional state associated with the correct belief. Eventually thoughts about the matter will evoke the positive emotional state associated with the correct belief, which will mean that you will have replaced the incorrect belief with the correct belief.

- Coincidence — Suppose you eat a particular food you enjoy on the first day you take a medication that makes you feel very sick. The likely short-term and possibly long-term result is that you may no longer enjoy the food as much or at all.

- Not putting things in the correct perspective — The best example of this is children watching movies that they are not knowledgeable enough about to understand and put in perspective. The same goes for some video games and some music videos.

- Drawing bad conclusions — A child who is not physically aggressive or good at insulting others can end up being excluded from the "in crowd at school." Children who are excluded are likely to conclude that they are not as good as other kids. This bad conclusion can last a lifetime if it is not recognized as a bad conclusion.

  Few adults would consider physical aggression and insulting others to be characteristics of a good person.

- Not viewing things based on how they directly and indirectly affect you — Make sure you accurately determine how something directly and indirectly affects you. Bright lights from a large SUV coming in your car's back window can affect you by making you angry. The lights could also affect you by getting you to not look in your rear view mirrors and ignoring the inconvenience. If your perception of reality is that things are always making you angry, you may experience the first of these two effects. If your perception of reality is that life has inconveniences that have to be dealt with as simply as possible, you may experience the second of these two effects.

- Advertisements — Companies want you to associate their product with other things you want. For example, car companies know that most people want to be respected for being financially successful, so their advertisements are designed to make people think that driving the companies' expensive luxury cars will result in respect for being financially successful.

Challenging Your Perception of Reality

You can challenge your perception of reality, as follows. Create a proposed theoretically sound perception of reality for yourself that you can consider when you think about something. Possibly, include your own version of the following in the overview of your proposed theoretically sound perception of reality:

- Human life is precious.
- Human existence is the highest form of existence, in at least our solar system, that we are aware of from a scientific perspective.
- Conscious thought is the highest level of human existence.
- Conscious thought is the reason human existence continues to advance in terms of knowledge and understanding.
- As a human being, your final legacy will be based on (1) how positive your impact was on the lives of family, friends, and others and (2) advances in knowledge and understanding credited to you.

  Note: If you figure out something that others want to understand, help as many of these others as possible to understand it.

- The most important part of your perception of reality is your perception of yourself. Define yourself based on what you do. When you discontinue making a mistake, the mistake is no longer part of your self-image that is based on what you do.

  Note: Do not let an incorrect perception of yourself hold you back from achieving worthwhile goals. Pursue the things that support your goals and notice if you are hindering yourself in any way. Examine the things you do that hinder yourself and clear them up so they no longer hinder you. If you are being hindered by the thought that something is not right concerning a matter you are thinking about, review your thoughts concerning the matter so you can identify and reconsider whatever does not seem right. If you are being hindered by wasted time spent worrying about things you cannot affect, convince yourself that the need to worry does not extend to situations you cannot affect.

  Keep an open mind concerning your goals and how they fit together. There are many goals to pursue simultaneously. Some of these goals will evolve and the importance of each relative to the others will fluctuate. When there is a hindrance caused by two goals that need the same resource, such as your time, find the most efficient way to use the resource for both goals. If the hindrance is being caused by something that is not in support of a goal, reconcile the rationalization behind the hindrance to the rationalization behind the goal you are pursuing.

BOOK FOUR

PRESERVING INCOME AND INVESTING FOR RETIREMENT

Money earned is the means to the end, not the end itself.

Preserving income and investing for retirement are necessary to maximize the benefit of money earned. Book Four explains the following with an emphasis on how to avoid the financial mistakes that many people make:

- How to curtail wasteful spending
- How to get the most from money spent
- How to maximize the purchasing power of money invested

Chapter 1

Saving and Spending

The purpose of saving is to preserve some of your money for use later. If you spend money as fast as you earn it, you will most likely have trouble meeting your financial needs after retirement.

The goal of saving is to be able to maintain a level or increasing standard of living throughout your life. It should be noted that the number of elderly people who cannot financially support themselves is growing. Many of these elderly people earned enough to have retired comfortably, but they did not save enough for their retirement.

"Savings" as used in this book refers to how much you put into saving/investment accounts. Price reductions on things for sale are deceivingly misleading when they are called "savings."

This chapter is divided into the sections listed below, which cover the importance of saving, spending wisely, and getting control over your finances.

- Saving Enough
- Compound Interest
- Getting the Most from Your Money
- Budgeting and Organizing Your Finances

Saving Enough

Compare your long-term saving goals to the following example in order to get an idea about how much you should be saving. Substitute your information in the calculation to get a better idea about how much you should be saving.

In this example, a married couple in their twenties have just bought a home, plan to have children, and need to start saving for retirement.

Based on the following assumptions, this couple needs to save 20% of their net pay every year so that they will have enough saved for retirement:

- Money saved/invested will grow at an average annual after-tax rate of return equal to the average annual inflation rate for the things that will be purchased with the money.
- Pay increases in excess of the inflation rate will generate enough extra money, after saving 20% of net income, to pay for all their children's non-college expenses.
- Their expectations are that employment will continue for the next 40 years and they need to save for 20 years of retirement.
- Annual retirement needs, stated in today's dollars, paid out of savings will equal 60% of their current net pay.

  Note: After retirement, living expenses should be lower than before, as the home should ideally be paid for and there should be no work-related expenses. In addition, there will be income from social security and possibly pensions.

The 20% of net pay that needs to be saved for retirement is calculated as follows:

Net pay multiplied by 20/60* multiplied by 60%** equals 20% of net pay.

*This part of the calculation sets aside one-third of net pay for the one-third (20 of 60 years) of their lives that comes after retirement.

**This part of the calculation, from the last assumption above, reduces the amount that needs to be saved in order to adjust for lower living expenses and other income after retirement.

Notes concerning the 20% of net pay that needs to be saved for retirement, are listed below:

- Increases in future amounts saved resulting from increases in net pay above the inflation rate will build up a reserve that will ideally cover emergencies such as losing a job.

- After the children grow up, the portion of income that was spent on their non-college expenses can be added to the amount being saved. This increase will hopefully not be needed to cover any shortfall in either amounts saved or investment earnings. Possibly, this extra savings could allow for an earlier retirement or build a reserve in case the couple outlives the 20 years planned for retirement. Ideally, they will not need to subsidize the income of their parents or their adult children.

- When totaling how much is being saved, untaxed income put into tax-deferred savings plans, including any company match, should be stated on an after-tax basis. See the Prioritizing Your Investments and the Choosing between Different Investments and Loans sections of the Investing chapter for information, respectively, on tax-deferred savings plans and information on converting before-tax amounts to after-tax amounts.

Continuing with the example above and its assumptions, suppose the couple wants to save an additional amount to pay for college expenses at the best state university available to their child.

Based on the following assumptions, the amount saved/invested each month needs to start at $200 and then increase with the inflation rate over the next 40 years for each child:

- The couple wants to spread college expenses evenly after adjusting for inflation, over their working lives. In effect, they will be dipping into retirement savings to pay for college expenses and repaying the money in later years.

- The current annual cost at the best state university for tuition, room and board, and books is $24,000, which will grow with the general inflation rate until the last child graduates from college.

The $200 per month that increases with the inflation rate for 40 years is calculated as follows:

Multiply the $24,000 by 4 years and then divide the total by 480 months (40 years) to get $200 per month.

If the annual inflation rate over the 40 years is 5%, the $200 per month will grow to over $1,400 per month in 40 years. In addition, a $75,000 annual salary with increases equal to the annual 5% inflation rate will grow to around $528,000 in 40 years.

To pay for college in less than 40 years, substitute the lesser year number in the formula. A 20-year period (240 months) would require an initial savings of $400 per month.

Compound Interest

Compound interest on savings and the effect of inflation on prices are the most confusing issues people face when planning how much to save.

As done in the preceding retirement and college expense savings examples, assume that money saved will grow at an average annual after-tax rate of return equal to the inflation rate for the things that will be purchased with the money. Based on this assumption, you can use today's costs for things you plan to purchase in the future as long as you increase the monthly amount saved by the inflation rate. If you feel that your after-tax rate of return may beat the inflation rate by almost 2%, do your financial planning projection using 0% inflation and 2% rate of return. If you feel that your after-tax rate of return may be short of the inflation rate by almost 2%, use 0% rate of return and 2% inflation rate.

The "Rule of 72" is a good way to approximate how long it will take savings and prices to double. Divide 72 by the assumed rate of return on savings or the assumed inflation rate, both expressed as a whole number, to get the number of years for savings or prices to double. You can also divide the 72 by the number of years to get the rate of return on savings or inflation rate that doubles savings or prices. The following shows both of these "Rule of 72" relationships.

Rate of Return/ Inflation Rate	Approximate Years for Savings/Costs to Double	Return/Inflation % Multiplied by Years
6%	12	72
12%	6	72
8%	9	72
9%	8	72
4%	18	72
18%	4	72

Getting the Most from Your Money

- Saving is not a matter of deciding to not spend or to spend less. Saving is a decision to spend the money later when you can put it to better use.

  A luxury car can cost as much as two regular cars that have the same basic utility as the luxury car. Instead of buying the luxury car, you would be better off buying a regular car now and saving the difference to pay for a second regular car after retirement.

Make sure you understand the difference between your *needs* (necessities of life) and your *wants* (desires). Minimize spending on your *wants* before retirement if there is a chance you will not have enough money for your *needs* after retirement.

- One of the purposes of advertising is to create wants in your mind that are more powerful than your desire to just satisfy current and future needs.

- Money paid to you by your employer has value because you can exchange it for goods and services. It is your decision whether to exchange it now or later.

- The earlier you start saving for retirement in tax-deferred accounts, the longer your money's growth will be compounded and the more you can earn on deferred taxes.

- If first generation immigrants from poor countries can work in the USA for 20–30 years and then enjoy a middle-class retirement, so can just about anyone.

- I hesitate to mention this, but it is a fact. Suppose there are two separate individuals starting retirement who are the same age and who have had the same income throughout their lives. Generally speaking, the one who spent the most in the past (saved the least) will get the most from the government in terms of after-tax retirement benefits. Currently over 25 million taxpayers are taxed on their social security benefits.

  Using the above as an excuse for not saving makes as much sense as not taking care of your health in order to get more health benefits from Medicare.

- Every couple of years, get form SSA-7005 from the Social Security Administration to verify that your earnings are being credited to your account.

- When I observe people flaunting or bragging about how much they spend, I am reminded of the following that my father used to say: "A fool and his money are soon parted."

- Measure financial success based on how much you save, not on how much you spend.

- When you see other people spending foolishly and you feel a need to compete, consider the competition as a matter of who will have enough money to retire at the youngest age.

- People who spend money to feel good about themselves will probably never have enough money to spend their way to happiness.

- Among the wealthy, people with "old money" are usually much more frugal than people with "new money." Unfortunately, it sometimes takes a generation or two of wasteful spending until the lesson of frugality is learned. In some cases, the wasteful spending keeps "new money" from becoming "old money."

- If you receive a one-time large sum of money, such as an inheritance or insurance payment, save it to pay for your future needs. If you have more than enough saved to meet your future needs, you should avoid the urge to *live it up*, and you should consider the following items to be higher priority than living extravagantly:
  - Set up trust funds to pay for your descendants' post-high school education and any supplementary education that may be needed during elementary and high school. Possibly, cover expenses for sports such as additional training and for school activities such as trips and exchange student programs.
  - Help your siblings and parents afford their current and future needs. Possibly, also help other relatives, friends, and worthwhile charitable organizations.

- Buy a home that meets your needs in a neighborhood where home values have a good chance of increasing in value more than in other neighborhoods that meet your needs. See the Buying and Selling a Home chapter.

  Do not decide to live in a rich, high-status neighborhood based on thinking that the higher cost of your home is an investment or will impress others, as explained in the following:
  - Investments should be diversified. While the gain on the sale of your home is generally tax free, within limits, the after-tax return on the extra money spent for your home is probably not any better than the risk adjusted after-tax return you can get in the financial market.
  - The *others* whom you will be trying to impress will include your rich, high-status neighbors, which will put additional pressure on you to spend money that should be saved. A big negative of raising a child in a rich, high-status neighborhood is that it will be harder to raise your children to be frugal adults especially if they grow up feeling poorer than their friends.

- It costs money to own things. In addition to repairs, maintenance, and insurance costs, there is the often-overlooked *opportunity cost* of money spent to buy things. Opportunity cost of money spent is what you could have earned after tax, if the money had been invested instead. If you have credit card debts or other similar debts, the opportunity cost includes the interest expense you could have avoided. Personal credit card debt is not tax deductible; therefore, the opportunity cost of purchases that result in increasing this type of debt is high.

  Suppose you take a $2,000 vacation that increases credit card debt by $2,000 for a year at an interest rate of 15%. Opportunity cost in the first year alone will add $300 to the cost of the vacation ($2,000 x 15%). The total opportunity cost will grow every year. When the $2,000 credit card debt is paid off, the annual opportunity cost gets based on earnings the $2,000 would be generating if it had been invested instead of used to pay off the credit card.

Before you buy a second home, third car, or a boat that will only get used occasionally, consider renting as needed instead. Make your decision based on the cost of ownership, including opportunity costs, versus the cost of renting.

- Take care of the things you own, as follows, but do not be pennywise and dollar foolish:
  - Change your automobile's engine oil, coolant, transmission fluid, and filters at least as often as recommended by the manufacturer, especially during the warranty period.
  - Purchase storm windows and insulation for your home if resulting utility savings will offset the cost over the next four years. Even if you may move, the improvements will possibly pay for themselves by increasing the sales price of your home.
  - Do not fix something that would be more economical to replace. Your decision whether to replace should be based on the repair's cost (money and time), the asset's added life resulting from the repair, and any differences in operating costs between the repaired and the replacement asset. Operating costs for a new furnace and air conditioner will most likely be significantly lower than for older units.

- Cheaper is better when you are getting the same goods or services as someone who paid more, such as with airline tickets.

For some goods and services, you can get better quality by paying more, such as for some clothes. You need to know when the increase in value is not worth the increase in cost. Also, avoid paying more just for the status of purchasing a particular brand. A watch only needs to be reliable and an automobile only needs to be reliable, safe, comfortable, and the right size and style to meet your needs.

- Do not make the mistake of thinking that since you overpaid $100 for something like an airline ticket, that saving $25 on a smaller purchase is not important. Mistakes happen, just make sure you recognize them and learn how to minimize the chance of repeating them.

- Do not mislead yourself into buying something you cannot afford by thinking that you can pay for it with future income. Keep in mind that the future income will be the same regardless of whether you make the purchase; therefore, the purchase will either increase your debt or reduce your savings.

- Credit cards are a convenient way to purchase things, as long as you pay them off each month.

Credit cards should be about the last source you use to finance debt. If you cannot get the money to pay off your credit cards, transfer the balance to the lowest rate card available and use a different credit card to make future purchases you can afford to pay off fully each month. Having the second card will save you the interest cost on these purchases, assuming you pay the credit card off in full each month.

Budgeting and Organizing Your Finances

- The less money that goes to pay expenses, the more money that can go into savings.

  There are two methods to reduce expenses. The simplest method is to minimize how much you spend on your wants and be as frugal as possible satisfying your needs. Budgeting is the more complicated method, but for most people it is more effective.

  Budgets can enable you to determine the following, which can be very helpful when it comes to reducing expenses:
  - How much you are currently saving or going into debt
  - Where you are currently spending your money, so you can determine where to best make cuts

- Guidelines for preparing a budget are listed below:
  - Select a time period you can best break your income and expenses into, for most people it is a month. If you are paid weekly and pay rent weekly, a week may suit you better. The rest of these guidelines are based on using a monthly time period.
  - Rough out a list of income and expenses for each of the last few months. Ideally, keep track of everything you spend money on for at least a month. Most of the information should be in your check register, bank account statements, and credit card statements. Categorize the expenses. It is better to have too many categories than not enough because later it will be easier to consolidate them rather than to break them out into different categories. Entertainment can be broken out into eating out, entertaining others, and weekend trips. The difference between total income and total expenses should be roughly equal to what you saved plus any changes in debt. Remember to count credit card finance charges as an expense.
  - Break out the income, expenses, and changes in net savings/debt identified above into an average month. For two-week pay periods, multiply net pay by 26 and divide by 12. For one-week pay periods as well as weekly expenses, multiply the amount by 52 and divide by 12. For expense paid twice a year, such as auto insurance, divide the payment amount by 6.
  - Identify how much you need to cut expenses each month in order to meet your savings goal.
  - Go through the monthly expenses and determine how much each one can be cut. If the budgeted expense and saving accounts are for a married couple, each person should separately make their own list of where expenses

should be cut. The two lists should then be merged, giving each person a fair say in the merged list. This joint effort will increase the chance that both people will work to make the budget succeed.
    - Do not assume that certain fixed expenses cannot be lowered. Home mortgages can be refinanced and insurance rates vary significantly.
    - Keep track of all future income, expenses, and savings/debt by month so you can fine-tune your monthly budget. Keep a list of expenses paid for by cash and keep an envelope with credit card receipts not yet billed.

- Sometimes you may decide to move money from one category in the budget to another. You may decide to sign your child up for a bowling league and pay for it with money from your entertainment category that is available because you grilled steaks at home instead of going out to a steak house.

- If you under spend one category in your budget and the other categories are within budget, add the under spent amount to the next month's budgeted amount for the category or add it to the amount you put into savings. Do not think that you have to spend everything in the budget. Sometimes the value of things available to purchase is not high enough to justify spending the money.

- Avoid spur-of-the-moment purchases. Always stop and consider where the expenditures fall in your list of priorities.

- Set up a file for everything that involves income, expenses, debt, and savings. It is better to have too many separate files than mixing similar things in one file. Typically, you will have a file for at least each of the following:
    - Bank accounts, one file for each account
    - Investments, one file for each investment company
    - Credit cards, one file for each card
    - Life insurance, one file for each company
    - Home
    - Home insurance
    - Property taxes
    - Automobiles, one file for each automobile
    - Automobile insurance
    - Employers, one file for each
    - Utilities
    - Income taxes, one file for each year
    - Medical and dental insurance claims
    - Medical and dental insurance information
    - Other insurances
    - Parts lists and instruction manuals
    - Warranty receipts and information
    - Other receipts

Note: It is generally better to save too much information in a file than not enough, though this strategy involves one risk. In the future, it will be hard to toss out the excess material in the files since it will be mixed with the material you want to keep.

- Have a place where you keep all bills you receive. Possibly, keep a list of these bills that also includes other payments you have to make.
- Keep a list of all checks you are expecting, such as rebates and expense reimbursements from work. Do not mark an item on the list "received" until you deposit the check and record it in your checkbook.
- When a store gives you a refund that will show up on your credit card statement, put the paperwork where you will see it when you file the next credit card statement.

Chapter 2

Investing

The purpose of investing is to preserve the purchasing power of the money you save. The more your after-tax rate of return exceeds the inflation rate, the more your purchasing power grows, and vice versa.

The goal of investing for most people should be to at least match average market returns without spending too much time managing and worrying about investments. If you can spend a minimum amount of time on your investments and match average market returns, you will have done well. Average market returns can be defined as the weighted average return for all stocks, bonds, and cash equivalents, based on your ideal mix of these three types of investments, as described later in this chapter.

This chapter is divided into the sections listed below. Contribution limits, laws, and information concerning investments in this chapter are subject to change and everyone's situation is unique; so you should consult with a competent investment professional before making any decisions concerning matters in this chapter.

- Prioritizing Your Investments
- Deciding Where to Invest
- Stocks (Equity)
- Bonds
- Cash Equivalents
- Balancing Your Portfolio

- Mutual Funds
- Buying Stock in a Company
- General Information about Investing
- Choosing between Different Investments and Loans

Prioritizing Your Investments

First priority is to invest enough in employer-sponsored savings plans so you get the maximum company match. The only possible exception is if you plan to quit the company before you will be significantly vested in the match.

Second priority is to pay off credit cards that have interest rates above 10%. Possibly, refinance them if you can get a home equity loan with tax-deductible interest expense.

Third priority is to invest the maximum in the three types of tax-deferred savings accounts/investments listed below.

- 401(k) plan contributions are before tax, where the income taxes on the wages contributed to the plan are calculated and paid when the contributions are withdrawn. Earnings accumulate tax deferred until withdrawn. Withdrawals before age 59 ½ may result in a 10% early withdrawal penalty. You can usually borrow some of your savings. There are 403(b) and 457 plans that are similar to 401(k) plans; the plan administrator can explain the differences to you.
- Traditional IRA contributions can be before tax or after tax. Earnings accumulate tax deferred until withdrawn. Withdrawals before age 59 ½ may result in a 10% early withdrawal penalty. After-tax contributions to this type of IRA should only be considered after you have contributed the maximum to 401(k) type plans and Roth IRAs.
- Roth IRA contributions are after tax and earnings accumulate tax deferred. Contributions can be withdrawn tax free. Earnings can be withdrawn tax free five years after the contribution is made if you are at least 59 ½ years old, or the withdrawal is made because of a qualified disability, or the withdrawal is used to pay up to $10,000 toward your first home. Consult with your tax and investment professional concerning both of the following. A Roth IRA may be better for you than a Traditional IRA. You may be better off converting your Traditional IRAs to Roth IRAs.

Note: Deferred taxes are like an interest-free loan from the U.S. Treasury that you can leave in your investment account to earn income. If you defer paying the tax until a year when your tax rate is lower, you will end up paying less tax than if you had paid the tax when your tax rate was higher.

Note: Insurance companies would argue that their annuity products should be included in the preceding list, for people who want more tax deferred retirement savings than the maximum allowed for the listed alternatives. I am not comfortable including annuities in the list because of the way their fees, other expenses, and surrender charges are presented and calculated.

Fourth priority is to invest the balance of what you can afford to save in the financial market (stocks, bonds, and cash equivalents), as covered later in this chapter.

If you are saving to buy a home in the next couple of years, avoid investments where you will have to pay a penalty to borrow or withdraw your contributions. As soon as you have saved 8% to 10% of your projected new home's cost, read the Financing or Refinancing a Home section of the Buying and Selling a Home chapter.

If you receive a one-time large sum of money, such as an inheritance or insurance payment, consider investing the maximum in the previously listed tax-deferred accounts. Then put the balance in investments that do not have withdrawal penalties, and draw out enough money each year to contribute the maximum to all these tax-deferred accounts. If you receive a large sum of money after marriage, you may be able to protect it in the event of a divorce, depending on the state you live in, by putting it in an account under your name that never gets touched. If you have accumulated a significant amount of money before marriage, consider a prenuptial agreement before getting married.

Put children's savings in custodial accounts so earnings will be taxed at the child's tax rate instead of yours. There are limits on how much a child can earn before the earnings are taxed as if owned by the parents.

Based on what I have read and heard, the general consensus among financial advisors who are independent from the insurance industry is — do not invest in any life insurance company investment that is combined with an insurance policy. I totally agree with this general consensus.

Deciding Where to Invest

A good place to buy and sell all your non-employer-sponsored investments is through a nationally recognized brokerage firm with access to all mutual funds. Discount brokerage firms generally have lower fees but provide less advice. Never invest with anyone who contacts you and claims to be with a reputable brokerage firm.

For all your investments, including employer-sponsored plans, you need to determine how much to invest in stocks, bonds, and cash equivalents.

Stocks (Equity)

When you buy common stock, you own part of the company. The other type of stock is preferred stocks, which is like a mix of common stocks and bonds. Preferred stock is generally too complicated for the average investor.

Large cap (capitalization) stocks refer to stocks in the big companies that make up the U.S. economy (Blue Chip companies).

Small cap stocks refer to stocks in companies with a market value under $500 million. Small cap stocks generally have a greater risk and greater potential return than large cap stocks.

There are two ways stocks can generate income for an investor. The price of the stock can go up (growth) and the company can pay dividends (income) to stockholders. Dividends are the portion of earnings not reinvested in the company.

Bonds

Corporations and governments borrow money by issuing bonds to investors. Bonds typically have a set maturity date and a set interest rate. When market interest rates go up, the value of outstanding bonds usually goes down because the bond interest rate becomes less attractive to investors relative to the market interest rate. When market interest rates go down, the value of outstanding bonds usually goes up because the bond interest rate becomes more attractive to investors relative to the market interest rate. The longer the maturity of the bond, the more it will tend to fluctuate due to changes in the market interest rates.

Investment grade bonds are the safest corporate bonds. Junk bonds have the highest interest rates, but you will also have the highest chance of losing all or part of your investment.

Government bonds generally have (1) an interest rate that is below the market rate and (2) interest income that is partially tax free. There are U.S. Treasury securities called I-Savings Bonds and TIPS that have adjustments for inflation. I-Savings Bonds have a two-part interest rate; one is fixed and the other adjusts for inflation. TIPS pay interest and adjust the principal invested for inflation. At www.TreasuryDirect.gov you can get information about I-Savings Bonds, TIPS, and other government bonds. There are mutual funds, described later in this chapter, that invest in government bonds.

Cash Equivalents

Generally, the safest place to put your money is in three- to six-month certificates of deposit (CDs) of less than $100,000 in banks and in saving and loan institutions that are covered by the Federal Deposit Insurance Program (FDIC). Treasury bills (T bills) issued by the U.S. Government are also just as safe, but are not as convenient to purchase.

The federal government does not insure money market funds at your brokerage house but they generally give you quick and more convenient access to your money.

Balancing Your Portfolio

The mix of stocks, bonds, and cash equivalents in your portfolio basically comes down to risk and expected returns, as follows:

- Stocks generally have the highest risks and highest expected long-term returns. Within stocks, small caps are more volatile than large caps. Both the risk and expected long-term return in stocks can be reduced by having a broadly diversified portfolio including approximately 25% invested in international stocks spread out across Europe and Asia. You should have no more than 2% of your stocks in any country other than the United States. Because of the risks, stocks are generally better for long-term investments.
- Cash equivalents generally have the lowest risks and the lowest expected long-term returns. Cash equivalents are more for short-term investments.
- Bonds generally fall between stocks and cash equivalents in terms of risk and expected long-term returns.

If you need to rebalance the mix of stocks, bonds, and cash equivalents in your portfolio, first change the mix in your tax-deferred accounts. Then, if necessary and if time permits, just redirect future investments, including dividend reinvestments. Selling investments in non-tax-deferred accounts can trigger taxes that are usually better left deferred. If you have to sell shares in a non-tax-deferred fund with a lot of deferred tax, consider identifying the shares for which you paid the highest price, and give your broker a letter with instructions on which shares to sell. It is probably best to consult with your tax preparer on exactly how to do this.

To illustrate how the ideal mix of stocks, bonds, and cash equivalents change, the following hypothetical example of a person's approximate investment mix is shown below:

- When right out of college at age 21–25
  - 90% in stocks, to go for compound growth without much to worry about concerning short-term market setbacks
  - 10% in cash equivalents, for liquidity

- When total investments equal approximately two years' current gross pay
  - 75% in stocks to keep investments growing
  - 22% in bonds to protect against market setbacks
  - 3% in cash equivalents
- When total investments equal approximately ten years' current gross pay
  - 60% in stocks to keep investments growing
  - 39% in bonds to further protect against market setbacks
  - 1% in cash equivalents
- Within five years of retirement with investments close to being enough to cover retirement needs
  - 25% in stocks is the most that should be at risk of a market downturn
  - 74% in bonds, since investments are close to meeting needs for retirement
  - 1% in cash equivalents
- After retirement
  - 10% in stocks to minimize the risk to retirement savings
  - 40% in bonds to protect retirement savings
  - 50% in cash equivalents to generate current income
- The mix percentages in the examples above are generalizations and will change based on factors such as the following:
  - Types of investments within each of the three categories, in particular the stock investments
  - Current and forecasted market conditions
  - Levels of current and expected future gross pay
  - Other income and expenses

Mutual Funds

Mutual funds are my preference for stocks, bonds, and cash equivalents. The main advantages of owning mutual funds rather than individual securities are professional management watching over your investments, diversification, and the ease of adding diversified international stocks to your portfolio.

- Confine your purchase of stock and bond mutual funds to the following:
  - Purchase no load funds. Short-term trading fees of up to 2% are not a problem assuming you are reasonably sure that you will be in the fund long enough to avoid paying the fee.
  - Purchase funds with a Morningstar rating of four or ideally five stars.
  - Purchase funds that have had good returns over the long term. Never invest based solely on a fund's good returns over a short time period. Risky funds often have good short-term periods followed by bad short-term periods.

- Taxes can take a big bite out of your mutual fund investment earnings that are in non-tax-deferred accounts. Even if you do not sell any shares or withdraw any money, you will have currently taxable income from dividends and from gains the fund realizes on securities it sells.

- There are two types of stock and bond mutual funds, as follows:
  - Index funds hold stocks or bonds in all, or a representative selection, of companies in a market, so your investment returns should theoretically match the market returns less fund expenses. Examples of markets where your investment returns can parallel the market less fund expenses are the S&P 500®, which accounts for about ¾ of the market value of the U.S. stock market, and the Wilshire 5000, which accounts for more than all stocks on the NYSE (New York Stock Exchange) and AMEX (American Stock Exchange). There are funds that specialize in markets such as small companies with good potential for fast growth. Generally, the broader the market, the lower the fees and the lower the risks.
  - Actively managed funds buy and sell stocks or bonds within limits set by the fund, with the goal of maximizing returns for the investors. You can find actively managed funds that specialize in many things, such as small or large companies in certain stages of development, different industries, and different regions of the country and world.

- Two main differences between index funds and actively managed funds are as follows:
  - First, index funds make fewer trades, which means they generate less current capital gains, which is an advantage for non-tax-deferred accounts, and their operating expense ratio (OER) is usually lower. Index stock fund OERs should be under .75 and actively managed stock fund OERs should be under 1.75. All bond funds should have an OER under 1.00. An OER of .75 means that if the investment in the fund earns 7% for the year, you will earn approximately 6.25% (7.00% less the .75% OER), assuming your investment remained relatively level throughout the year. A fund's OER can be found in its prospectus.
  - Second, index funds are generally broader and more diversified, which reduces both risk and potential return.

- An index stock fund that emphasizes growth over dividends and tries to minimize capital gains caused by turnover within its portfolio is generally preferable for stock investments in non-tax-deferred accounts.

- An actively managed stock fund seems to be better suited for tax-deferred accounts. If you plan to buy and sell different actively traded stock funds using your tax-deferred accounts, you have to decide if the higher OER and generally lower level of diversification is worth it. If you plan to leave your investment alone, an index fund may be more appropriate.

- Buying and selling mutual funds or stocks in an effort to "time the market" is not as easy as it seems.
- The greater the percentage of your portfolio that is invested in bonds, the more appropriate a broad-based bond index fund would seem.
- The lower the percentage of your portfolio invested in cash equivalents, the more appropriate money market mutual funds at your broker would be. The greater your investment in cash equivalents, the more that treasury bills and certificates of deposit would be appropriate.
- There are mutual funds that invest in a combination of stocks, bonds, and cash equivalents.
- Tax managed funds invest in federal government obligations, which are generally not taxable by states, and invest in state/local government obligations, which are generally not taxable by the federal government. These investments generally pay a lower before-tax return than other investments with comparable risks. Usually only taxpayers with the highest marginal tax rate will get enough benefit from these tax advantages to more than offset the lower before-tax return.

Buying Stock in a Company

Buying shares of stock in a company takes more time and effort to do correctly than buying shares in a mutual fund. In the long term, it is hard to match the market returns by investing in individual company stocks unless you know something significant that is not known by the general investing public. If you decide to buy shares of stock in companies, consider the following:

- Avoid "penny stocks."
- Do not put more than 10% of your investments in any one company.
- Find out what percentage of the company's stock is held by the company's managers and if there are any restrictions on their sale of the stock. A high percentage of the stock being voluntarily held by management is an indication that the people who are running the business feel that it is a good investment. In addition, the greater the percentage of stock held by management, the greater management's incentive to make the stock price grow.
- Earnings per share (EPS) is net income, less preferred stock dividends, divided by the number of common stock shares outstanding.
- Price/Earnings ratio (P/E) is the current price of the stock per share divided by its earnings per share (EPS) in the last year.
- When analyzing a company's earnings per share (EPS) and price/earnings ratio (P/E), you need to consider where the company is in its life cycle. Is it in its

startup phase, its rapid growth phase, its mature phase, or is it between two of these phases?

- When you sell stock that is not in a tax-deferred account, any gain on the sale is currently taxable.

- When you get a "hot tip" from someone concerning a stock, you should consider the source. Has the source been reliable in the past? Before you invest, keep in mind that the desire to "make a killing in the market" has caused many investors to foolishly risk their investment funds. Usually by the time you hear about something that affects a stock's price or the market in total, the market has already been affected. Whenever someone brags about "making a killing in the market," I am reminded of how people who go to Las Vegas usually talk more about how much they win than how much they lose. In both the stock market and the Las Vegas situations, I am either not talking to a representative sample of people or I am not getting the whole story.

General Information about Investing

- Bear and Bull markets refer to markets that are down and up, respectively. It is easy to remember which is which by thinking about how a *bear* will knock you *down* and a *bull* will toss you *up*.

- The financial market works efficiently, though investors often act irrationally, as follows:
  - Investors over react to major good and bad news, driving stock prices artificially high and low for short periods of time.
  - Investors have a tendency to keep falling investments too long and to sell rising investments too soon.
  - Investors sometimes hold on to an investment that has crashed with the idea that it will someday creep back up to the price they paid, even though they could sell it after it crashed and put the proceeds into a better investment.

    Note: You should always look at your portfolio as if someone just handed it over to you for the first time, except for tax considerations.

- The less you have to invest, the less an investment advisor is economically justified. Some people never use investment advisors and others have the need to hire one when investments exceed $100,000 or $150,000.

  Only use fee-based investment advisors. Fees range from 1% for large portfolios to 3% for small portfolios, of the assets managed. Under this arrangement, what is best for the investment advisor, to increase the total value of assets managed, is also best for you.

  Never hire an investment advisor who is paid via commissions on the financial products you buy. Under this arrangement, what is best for the financial advisor is much less likely to be what is best for you, compared to using a fee-based financial advisor.

- If you want to invest in real estate, consider buying shares in real estate investment trusts (REITs) that invest in commercial and/or residential properties. You can diversify your investment in REITs by buying shares in mutual funds that invest in REITs. Buying, managing, and selling properties on your own is riskier and much more time consuming than buying shares in a REIT, but the potential earnings are higher.

- Investments in gold, art, and other collectibles may seem appealing, but keep in mind that as a casual investor you are at a disadvantage relative to the professionals who specialize in buying and selling these assets

Choosing between Different Investments and Loans

In order to choose between different investments, such as real estate deals, or different loans, such as refinancing your home, follow the three steps below:

- First, identify all the alternatives for the investment or loan you are considering, and determine the projected before-tax cash flow by year for each. Exclude cash flow items that have the same after-tax cash flow amounts in each alternative being compared. After-tax cash flows are covered in the next bullet.

- Second, if the cash flow is taxable income or tax-deductible expenses, reduce the cash flow by your marginal (incremental) tax rate to get the after-tax cash flow by year. Determine your marginal tax rate by taking your prior year's tax return, assuming future income will remain relatively constant, and determine how much your total federal and state income taxes would have changed for a $1,000 change in income. A $350 change in tax for a $1,000 change in income means you have a 35% marginal tax rate. Using this rate, a $500 before-tax cash flow will equal $325 after tax ($500 less $500 x 35% equals $325).

  An alternative method to convert taxable/tax-deductible before-tax cash flows into after-tax cash flows starts with your last year's taxable income along with your federal and state income tax expense in the tax tables. Adjust the taxable income by the amount of the before-tax cash flow and see how much the tax expense would change. Subtract this change in tax expense from the before-tax amount to get the after-tax amount. If your projected future taxable income, excluding the before-tax cash flow being analyzed, will be increasing or decreasing, change the taxable income starting point of this alternative method by the amount of this increase or decrease. Changes in future tax rates also have to be taken into account.

  If your choice between alternatives is not obvious after this step, continue with the third step below.

- Third, subtract each year's after-tax cash flow in one of the alternatives being considered (call it A) from a different alternative being considered (call it B). If the resulting positive balances more than offset the resulting negative balances, alternative B is a better choice. Determine if the positive balances offset the negative balances, as follows. If the positive balances come first in the earlier years, assume they grow with interest and determine if they will grow to an amount that will exceed the negative balances in the future. If the negative balances come first, assume they grow with interest and determine if they will grow to an amount that will exceed the positive balances in the future. The growth rate for positive and negative balances in the early years should be based on what the money will get used for or where it will come from, respectively, and should be calculated as follows. For increases or decreases in debt, use the after-tax cost of interest expense, which for personal credit cards is the full credit card interest rate since the interest expense is not tax deductible. For increases or decreases in savings, use your after-tax rate of return on savings. For example, a $5,000 positive after-tax cash flow will more than cover a $7,000 negative after-tax cash flow four years later based on the first scenario below but not based on the second scenario below. In the first scenario, the $5,000 gets used to pay off personal credit card debt, with a 10% interest rate, that would otherwise not be paid off. In the second scenario, the $5,000 is saved in an account that earns 5% interest after tax.

Note: You can adjust the comparison in the preceding steps for risks, by calculating the expected before-tax cash flows based on the weighted average of the different possible scenarios' cash flows.

Note: For more on choosing between different investments and loans, see the Projecting the Financial Benefit of an Investment section in the Financial Decision Making chapter of Book Two.

Chapter 3

Insurance

The concept behind insurance is simple. A group of people pays money into a fund that gets used to pay expenses for anyone in the group who has a covered loss.

This chapter is divided into the basic types of insurance that all individuals should at least consider.

- Life Insurance
- Health Insurance
- Automobile Insurance
- Home Owners/Renters Insurance
- Disability Insurance
- Long-Term Care Insurance
- Personal Umbrella Insurance

Life Insurance

The two most important things to remember about life insurance are as follows:

- First, only buy term insurance, without any investment/savings plan or return-of-premium-paid plan attached to it. Life insurance companies keep coming up with new non-term policies that agents keep saying are as good as or better than term insurance. I have never seen any non-term insurance policies that are as good as term insurance, and I doubt I ever will. If an insurance agent tells you about new tax law changes that affect non-term life insurance policies, check with a tax preparer who does not sell insurance. I would not even consider looking at a non-term policy until I see competitive advertisements for non-term insurance like the ones you see for term insurance. By competitive, I mean advertisements that give the effective interest rate earned by average non-term policyholders. Effective interest rate would have to be based on cash value accumulation that policyholders receive and the net premiums they pay. Net premiums paid would be total premiums paid less the lowest cost for term insurance the insured person could have gotten from an equally rated insurance company. Insurance companies will never release this information because it will clearly make term insurance the obvious choice for life insurance. Non-term insurance includes term policies combined with annuities and with any other savings/investment plan.

- Second, buy at least enough life insurance so your death will not cause your dependents to suffer financially.

Life insurance is needed to replace lost income for your dependents. At a minimum, you need a current death benefit equal to the total of all your projected income from now until your youngest child finishes college. Be conservative in projecting this minimum insurance requirement. Assume your wages will increase by 10% a year and the life insurance death benefit will not earn any interest. Possibly, increase the life insurance death benefit so your spouse will not have to work and your dependents can live a better life financially than if you had lived.

If you need insurance for the next 10 or 20 years, buy a 10- or 20-year level term policy where the premium amount never increases. Only buy insurance from companies that the rating firm A. M. Best rates as A+ or A. Compare quotes from at least two different salespeople or web sites with access to the A+ and A companies. Web sites include www.termbuster.com, www.insurance.com, www.insweb.com, and www.insure.com. If you contact a salesperson, you may be subjected to a well-thought-out sales pitch for non-term insurance.

Credit life insurance pays debts, such as your mortgage, if you die. This insurance is usually more expensive than a regular term policy.

If you are replacing your insurance, make sure your new policy is in effect before you cancel the old policy.

If your children or other non-spouse are the beneficiaries of your life insurance policy and the death benefit would result in significant estate taxes, have the beneficiaries own the policy and make the policy premium payments.

Leave instructions with the original copy of your insurance policy that detail how the life insurance death benefit should be invested. See the Investing chapter. First thing on the list of instructions should be to ask the insurance company for a full payment of death benefits. None of your death benefits should be invested in the insurance company.

Health Insurance

Health insurance should be in effect at all times for all members of your family.

When changing insurance companies, it is better to overlap coverage than to risk not having coverage for one day. One day without coverage can cause pre-existing conditions to not be covered. If the new insurance company excludes pre-existing conditions, possibly keep your old insurance in effect until any pre-existing condition is cured or the new insurance company covers pre-existing conditions.

Automobile Insurance

Automobile insurance liability coverage should be in effect at all times your vehicles are driven. The additional cost for higher liability limits is usually worth the additional protection it provides, especially if you have significant wealth. The higher cost of lower deductibles for collision and comprehensive coverage should be evaluated based on the likelihood of you having a claim where your insurance company will end up paying for damages to your car. Comprehensive coverage is for theft and vandalism.

Make sure your policy fully covers you when you rent a car so you can decline all the insurances that car rental companies try to talk you into buying. When you rent a car and decline the insurance, make sure you get a copy of the inspections that show all marks on the vehicle when you picked it up and when you returned it; make sure the inspections are accurate, indicate the date of the inspection, and are initialed by the inspector.

Shop around for lower insurance rates.

Home Owners/Renters Insurance

Home Owners/Renters insurance is usually cheap and should always be in effect if you own or rent. Make sure your policy pays replacement value on claims rather than original cost less depreciation.

If your policy does not cover floods and earthquakes, consider separate flood and earthquake insurance policies.

Disability Insurance

Disability insurance should be provided by your employer; some small companies do not provide it. If not provided by your employer, you should at least buy long-term disability insurance.

Short-term disability coverage should pay what you were earning before the disability and usually lasts three to six months.

Long-term disability should start when the short-term disability coverage ends. Long-term coverage typically is for less than your full pay before disability. In addition, it usually does not go up for inflation and it usually ends when you get to a preset retirement age, such as 65 years old.

Long-Term Care Insurance

Long-Term Care insurance can pay for some or all of your long-term care expenses in the event you can no longer take care of yourself.

Personal Umbrella Insurance

Personal Umbrella insurance can cover you for liabilities greater than the liability coverage on your auto and home policies. Make sure your automobile and homeowner insurance policy liability limits meet the requirements of the personal umbrella insurance policy. The more assets and income you have, the more likely that the personal umbrella insurance is worth the cost.

Shop around for this insurance. Start by contacting the insurance companies that insure your auto and home.

Chapter 4

Buying and Selling a Home

This chapter covers the major items involved with buying, selling, and financing a home.

Buying a Home

- Understand the housing market in the general area you want to live, so you can find all the neighborhoods that meet your needs. Try to buy a home in a neighborhood where home values have a good chance of increasing in value at least as much as in other neighborhoods that meet your needs.
- Make a list of things you want in a home. List could include things like two-car-attached garage with street access, backyard on south side of home, four bedrooms, and basement.
- If you plan to have children, it may be worth paying extra for a home in a neighborhood with good public schools your children can attend rather than paying for private schools.
- Make sure the neighborhood is safe for your family.
- Determine how close you want to live to relatives and friends.
- If you drive to work, you could save a lot of time and fuel by living close to work. Driving an extra 30 minutes each way to and from work adds approximately 250 hours a year to your commute.

- If you take the train to work, it usually is financially advantageous to be able to get to the train without using a car. Maintaining a car just to drive to the train is very expensive.
- Do not buy a home in a flood zone.
- Avoid living on a busy street or on a street that may someday be widened, especially if you plan to have children.
- Expressways can be noisy for everyone living within a half mile.
- If there is vacant land nearby, possibly consult with a local land use attorney to get an idea about what may end up being on the land. Nearby factories can lower your property value. Retail stores can bring in a lot of traffic. Car dealers often use loud outside paging systems. Grocery stores often have late night deliveries by trucks that leave their engines and refrigeration systems running.
- Check out the homes that are close to any homes you are thinking about buying. Are any of them run down, full of junk, or is there anything else that would bother you?
- Are there train tracks nearby with crossings where trains blow their whistle at night?
- Try to get a warranty paid for by the seller. Prior to the warranty expiring, you should inspect everything that is covered.
- Moving to another home is expensive, especially if real estate brokers are handling the sale of both homes, so avoid buying a home with the idea of upgrading to another home in a few years.
- The agreement (contract) to buy a home will typically have a daily rate the sellers pay to you if they do not move out by closing. Set this rate as high as possible to reduce the chance that the sellers stay in the home after the closing date.
- Have an attorney review anything in the agreement you do not understand.
- Condominiums and townhouses usually have monthly charges to cover common area expenses. Figure in the monthly charge when you compare properties. If the roof or HVAC system looks old, have it inspected. Also, make sure there are no unpaid tax assessments.
- When you plant trees and bushes, space them based on their eventual size. When trimming existing trees and bushes, cut small amounts at a time because you can always cut more but you cannot reattach.
- If you are having a home built, also consider the following:
  - A basement is usually worth the cost unless you live in an area where basements are rare or they commonly flood.

  - Wiring for ceiling fans, extra electrical outlets, and cable outlets can be easily accommodated before the plasterboards are attached to the walls.
  - Builders often just paint the walls with one coat of cheap paint. Selecting your own paint and having two coats applied before you move in is advisable. Possibly, have the builder apply a good primer before painting. Get the unused paint, or buy some, so you can do touch ups as needed.
  - Your builder may be willing to build a deck and pour a cement patio at a cost lower than if you had the work done later.

- If you are buying a used home, also consider the following:
  - The older the home, the more important it is to get it inspected before you buy. You can check some things for yourself such as watermarks on basement walls or on ceiling; fresh paint on ceilings can be a sign that watermarks were covered up. Check the plumbing for leaks and make sure the foundation is solid with no cracks or decomposed wood.
  - Roofs and furnaces typically last around 20 years.

Selling a Home

- Selling by owner or with a discount real estate broker can save a significant amount of money, but it may take longer to sell.

- The agreement to sell your home will typically have a daily rate you pay if you do not move out by closing. Set this as low as possible if there is a chance you may need to stay awhile after closing.

- Have an attorney review anything in the agreement you do not understand.

Financing or Refinancing a Home

When saving money to buy a home, see if you qualify and can afford the following when you have saved 8% to 10% of what your new home will cost:

- Get an 80% mortgage with <u>no</u> mortgage insurance.

- Get a 15% home equity loan with <u>no</u> mortgage insurance.

Note: Loans above should have no points and minimal closing costs.

Use the extra amount saved, 8% to 10% saved less 5% down payment and less the closing costs, to help with the mortgage payments in the early years.

Possibly, rent out one of the bedrooms. You can usually charge more rent if the renter gets exclusive use of a full bathroom.

When comparing two financing options, lay out the payments for each, including up-front costs, by year until the home is paid off or until the time you tentatively plan to sell the home. See the Choosing between Different Investments and Loans section of the Investing chapter for information on how to compare different loans.

Adjustable rate mortgages and mortgages that have to be paid off in five years are very risky. It is usually a good idea to pay a slightly higher interest rate and get a 30-year fixed mortgage, unless you plan to sell the property in a few years.

The longer you plan to own the home, the more financially justified it is to pay higher up-front cost to get lower payments over the life of the mortgage.

When you refinance your home, make sure the release from your old mortgage is recorded.

Chapter 5

Buying and Selling an Automobile

This chapter covers the major items involved with buying and selling an automobile.

Buying an Automobile

When you purchase an automobile, you are satisfying your need for transportation that is reliable, safe, comfortable, and the right size and style to meet your needs. Advertisements for expensive luxury and sports cars are designed to make people think that they will feel better about themselves while driving the expensive cars and that others will be impressed. Do not be fooled by advertisements into spending more than necessary to meet your transportation needs. In addition, the more expensive an automobile is, the more expensive the insurance usually is. In addition, the larger and faster an automobile is, the more you will probably pay for fuel and repairs.

New Automobile

- Your goal should be to not pay more than the dealer invoice price. At www.kelleybluebook.com, you can get the dealer invoice price that includes destination charges and all optional equipment on the automobile you select. Subtract all factory rebates and incentives from the dealer invoice price to get your price.

- Do not pay any other charges the dealer may add to the cost, such as transportation charges and dealer preparation costs. Often salespeople do not mention the other charges when you discuss the price and then they include them in the written contract and say these are normal charges for all new car sales.

- Get prices from more than one dealer.

- Look in the transportation section of the newspaper to get a list of auto loan interest rates being offered by local banks. Bring the list to the dealer and say you will only accept dealer financing at the lowest rate on the list.

  Note: The title of the vehicle will be held by the financial institution that loans the money to you until you repay the loan in full.

- If you are getting prices from different dealers, get (1) Amount Financed excluding down payment and trade-in allowance; (2) interest rate, you will need to submit a credit application; and (3) the monthly payment. Make sure all three of these items are in the Federal Truth in Lending Disclosure section of the sales agreement (contract) before you sign.

- You should also check the following in the sales agreement before you sign:
  - Are the model, make, and year of the auto correct?
  - Does the VIN number match the auto?
  - Every option on the auto should be listed, especially options not already on the auto that will be added before you take delivery.
  - If you do not want the dealer sticker on your automobile, get it written in the sales agreement. If it is put on, you can make the dealer remove it. Stickers can usually be removed by heating them with a hair dryer to loosen the glue. Never try to remove stickers by scraping them or by using chemicals.
  - If you sign the sales agreement, get a copy signed by the salesperson or dealer before you leave the dealership.

- It is better to buy than lease an auto that is for personal use.

- After you buy your automobile, make sure the insurance is in effect before you take possession.

- Make sure you keep your warranty in effect by getting all required maintenance, keep receipts and make sure they accurately reflect mileage and date. Do not panic if you go over the mileage or time period requirements for oil changes by a little; just find an oil change shop that will use the mileage total and date you provide. Ask the attendant before the oil change and leave if the response is "no."

- If you want to protect your car in parking lots, remember shopping carts roll downhill and strong winds from behind can cause car doors to open more than intended.

Used Automobile

- Seriously consider spending more and buying an inexpensive new automobile. The resale value of most used automobiles, in my opinion, is overstated because most buyers of used automobiles do not adequately consider the cost and time to keep the automobile running reliably and safe. Buying a used automobile that is still under warranty is less risky, assuming the warranty is transferable and you get and check all the receipts for required maintenance.
- Consider having a reliable mechanic inspect any used automobile you are thinking about buying. The older the automobile and higher the mileage, the more an inspection is important.
- Check the asking price against the retail and wholesale price that you can find on the internet, such as at www.kelleybluebook.com.
- Most sellers ask for more than they usually end up accepting.
- When you pay, you must immediately get the title and receipt.
- Title you receive should be as follows:
    - Properly describe the vehicle — In particular, make sure the VIN (Vehicle Identification Number) on the title matches the automobile. VIN on automobiles can usually be seen by looking in through the front windshield on the driver's side.
    - Be signed where it says sellers, by everyone who is listed as an owner
    - Not have any erasures or evidence of alteration
    - Not show any outstanding loans
    - Be signed by a notary public if there is a space for the notary to sign
- Receipt you receive should contain the following:
    - Date
    - How much you paid and that it is the full price
    - What you bought, describe auto and include VIN number
    - Signature and printed name of all the owner(s), as shown on the title, acknowledging receipt of your payment — Check the signer's name against a drivers license and write down the drivers license number and address on the receipt.
- You may have to pay sales tax when you take the signed title to the currency exchange to get the title transferred.

Selling an Automobile

- Make sure the buyer is at least 18 years old; buyer's drivers license has date of birth. Age to purchase an automobile may be different in some states.

- Only accept cash.
- If the buyer asks for a receipt, write on the receipt "sold as is" and "no warranty or guarantee." Keep a copy of the signed receipt.
- Remove your license plate and window sticker.

Chapter 6

Other Purchases

When it comes to purchases in general, you need to be aware of the ten items in this chapter.

1. Often the more complicated a sales decision is, the less likely people are to check the details. This is the opposite of how you should act. Companies know that people have this tendency and sometimes overcomplicate things they do not want people to question.

2. Always get a receipt to prove your ownership and to prove a debt has been paid, especially when you pay with cash.

3. Cash is the least safe way to pay for things. A cashier or bank check is basically just as good as cash and safer to pay with; make sure you put the name of the person you are paying on the check and get a receipt with the amount that is signed by the person whom you paid.

   The safest way to pay is with a credit card. If the product is no good and the vendor will not give you a credit, contact the credit card company and stop payment to the vendor.

4. An attorney should ideally review agreements (contracts) before you sign them. Standard agreements you buy in an office supply store are safer than an agreement written up by the other person who will be signing the agreement with you. Do not sign an agreement if there are any blank spaces or if you have any questions.

Make sure whatever the salesperson says, such as "there is a full three-year warranty," is in the agreement. You may have three days after signing to have an attorney review the agreement and, if necessary, void it. If you do have three days, it should be written in the agreement. Handwritten changes to a typed agreement must be initialed by all people who sign the agreement. Always get a copy of the agreement signed by the other person; do not leave without it. If there is more than one page, each page other than the signature page should be initialed by everyone who signs the agreement.

When you drop your car off for service at the dealer or at a service station, you will sign a work order and will not get a copy. You may want to draw a vertical line through the blank spaces at the end of the section of the work order where requested work is listed. For car repairs, it is best to only deal with established businesses that have honest reputations.

5. When you compare two different financing options, compare their APRs (Annual Percentage Rate). The APR, along with other important information, is in the Federal Truth in Lending Disclosure Statement that should be part of any financed purchase agreement you sign.

6. Sometimes negotiating a lower price or longer warranty on something is as simple as asking for it.

7. Remember, you can usually shop around and find the same merchandise at more than one store, though it is not worth spending all afternoon to save $20. Be sure to check prices on the internet.

8. Whenever you hire people to do work on your property, make sure they are insured and bonded in case they get hurt or they damage your property. Also, if applicable, get a guarantee that the work will pass all applicable building codes. All three items above should be in any agreement you sign. Possibly, ask contractors to have their insurance company send to you a Certificate of Liability Insurance. When you get the Certificate of Liability Insurance, make sure the insured party is whom you are hiring to do the work, the policy's effective date is current, and the policy includes an adequate amount of general liability and workers compensation insurance.

   In addition, whenever you hire someone to do something like remodeling a bathroom or putting up a fence, avoid paying in advance. There is no need to pay for materials in advance because all reputable contractors buy on account. You could offer to buy the materials yourself, but the contractor would have to reveal the markup on the materials. You could offer to pay enough to cover the materials when the contractor brings them to your home. If you are having a fence put in, consider paying one-third when the posts are set and the balance when the fence is finished. If you make an advance payment that is greater than the contractor's profit on the job, the contractor will not be in a hurry to buy the materials and complete the work for you.

If you are not dealing with a local home center or established business, ask for the names of previous customers you can contact.

9. The following five situations are a strong indication that someone may be trying to cheat you:
   - You have to decide today, it cannot wait.
   - You are not supposed to tell anyone else about it.
   - You pay with cash.
   - The deal seems too good to be true.
   - The deal is based on a tax loophole that hardly anyone else knows about. Note: You can always find someone who knows about taxes to ask about the loophole.

10. The following is an example of fraud.

    Someone who claims to have found $25,000 contacts you. The person says that for $2,000, which cannot come out of the $25,000 and has to be paid quickly, an attorney will make it legal to keep the $25,000. If you give the person $2,000 now for the attorney, you will get half of the $25,000 after the attorney has made it legal to keep.

Chapter 7

Other Financial and Legal Matters

This chapter covers the following miscellaneous financial and legal matters.

- Protecting Your Financial Assets
- Managing Debt
- Gambling
- Paying Income Taxes
- Having a Will (Last Will and Testament)
- Your Legal Rights

Protecting Your Financial Assets

- Your ATM card should not be linked (allow access) to your savings account. Also, consider limiting the daily ATM withdraw amounts from your checking account.

- Your ATM PIN and the password to transfer funds between accounts should not be the same.

- Frequently change your PIN and bank password.

- When you use the mail to pay bills, put payment envelopes into a post office mailbox. The worst place to put the envelopes is in your mailbox at home with the flag up for potential thieves to see. If a thief gets your payment envelope, the thief can soak the ink off part of the check and rewrite it. There are pens with ink that cannot be easily soaked off, such as some uni-ball ® gel pens. You should test the ink in these pens by letting it dry on regular paper and then trying to wipe it off with nail polish remover that has acetone.

- Know when your bank statements and credit card statements usually arrive in the mail. If you do not receive them, contact the banks or credit card companies and find out why. Possibly, someone sent in a change of address form, so it will take longer for you to catch an unauthorized transaction on your account. Ideally, have all these statements emailed to you instead of sent in the regular mail.
- Bank statements and credit card statements should be reviewed as soon as you receive them. If there are any unauthorized charges or if any deposits/payments are missing, immediately contact the bank or credit card company.
- Review investment account activity frequently. Put restrictions on how withdrawals can be authorized and where withdrawn funds can be sent.
- Ideally, manage your bank accounts, credit cards, mortgage, and investments online so nothing is mailed.
- Maintain a list with all your credit, debit, ATM, and check cashing card numbers along with the phone number to call if they get lost. Do not include expiration dates or PIN numbers on the list. Keep copies of the list in a safe place that you can easily access. When you call to report a lost or stolen card, write down the name of the person you talked to and the time of your call. Ask the person what else you need to do and then do it. Make sure that what you are told to do is what your card member agreement (contract) says you should do.
- Cancel and cut up old credit cards.
- Credit cards that are infrequently used should be left at home in a secure location.
- Consider calling (888) 567-8688 and requesting that unsolicited credit card applications not be sent to you. If you do receive them, shred them.
- Make your signature hard to forge by forming each letter while writing quickly and not lifting the pen, except between names. Adding your middle name can also help.
- Be careful about who gets your social security number, date of birth, bank account information, mother's maiden name, drivers license number, and other similar types of information.
- Never give your credit card number and expiration date to anyone who contacts you.
- At least once a year, get a copy of your credit report and verify the information. Once a year you should be able to get a free copy from each of the three credit

reporting agencies, by requesting them at www.annualcreditreport.com. Make sure there are no unauthorized credit cards or loans listed.

- Read the Insurance chapter and make sure you adequately insure your assets.

Managing Debt

- If you ever borrow money to cover a period of negative cash flows, do not increase your spending just because you have more money in your pocket.
- When people's bills get too high, they should not be too embarrassed to look into filing for bankruptcy. If you know people in this situation, do not loan them more than a small amount of money. If they file for bankruptcy, you will only remain friends if you are not one of the people who lost money that was loaned to them.

Gambling

- When it comes to gambling, state sponsored lotteries have a very low after-tax payout to amount bet ratio, unless the pot has rolled over a few times. Best bet, in my opinion, is with a friend on a sports game. You can use the line (point spread or odds) in the newspaper before the game. Make sure the person you are betting against is not better informed than you are concerning what you are betting about, such as knowing that a key player on one of the teams is injured.
- It is not good for children to see adults in their family engaged in gambling.
- If you have to gamble, gamble in the stock market.
- When it comes to winning streaks based on pure chance, remember that it is nothing more than random occurrences. Flip a coin a 1,000 times and get close to 500 heads and 500 tails. During these flips, there will be a number of times when you get five heads or five tails in a row; statistically this is just random occurrence. No matter what the previous result of the coin toss was, each flip has a 50% chance of being a head or a tail.

  It may be a different matter than the above, when it comes to skill versus pure chance. If you are doing better than you usually do concerning a skill, possibly you are mentally sharper than you usually are.

Paying Income Taxes

- When it comes to income taxes, you should practice tax avoidance but not tax evasion. Tax avoidance is taking advantage of tax breaks built into the tax law. Tax evasion is breaking the law. When you hear people bragging about cheating on their taxes, keep in mind that the IRS sometimes takes a few years to catch cheaters.

- Keep a copy of all income tax forms you file, along with the instructions and supporting documents.
- If you anticipate getting a tax refund for the year, you are in effect loaning money to the government interest free. In this situation, you should consider decreasing the amount withheld each pay period.

Having a Will (Last Will and Testament)

Always have a will. The cost should be around $200–$250 for a simple will. The two main advantages of having a valid will when you die are as follows:

- Things will be much simpler and less costly for your heirs.
- Your estate will be distributed as you desire, subject to state law.

If you have under-aged children, you will need to determine who will be their legal guardian, who will control your children's money, and when your children will get the money that remains after they are raised.

Possibly, leave a note attached to your will with burial/cremation instructions and a final farewell to your loved ones.

Your Legal Rights

- For good information on your civil and criminal legal rights, go to the American Bar Association web site at www.abanet.org.
- Small claims court can be used to settle financial disputes inexpensively. When filing the claim, use the defendant's official legal name and clearly state the basis for the amount you are seeking. At the hearing, bring any physical evidence and impartial witnesses.
- If you are traveling in a foreign country and you get into legal trouble, immediately insist on talking to the U.S. Consular at the U.S. Embassy. You have this right per the 1963 Vienna Convention. You do not have to answer any questions from the local police until after you talk to the U.S. Counselor.

Chapter 8

Health

Poor health will increase your expenses and will likely decrease your earnings. Health and longevity are more important than money; just ask any rich person who is in poor health. This chapter includes some basic information on improving your health and living longer.

Taking care of your health is not an all-or-nothing type endeavor. You can do it well without being a fanatic. Talk to your doctor before doing any of the following so you can make sure you do what is right for you.

- Do not over or under eat. The purpose of eating is for nutrition, nothing else. The urge to over eat probably goes back to when food was scarce and seems to be ingrained into our minds. The urge to under eat in order to be very thin is ridiculous and should be resisted just like the urge to over eat. Food, like everything else that is good for you, has a point where more is actually bad for you. In the short term, too much food can make you tired. In the long term, too much food can cause excessive wear and tear on your body.

- Take a multiple vitamin and mineral supplement every day plus other supplements based on the latest research. Do not take anything in doses that legitimate health experts say may be harmful.

- Drink a half gallon of water a day, plus more when you exercise. Avoid drinking unfiltered well water. Water in your food counts the same as water you drink.

- Do aerobic exercises at least every other day, for at least 30 minutes each time, to the extent that you are breathing at least moderately hard throughout. Ask your doctor how high you can let your heart beat go while exercising.
- Stretch all the major muscle groups of your body at least once a week.
- Exercise all the major muscle group of your body at least once a month. Check with your doctor first.
- Lift with your legs, not with your back. If you are bent over while holding a heavy object, do not move your upper body to either side. Turn by walking, while keeping your lower back and pelvis locked in position together.
- Minimize the curve in the small of your back, as follows:
    - When you walk or stand, pivot your hips forward and pull in your stomach.
    - Once a day put your heels, calves, and the back of your shoulders against a wall and bring the small of your back as close to the wall as possible for 30–60 seconds.
    - Before going to bed, lie face up on the floor while holding your knees and then rock on the small of your back 10–15 times.
- Do not allow your posture to become hunched over as can happen from playing the guitar. Exercises that pull your shoulders back can help offset this problem.
- Keep your stomach muscles strong so you can reduce the chance of getting a hernia.
- Keep cuts covered until they heal.
- Wash your hands before touching your food or touching any part of your body that has an opening, such as your eyes or your mouth.
- If something hurts or you just do not feel right, check it out and treat it accordingly. See a doctor concerning anything that could be serious.

    I have known people who are more inclined to take their automobile in for service when it does not sound right than they are inclined to go to the doctor when they do not feel right. You can easily replace your automobile, but you cannot replace your body.

- If you have a genetic health condition or if you have injured something like your lungs, research the condition so you know the early signs of problems. Also, research what you should be doing and not doing to reasonably minimize any problems.
- Do not take foolish risks with your health, such as not wearing a seat belt or riding with a drunk driver.
- Avoid suntans, and wear sunglasses that block 100% of ultraviolet light.

Book Five

Raising Successful Children Who Are Prepared For The Career Fast Track

The overall emphasis in Book Five is on the following:

- Children need to learn how to be successful in whatever they decide to pursue. The earlier they learn how to do this, the greater the chance that they will lead successful lives.
- Children need to develop the self-esteem that comes from being successful. Parents need to bolster this developing self-esteem by (1) minimizing the credit they deserve in their children's successes, (2) acknowledging the significance of the successes, and (3) encouraging their children to reflect upon what led up to the successes.

Book Five will prepare children for the career fast track by helping their parents instill the following basic characteristics of people with successful careers:

- They understand the importance of having a successful career
- They are willing to work hard enough to be successful
- They have the skills, knowledge, and abilities to be successful

References to parents refer in general to primary caregivers.

Chapter 1

Getting on the Right Track

It is easier to get on and stay on the right track in the first place than to switch over to it later. People tend to (1) view things as they have previously viewed similar things, (2) handle things as they have previously handled similar things, and (3) expect things to be the same as they have previously been. This tendency to stay on the same track applies to many things, such as understanding things, working, approaching challenges, questioning things, and pursuing knowledge. It should also be noted that children often get on the same track as others whom they look up to and admire. Children who observe that their parents enjoy reading and enjoy the company of others will likely also enjoy reading and enjoy the company of others. As detailed in this chapter, the younger children are, the easier it is to get them on the right track.

People, like most living organisms, adapt to their environment. Rapid and difficult to reverse adaptation begins at birth and continues for a few years, after which it tapers off for the rest of the person's life. This rapid adaptation occurs in response to the baby's environment. Parents have an absolutely critical responsibility to provide an environment that results in a child who is well adjusted (adapted). A well-adjusted child is one who is on track to be a good, happy, and successful adult.

Adaptation involves forming links, called neural circuits, between neurons (electrically excitable nerve cells) throughout the brain. There are approximately 100 billion neurons at birth, and this total may not grow.

Neural circuits guide the thinking process (thoughts, decision making, emotions, and the like) and are formed as follows:

- Instincts are always automatic so they have to be rooted in neural circuits that are formed before or right after birth.
- Thought processes involve links between neurons in different parts of the brain. The more that a particular thought process is repeated, the stronger the link between the neurons involved with the thought. The stronger the link, the faster the thought process occurs. For example, solving addition problems involves a link between neurons. The more times that addition problems are solved, the stronger the link and the faster that addition problems can be solved. An example that starts much earlier is curiosity. A child whose curiosity is encouraged will develop stronger neural circuits involved with identifying questions, asking questions, pursuing answers, and analyzing information.
- Learned information can directly form a neural circuit. If a mother shows fear in front of her baby and runs away from a wave at the beach, the baby may form the same neural circuit and be afraid of waves. If a parent says motorcycles are too dangerous to drive, the child may make a neural circuit that links motorcycles to significant danger. If children see and understand why their parents help others in need, the children will be inclined to link helping others with the good feeling that results from it. Additionally, if parents react violently when they are angry, their children may link being angry with getting violent. This learned behavior might likely explain why some victims of child abuse have a tendency to become abusive parents. It should be noted that many victims of child abuse have the opposite tendency and are more nurturing than the average parent is; possibly, they linked the abusive behavior to how they felt while being abused.
- Some genes are turned on and off by environmental factors; these genes adapt the baby's neural circuits to the environment. In a safe and secure environment, the genes facilitate neural circuits that open the baby's mind to maximum interaction with the environment. In a hostile environment, the genes facilitate neural circuits that (1) put up defenses that block some interaction with the environment and (2) can lead to aggressive behavior. The longer that neural circuits are in use, the harder they are to change.

  Note: As part of making babies feel safe and secure, parents and other family members need to always act as if they are delighted to see the babies, starting when the babies first open their eyes. This will help form strong neural circuits that will (1) create emotional attachment by the baby to the family members and (2) enable the baby later in life to form emotional attachments to others. If babies cannot form emotional attachments to their family members, they may never be able to form emotional attachments to others.

The first time a neural circuit is created, it can become the root of a first impression and have an excessively strong effect on how future similar input is processed. For example, suppose a baby encounters a dog for the first time. Imagine the two following different scenarios. In the first, the dog licks the baby and the baby laughs. In the second, the dog barks and scares the baby. The next time the baby encounters a dog, each of these two different scenarios will likely result in opposite reactions from the baby.

As a parent, you will inevitably make mistakes and others will have contact with your children, such as when they go to daycare or preschool. If you notice your child do something wrong like hitting or insulting others, explain why it should not be done. The sooner you discourage this type of behavior, the easier it will be to form a more appropriate neural circuit.

The younger children are, the more impressionable they usually are. The more impressionable they are, the more important it is for parents to make sure their children get a good understanding about new things they learn and experience. This will help ensure that neural circuits make the appropriate links. Even when children are older, watching "PG-13" and "R" rated movies before they are 13 and 17, can easily lead to inappropriate understandings about life. This is especially true of "R" rated movies that often portray swearing, violence, casual sex, and breaking the law as normal acceptable behavior. If a picture is worth a 1,000 words, how many words does it take to offset a movie that glorifies people doing things you do not want your children to do? A good understanding about life is critical for decision making concerning where and how to pursue success.

Neural circuits are the basis for generalizations about similar and related things. Generalizations simplify the thinking process. For example, if the first schoolteachers encountered are associated/linked with kindness, caring, and helpfulness, then all schoolteachers may likely be assumed to be kind, caring, and helpful. Unfortunately, these generalizations about groups can create negative stereotypes where similar and related people and places are prejudged to all have the same preconceived negative characteristics. To make matters worse, these preconceived characteristics may have been based on non-representative first impressions or based on faulty opinions expressed by others.

The less that children hear generalizations, especially from their parents, about people's races, nationality, religion, sexual orientation, body size, and the like, the less that the children will develop generalizations about these groups of people.

Parents should demonstrate, with their actions and comments, the beliefs that (1) people should be judged individually based on their character and (2) generalizations their children hear about people in a group are irrelevant when it comes to assessing the character of any member of the group.

Chapter 2

Learning the Fundamentals of Being a Person

Your children need to learn the fundamentals of being a person, as listed below. This chapter covers how to help your children master these fundamentals:

- Get control over their bodies and thoughts
- Realize they are people like everyone else
- Learn how to take care of themselves
- Learn how to take care of their belongings
- Learn how to interact with their environment, primarily other people
- Develop self-esteem

Learning the fundamentals of being a person is a lifelong endeavor that needs to start as soon as possible because there is a lot to learn at first. Parents can start this learning process by doing things similar to what is described in the remainder of this chapter.

When you do things for and with your children, always remember that you cannot spoil them by taking care of their needs, such as the need for love and attention. Children whose needs are met will be better able to entertain themselves without parental involvement. During these times of self-sufficiency, parents should avoid the urge to be a part of whatever the child is doing.

Human Contact Is Very Important for Babies/Children

- Hold them so they feel safe and secure.

- Rock them, side to side is the most comforting.
- Hug them.
- Hold hands with them.
- Talk to them from day one in a normal voice. Use short simple sentences with each word pronounced correctly. Vary the tone and emphasis of words in the sentence to show your excitement/joy/interest in the child and in the subject of your sentences. Use exaggerated body language, facial expressions in particular, to go along with the words. Children can learn to recognize and make a wide range of sounds. It is very important that they hear speech as soon as possible, ideally male and female as well as young and old, so they recognize and learn the sounds involved with speech. Different languages have different sounds, and children adapt their language skills to the sounds of speech they hear. Do not make baby sounds even to a newborn.
- Make eye contact while talking to babies because they need to focus on your face in order to learn and understand facial expressions. Also, try facing a mirror together with your babies and copying their facial expressions; smiling, laughing, and looking excited whenever they show these expressions. Babies need a framework to fit new knowledge into; a human face and voice is the ideal centerpiece of their framework.

Enable Your Babies/Children to Get Control over Their Motor Functions

- Have a carousel on their crib that rotates hanging objects they can follow with their eyes.
- Have colorful pads on the inside of their crib and point out the objects.
- Let them grab your finger.
- Put toys in their hands that they can grab.
- Play games where you point to your nose, ear, and mouth and help your children point to and name their own nose, ear, and mouth.
- When your babies make a noise that sounds like a letter or part of a word, make the same sound and look at your babies as if you are waiting for them to repeat it or say something else.
- Sing and sway to music with your children.
- Play games that involve all the senses such as the following. Taste the difference between sugar and salt. Smell the difference between a real and an artificial flower. Select the largest ball based on sight. Determine which of two music

boxes is playing. Pick the ball out of a bag that has the ball and a block. Select the piece of sandpaper out of a bag that has sandpaper and writing paper.

- Play catch where your child learns to catch and throw under- and overhand with each hand.
- Children should be able to clench your finger with either hand as hard as they can without clenching any other muscles at the same time, such as their jaw or their other hand.
- All children should complete swimming lessons up to and possibly through the life saving course.
- Gymnastics, dancing, and skating should be considered if the child is interested.

Enable Your Children to Explore Their Environment

- Get crayons and paint for your children to use. Have blank paper and paper with outlines they can use.
- Pick a flower with them, and smell it.
- Pick a leaf off a tree with them, and feel it.
- Get a picture of a rainbow with all the colors and explain how primary colors (red, blue, and yellow) make up all the colors.
- Turn on two different music boxes, and have your child listen to both at the same time; increase it to three and four if your child is interested in listening to more. You should hum along with each of the music boxes one at a time. Ideally, your child will do the same thing. Being able to pick out each music box's sounds and concentrating on each is a good experience for listening and concentrating on things in the future.
- Listen to music. Get a Baby Mozart or a Baby Beethoven DVD from Baby Einstein®. Possibly, record a symphony performance on TV and point out each instrument and the sound each makes.

Explain Things to Your Children As Much As Possible

- Let them know what you are planning for them and if possible give them options to choose, such as what to do first.
- Let them pick out clothes to wear based on what they will be doing after they get dressed. Explain about outside temperature; look at a thermometer and look on the internet.

- Explain the importance of putting games and toys away neatly so they are ready to be used next time; help your children get into this habit.

- Encourage your children to speak their mind. Ask them questions so they learn to think out their thoughts and express them clearly. Your questions should focus on things they may not have considered. Your questions should be well balanced, and not asked in an attempt to get your children to share your conclusions about the subject being discussed. It is very important that children learn to compare and contrast things as well as draw well thought out conclusions about them. It is also important that children are confident enough in their abilities to draw conclusions, to express them, and to discuss the rationale behind them. Success in life often comes down to figuring things out and explaining them to others.

- Explain how actions have consequences. For example, playing in snow without gloves will result in cold wet hands.

- Explain how your children, like all children, have a right to be safe and secure at school and everywhere else. Also, teach your children to recognize, avoid, and tell you about situations where others try to exert inappropriate control over your children.

- When something good or bad happens to someone, ask your child how the other person probably felt. It is very important that your child develops the natural empathy felt for other people. It is critical that your child can feel other people's sorrow and share in their joy; this link between people is what connects people together. This connection with others is needed for people to be at peace with themselves and with others.

- When your child physically or verbally hurts you or someone else, explain about the golden rule, which, as taught to me by my mother, is — "treat others the way you would like them to treat you."

- Explain the importance of standing up for themselves when other children are not following the golden rule. The fair solution to a conflict should be rationally thought out and explained to the other person. Teach your children to settle conflicts verbally, ideally without contacting an adult to determine who is in the right.

- If you have to tell your children to stop doing something that is wrong, tell them that what they are doing is wrong rather than that they are wrong. Also, explain why it is wrong.

  Note: Self-esteem can be easily crushed, especially by parents that children admire. A low initial self-esteem can be like a bad first impression that is not questioned before it leads to bad decision making that reinforces the bad first impression. Children, like everyone else, try not to do things that lower their self-esteem, and eventually base their self-esteem on what they have done. The higher a child's self-esteem, the better the child's decisions will be concerning the child's character. A child whose self-esteem is high due to successfully taking on challenges in the past, will most likely continue to successfully take on challenges in the future.

- Rules should be explained as being in the children's best interest for safety, health, or their well-being in general. The more that children realize rules are for their well-being, the better able they will be to make their own rules later in life. The more that children feel rules are arbitrary, the more they will rebel against them. Rules should be consistently applied.

- If your child is misbehaving and making you unhappy, try to explain to your child that you, just like your child, have a right to be happy.

- When your children do something on their own that is good, be sure to make a point of noticing and appreciating it. Children who do not get enough attention for doing good things may start doing bad things to get needed attention.

- Explain to your children how lucky each of them are to be a person and all the wonderful things they can do and think.

- Encourage your children to use their imagination. Make sure your children distinguish the difference between reality and what they imagined, assumed, or dreamed. If your children ask if there is any truth to alien abductions, ghosts, psychic healers/advisors, superstitions, lucky numbers, moon's and star's effect on people, witchcraft, horoscopes, astrology, fortune tellers, tarot cards, levitation without magnets, communication with others in dreams or with the dead, and the like, explain that nobody has ever proved any of these things to be true. If there was any truth to these things, it would have been analyzed and reported on in a peer reviewed scientific journal and everyone would know about it.

  If your child says something happened that could only be explained by the aforementioned, point out how magic tricks make impossible things appear to happen. If your child points out a coincidence and says it has to be more than a coincidence, explain the following. With all the different things in this world, coincidences are going to occur.

  There is nothing wrong with your child having imaginary friends and there is nothing wrong with you playing along, as long as you do not encourage it. For example, if your child is working on the computer with an imaginary friend, you can ask your child what they are working on, but do not address any question or comments to the imaginary friend. If your child asks if you believe in the imaginary friend, do not say "yes" or even "maybe," and try to avoid saying "no." Possibly, tell your child that you had an imaginary friend when you were a child, assuming you did.

- It is very important that your children learn how to do multiple tasks at the same time, as in the following examples. It seems that when older people start to have trouble thinking, they are having trouble thinking about more than one thing at a time.
    - o Child should have two separate conversations with two separate people simultaneously.
    - o Child should be able to do math problems while discussing an unrelated subject.
    - o Child should be able to walk, talk, and catch a ball with either hand all at the same time.

Bullying

You do not want your children to be bullies or to be victimized by bullies. The root for both these patterns of behavior can often be found in how you handle the following situation. Around age two or three, your children will realize that there are so many new things they can do, and they will not want to accept any limits from others concerning what they do. As a parent, you must set limits. The struggle of getting children to accept limits results in what is sometime called the "terrible twos" or the "terrible threes." Ideally, your children will eventually realize that the limits are for their own benefit, directly and indirectly, and will not feel coerced into accepting them. Direct benefits include safety in the example of limiting where they play. Indirect benefits include having others respect their rights in the example of limiting their actions to things that do not violate the rights of others. If, on the other hand, your children feel coerced, they may view themselves as "being forced to do what someone else wants them to do"; this is where the roots of bullying or being victimized by bullying can get started. Children who never stop fighting with their parents about "being forced to do what others want them to do" may tend to become bullies who feel the need to "force" others to do what they want them to do. Alternatively, children who stop fighting with their parents and accept "being forced to do what others want them to do" may tend to fall into a pattern of accepting "forced" behavior and become victims of bullies.

This book includes factors that affect the tendencies above, as summarized in the following. The tendency to be a bully can be mitigated by (1) developing the natural empathy that a child has for others; (2) encouraging rational, peaceful resolution of disputes; (3) developing self-esteem in the child that is not dependent upon reducing someone else's self-esteem; and (4) explaining about the rights that everyone has, including the child. The tendency to be bullied can be partially offset by (1) helping the child recognize and avoid situations where others try to exert inappropriate control over the child, and (2) teaching the child how to deal with bullies.

When confronted by a bully, a child should be courteous, to avoid a conflict, but should not do anything that the bully wants done. Even being extra friendly or helpful can be viewed as fear causing the child to do what the bully wants done, which is exactly what the bully is looking for in someone to victimize. The more bullying that a victim submits to, the more control the bully feels over the victim. The more control felt by the bully, the harder the bully will fight to keep the victim under control. A child should tell parents and school authorities when a bully starts using physical violence to force the child to do anything. Bullies are less likely to attempt bullying children who (1) are good students, (2) do not get into trouble, (3) get along with most everyone else, and (4) are able and willing to defend themselves against the bully.

Being bullied can be harmful to a child for many reasons, three of which follow. First, being bullied will lower self-esteem. Second, being bullied creates frustration that will consume a lot of mental energy. Third, being preoccupied about being bullied after school will make it difficult to pay attention in class.

Chapter 3

Getting a Good Formal and Informal Education

Get your children off to a good start in school with the confidence and desire to always remain in the top of their class. This chapter includes (1) things you can teach your children so they start in the top of their class, (2) ideas on how you can keep your children motivated to stay in the top of their class, and (3) information on going to college.

Reading

- Read to your children while they look at each page with you. Go slow enough so they always follow the story. Use books with enough pictures so your children can picture-walk through the story while you read it to them. Point out things in the pictures as you read about them. Discuss the story with your children.

- When your children can recognize, say, and write each letter of the alphabet, upper and lower case, modify your reading to them as follows. Point out the words as you say them, making sure the meaning of each word is understood. If your children try to say a word with you, help them sound it out by pointing to specific letters, with something smaller than your finger, as you pronounce them. Do not move on to the next word until they are done thinking about the one you just helped them pronounce. At first, you may need to make sure they recognize the letters you are pronouncing. Later, after your children are reading some of the words by themselves, you may need to explain the rules of pronunciation, such as when there are two vowels together or there is a silent "e" at the end of a word. There are only around four dozen different sounds represented by letters in the English language. Most educational bookstores have books that contain a picture with a name for each of sound.

- Keep reading with your children until they enjoy reading so much that they will pick up a book on their own and read it, ideally aloud to you. When the opportunity arises, ask them to tell you about the book they have just read. It is important that children can summarize and retell a story they read.

- Instill an appreciation of the written word by commenting about all the wonderful stories and information available to anyone who can read. Explain how well written stories and information usually do a more accurate job conveying thoughts and information than the spoken word.

Note: If your children see you reading and enjoying it, they will be more inclined to enjoy reading.

Note: Being a proficient reader is very important when it comes to taking standardized tests and doing well in school.

Grammar and Writing

- It is very important that children learn how to speak and write without making grammatical errors. It is also important that they learn how to write an email that is concise, covers everything that needs to be conveyed, and is easy to read. Adults who make grammatical errors and who cannot write a decent email are often categorized as being poorly educated, which has a major negative impact on getting hired and promoted.

- Parents and other family members should always use proper grammar in front of the children. For example, from the Business Writing chapter of Book One, the word good goes with a noun, and the word well goes with a verb. An easy way to remember both of these is as follows. The second letter of *good* and *noun* is an o. The second letter of *well* and *verb* is an e.

  If a child learns to speak grammatically correct, it is much easier to learn how to write grammatically correct.

- When grammar and writing are covered in your children's school, be sure the lessons are fully understood and learned.

- Make sure your children understand that the purpose of writing is to convey information in a manner that is easy to understand.

Math

- Children are ready to learn about numbers anytime after they have learned to recognize, say, and write all upper and lower case letters of the alphabet. Only work on math when children want to work on it and stop when they lose interest. Whenever you are working with them and they grasp a new concept, pause to give them enough time to savor the moment and digest what was learned. If they explain to you what they just learned, subtly express your admiration.

- Teach them to count to ten verbally and then to write each number one through ten. Next, get ten pennies, or similar objects, and teach them to understand the quantity that goes with each number. Pennies up to ten should be counted in a row, with a slightly larger gap between the fifth and sixth penny. Numbers over five would be counted as five plus whatever else is needed to reach the number being counted.

- Next, explain that two 10s equal 20, three 10s equal 30, and so on up to 100. Teach your children to count verbally to 100 and to write each number 1 through 100. The numbers should be written in ten separate rows of ten numbers each across the page so that the numbers on the left margin going down are 1, 11, 21...91. Possibly, you should write the numbers at the same time, on a separate piece of paper. Use pennies to show the quantity that goes with each number 1 through 100. Arrange 100 pennies in a square with each penny touching the pennies next to it. Use a ruler, or other flat surface, to make sure both the ten pennies across the top and the ten pennies down the side are straight. Review with your children how the 100 pennies match up to the 100 numbers they wrote. Randomly select a number from 1 through 100 and ask your children to show you how many pennies the number represents. Children should show you how many pennies it represents by using two sheets of paper to cover up the pennies that come after the number. For example, 73 pennies would be shown by covering up the 74th through the 100th penny. Make a game out of this and leave the pennies out for whenever your children are interested. When your children can easily do this and have lost interest in doing it anymore, briefly introduce them to the concept of percents. Use the pennies and explain that 25, 50, 75, and 100 are 25%, 50%, 75%, and 100%, respectively, of 100. Then explain that 1, 2, 3, 4 are 25%, 50%, 75%, and 100%, respectively, of 4.

- Next, explain that two 100s equal 200, and three 100s equal 300, and so on up to 1,000. Show them what the number 1,000 looks like, and always use a comma.

- Next, teach them to add and subtract on paper, using the pennies at first to explain the process and then to check the answer. Be sure to explain that adding and subtracting are just the opposite of each other. The more addition and subtraction problems they solve, the faster they will get at this. Eventually they need to be able to add and subtract numbers up to 100 in their head (without using paper or a calculator).

- Next, teach them to multiply and divide on paper, using the pennies at first to explain the process and then to check the answer. Be sure to explain that multiplying and dividing are just the opposite of each other. Also, introduce them to squaring numbers and finding square roots. After the concept of multiplying and dividing is understood, the multiplication table through 12 multiplied by 12 should be looked at and eventually memorized. The more multiplication and division problems they solve, the faster they will be able to do multiplication and division problems.

- Whenever you and your children are in the mood, give them math problems (adding, subtracting, multiplying, and dividing) to do in their head. Possibly, get your children to give you similar problems to solve.

- Teach your children the basic shortcut about multiplying by 10, 100, and 1,000 (just add 0, 00, or 000, respectively, to the number being multiplied), then explain the following. 10 thousands is 10,000, 100 thousands is 100,000, 1,000 thousands is 1,000,000 (million), 1,000 millions is 1,000,000,000 (billion), and 1,000 billions is 1,000,000,000,000 (trillion).

- Always make sure your children are ahead of their class in math. Possibly, ask the teacher at the beginning of the year what will be covered. For example, your child should have memorized the multiplication tables before they start working on them in school.

- Depending upon your children's interest and your knowledge concerning math, you may want to get self-taught math programs for your children to use concerning the following:
    - Algebra — mathematical problems are expressed in formulas that can be easily simplified
    - Geometry — studies shapes, lines, and points
    - Trigonometry — branch of geometry that deals with triangles and their parts
    - Analytical geometry — applies algebra to geometry
    - Logarithms — simplified method for multiplying and dividing large numbers
    - Calculus — method to determine quantities while they are changing
    - Probability — likelihood that something will occur
    - Statistics — method of collecting, organizing, and interpreting large quantities of numbers

Note: Math formulas should be understood, not just memorized. Understanding formulas makes them easier to remember and will form building blocks that will make it easier to understand more complicated math concepts.

Money

Explain about the monetary value of pennies, nickels, dimes, quarters, and dollars. Let your children pay for some small purchases at the store and encourage them to verify that the change received is correct.

Telling Time

Teach your children how to tell time on a dial type clock. Explain (1) the relationships among seconds, minutes, and hours; (2) the difference between a.m. and p.m.; and (3) that 24 hours is the time it takes for the earth to spin around one time. Use a globe and a light to explain why each day has daylight and darkness. Explain that it takes a year (365 ¼ days) for the earth to go around the sun. Explain how the year is broken up into months and weeks. Explain that the earth's axis (line between the north and south poles) is not perpendicular (at a right angle) to a line from the center of the earth to the center of the sun. This non-perpendicular alignment causes seasons because the northern half of the earth has the sun directly overhead for six months and the southern half of the earth has the sun directly overhead for the other six months of the year. The sun's hottest effect on the surface of the earth is where the sun is directly overhead because the sun's rays are going through the least amount of atmosphere.

Measuring

Teach your children the basics about the English and the Metric measurement system. Measuring your children's and your own weight and height is a good way to give your children something they can relate to the measurement systems. In addition, you can look up your automobile's weight and explain the length of something like a football field.

Encouraging Your Children to Learn and Accomplish Things on Their Own

The following concerns children and schoolwork. Consider these things when planning for your children's success in school.

- Recognize and congratulate your children for all their academic accomplishments, no matter how small. You should not over do it to the point of losing credibility.
- Children should know that success at school is usually just a matter of who works the hardest. When your children are working hard on something, congratulate them for being hard workers.

- Children's desire to learn will be easier to sustain in the following instances:
    - When they have input concerning what they learn about
    - When they are making progress learning
    - When parents and teachers acknowledge and congratulate them for their academic accomplishments
    - When they feel that their parents still enjoy learning new things, such as when you share an interesting newspaper article with them

  Note: Children are turned off about education when they feel that they cannot live up to expectations set by parents and teachers. Be patient with your children when they have difficulty grasping something you think is easy to understand; try to figure out what is confusing them. Never ever give your children the impression that you think they are not smart. Self-esteem is much harder to bolster than to crush.

- When your children need your help with their schoolwork, always remember that the more they do themselves, the better. Try to confine your help to asking questions, such as "what directions did your teacher give?" and "what is it that you are trying to accomplish?" Parents should be enablers, driving to places like the library or a store, making resources available, and providing guidance only when needed.

- Keep all school projects your children bring home, especially the ones where you were involved.

- When the opportunity arises, often in math and science, explain to your children how it took years and years for people to discover the information and knowledge that is being explained to them in school. Comment about how exciting it must have been for the person who put it all together and discovered this new information.

- Make sure your children see the connection between doing well in school and having a good life as an adult. Children should know that just about everyone wants to be successful in life, but most people do not work hard enough to be successful.

- Explain how grades are important, but how fully understanding the material is more important, especially in math and science where classes are often continuations of previous classes.

- Help your children figure out how to overcome adversity at school, so the adversity does not turn them off about school.

- If any of your grade school children say that high school or college will be too hard, explain that every year when they move to the next grade level, it is like taking the next step up a staircase.

- A brain is like a muscle in that the more you use it, the stronger it gets. It is believed that mental stimulation can activate unused neurons and improve the functionality/performance of neurons.
- Some children take longer to get going academically. These children have the same potential as others, assuming their parents do not give up on them. If children feel that their parents have given up on them, there is a good chance that they will give up on themselves.
- Children who have it too easy academically can run the risk of not learning how to work hard. They need to be aware that there will be times when they will need to work hard to stay ahead of their peers who have always had to work hard.
- Participation in sports will increase competency in sports, which will make it much easier for children to fit in with their peers. Participation in other school activities such as band, debate club, theater, and the like, can have the same effect.
- Going to college should always be a foregone conclusion in your children's minds. It should just be a matter of where they will go to college, not if they will go to college.

The following list concerns things your children should understand and consider. Work these things into conversations with your children. Older children can just read this list, when they are interested. "You" as used in these bullets, refers to your children.

- You should plan how to accomplish particular goals, and make changes to the plans as more is learned. After accomplishing goals, look back at your plans and try to identify improvements that can be used in future plans.
- The more complicated something is, the more time you can likely save by planning and organizing the work in advance. If you are going to need something from someone else, request it as soon as possible.
- For most things you do in life, it takes less time to do them right in the first place than to do them wrong and fix them.
- Get things done as efficiently as possible. Only get involved with the details to the extent necessary.
- Prioritize the different things you want to accomplish. The less time you spend on unimportant things, the more time you can spend on important things.
- Keep your objectives in mind whenever you go into a situation.

- Look for opportunities where you are better off working with others than working alone.
- When working with other students on a project, it is usually more efficient to split up the work into parts that each student can do, rather than for everyone to work together on each part.
- The decision to take on a new project should be based on whether the benefit of completing the project is greater than the work to complete the project.
- The decision to stop working on a project should be based on whether the benefit of completing the project is greater than the remaining work to complete the project. Work already done on a project is irrelevant when it comes to deciding whether to complete the project.
- When you work on a project, your goal is to "accomplish it," not to be able to say, "I tried but…"
- When you present something that you worked on, start with an overview and end with a summary.
- Make sure the things you write are organized, clear, and concise. Make sure your writings accomplish your goal. Beware that when you proofread your own work, you may *see* what you meant to write, not what you actually wrote. Get in the habit of using proper grammar.
- It is easy to work hard on something you enjoy, especially if it makes you feel good.
- When you learn from others, ask questions to clear up anything that does not seem right.
- When you learn to do something new like writing cursively, go as slow as needed to do it correctly; eventually you will get fast while still doing it correctly. If you start off going fast, you may never do it correctly.
- Learn from your mistakes, or you will keep making them.
- When you make a mistake, you should work extra hard to fix it.
- Frustration creates a barrier that can be overcome with patience.
- Successful people are often people who failed at first but kept trying.
- Take advantage of the hidden opportunities in life such as learning about something that interests you.
- Avoid the hidden pitfalls in life such as following the crowd too much.

- If you are friendly and cooperative with others, others will generally be friendly and cooperative with you.
- Treat others fairly and they will likely treat you fairly.
- When you negotiate with others, keep it friendly and never act as if you received more than the other person received.
- If you are trying to talk someone into something and the person says "okay," say "thanks" and do not give any more reason for the person to agree because it just opens the door for the person to reconsider.
- If you agree to something you should not have agreed to, then as soon as possible, you should explain that you misunderstood the situation and you are not agreeing.
- Helping other people overcome their misfortunes is a good thing to do, within reason. Helping people who do not help themselves may create a dependency where these people become less likely to start helping themselves.
- If two of your friends are having a conflict that does not involve you, try to avoid agreeing with either of your friends' side of the conflict.
- Before you react with anger concerning something someone said or did, make sure you are not over reacting.
- When you get older, remember the following, which my brother once said: "When you call yourself an adult, the statute of limitations runs out on what you can blame on your parents."
- Familiarize yourself with the content in Book Three, so you will know what information is available when needed.

The following concerns learning in general. Consider these things, which can help your children understand the world around them.

- Curiosity should always be encouraged. Sometimes a question or comment on your part can stimulate your children's curiosity. Curiosity begins as soon as babies start looking around and should never be stifled. If you do not have the time to answer a question from your children, always get back to them as soon as possible. Never act as if your children are not smart enough to understand an answer. Keep your answers simple unless your children ask for more details. If you do not know the answer, look it up, ideally with your children. Never guess or make something up, as children need to form solid building blocks of information and they start off believing everything their parents tell them.
- Encourage your children to explore anything good they are curious about, such as sports, scouts, musical instruments, foreign languages, and debate club.

Without necessarily encouraging it, you should make sure your children are aware of any of these types of opportunities you can fit into your time schedule and financial budget. Find out about these types of opportunities by checking with your children's teachers, local library, park district, recreational center, social/religious organizations, and ask other parents.

- Your children should know that they can learn and understand anything that others have learned and understood, as long as your children are willing to work hard enough at it.
- When your children notice differences between things that are similar and notice similarities between things that are different, let them know how impressed you are and, if appropriate, ask them for further details. People who notice and understand things like this often find breakthrough discoveries in life. I believe this is one of the keys to being a genius. As a parent, you should not worry about your children thinking and talking about things that others do not think and talk about and you should not discourage your children from doing it.

College

Going to college and getting at least a four-year college degree will open a world of opportunities that will make success in life much more likely.

Never assume your high school child will not be able to make it in college. It is believed that the brain activates unused neurons when children are in their late teens to early twenties. These neurons can noticeably increase intelligence if the child continues studying and learning new things; without this stimulation, these neurons will end up under developed at best.

Going to a junior college for two years and then transferring to a four-year university is a good way to save money on college and it reduces the chance that the student will fail freshman year.

Going away to college directly from high school and living in a large freshman dorm is an unbelievably maturing experience. High school becomes a distant memory, as students take responsibility for their own life and settle in with the other students who have also made it to this major plateau in life.

The key to graduating from college is to have a good start freshman year. Students who go off to college and party too much are often those students who did not have enough freedom at home. The summer between high school and college is a good time for parents to ease up on the rules so their students will have less resentment over rules to get out of their system.

Freshman students in a dorm may be better off their first semester/quarter by (1) not taking any classes that meet before 10:00 a.m. and (2) not taking a heavy course load.

Going to a state university is usually a good value for the money. If students are not accepted into their first choice for school, good grades at a lower rated university may make a transfer possible to their first choice.

Complete the federal financial aid form (FAFSA) as soon as all federal tax returns are completed for the year prior to the student's first school year. School years typically begin in the fall and go through the following summer.

Certification schools in Information Technology provide a quick way to get into the work force, but do not provide the job security or advancement potential of a traditional four-year Information Technology Degree.

Chapter 4

Learning to Take Responsibility for Actions Taken

By the time your children are adults, they must be able to make good choices concerning their future and understand that they are totally responsible for the choices they make. As covered in this chapter, parents need to make sure their children have enough experience (1) making good choices for themselves and (2) living with or at least understanding the consequences of their choices.

Children need to learn how to set goals and how to determine the necessary steps to accomplish them. Parents should not suggest goals or suggest how to accomplish goals. Parents should just be available to answer questions about what works and what will not work. The younger the children are, the more their parents might need to guide them with hints. Children need to feel ownership of their goals and of the plans to accomplish them. They should be encouraged to always persevere when the steps in their plans are harder than anticipated. Sometimes plans need to be modified based on information not available when the plans were made. Children should also be encouraged to look back at executed plans for "lessons to be learned" that can improve future plans. They should also reflect upon what led up to each success, which will help ensure that their self-esteem takes into account the entire success.

Sometimes changing circumstances make it impossible to achieve goals that are being pursued. In these instances, the goals should be modified, not necessarily dropped.

It is hard for children to stay focused on long-term goals and short-term goals at the same time. They need to enjoy life but they also need to keep working toward long-term goals such as getting into a good college/university.

A good long-term goal in life is to be able to look back on your life, when you are old, without regrets. Everyone is going to make mistakes, but you will want to look back at your life and know that you were a good person, led a good life, were well respected, and had a significantly positive net impact on family, friends, and others. If your children can adopt this long-term goal from you, they will have a good long-term goal to consider when making plans to meet their other goals.

Successful people will often say that the keys to their success are (1) identify your goals, (2) identify plans to achieve your goals, and (3) execute the steps in your plans.

Children need to be aware that for every team project, from a school project to building a fort in the woods, there is a team leader who does most of the figuring out concerning how to complete the project. Team leaders are those who come up with the best plans and communicate them in a convincing way to others in the group. Team leaders can develop into natural leaders if their plans prove to be good and if the members of their teams do not feel belittled either by the leader or by how credit for the completed project is spread to all team members.

Children need to learn that when they encounter something new, they should start with an overview before getting into the details. Details should always be viewed as they fit into the overview. In addition, details should only be looked into to the extent necessary.

As previously mentioned, you should encourage your children to participate in things that interest them, as long as the things fit into your time schedule and financial budget. Before they sign up, you should explain the commitment on their part and then let them decide whether to proceed. Explain about the cost (money and time) of quitting, and possibly tell your children that they will have to bear some or all of the cost. It is a bad precedent to join something without adequately considering the commitment involved and then quitting because it is too hard. Children should learn that they should never quit anything for reasons they should have anticipated in advance.

Understanding and living with the negative consequences of choices made can be a good learning experience for your children, but parents need to be careful, as follows:

- Lessons learned from direct consequences of choices made are much more effective than lessons learned from indirect consequences. Direct consequences include lost pieces from a game that was left spread out on the floor. Indirect consequences include being punished for having a messy room caused by game pieces being left spread out on the floor.

- If you cannot or decide not to offset negative consequences caused by your children's choices, be sympathetic and offer to help, if appropriate.

- If you decide to offset negative consequences caused by your children's choices, make sure your children understand (1) how they caused the consequences and (2) the cost of the consequences.
- The best way to explain about potential negative consequences is to use an example of someone in your children's situation.
- Never say, "I told you so." Children are much more inclined to take advice from a parent who is helpful rather than critical, especially when the criticism is accompanied by an "I am smarter than you" attitude.

  Note: There is nothing wrong with constructive criticism, as long as your children know the intention is to be helpful. Constructive criticism should ideally be explained as a better way that someone in your children's situation could have handled things, rather than telling your children what they should have done or not done.
- Lecturing about potential negative consequences your children are well aware of can result in an "I do not care" response that could increase the likelihood of the potential negative consequences.
- If the potential negative consequences of a choice being considered are known to your children and are not significant, it may be best for you to just say, "The choice is yours."

Children, like everyone else, learn how to fit in with their peers through a combination of the following two methods:

- Doing what their peers do
- Figuring out how they want to fit in and how to make it happen

Note: The more your children talk to you about what is going on in their lives, the more you can help them rely on this second method. It should be noted that it is hard for children to express their individuality until they feel accepted by their peers. Children also need to feel accepted at home for who they are. They should not have to alter what they think and feel in order to be accepted. As a parent, you need to understand what your children think and feel so you can better guide them. The less that children feel they are accepted at home, the more they will feel the need to be accepted by their peers, which makes them more susceptible to peer pressure. Make sure your children understand that it is much more important how they fit in with their peers as adults, than how they fit in with their peers when they were children.

Children need to learn and understand the following, so they can start to see how their childhood leads to them becoming adults:

- The problems they face while growing up are not unique to them and they will get past them just as others have. In the future, most of these problems will seem trivial.
- They are each unique individuals and no one else thinks or feels the same way they do.
- Ultimately, they are responsible for their own successes and failures. The sooner they take responsibility for themselves, the better off they will be.
- When they become adults, they will need to be capable of being totally independent, though they should help and accept help from others.

Note: Your children, like everyone else, need to have a self-image of themselves that is based on how an objective person would view them. Having this self-image will lead to better decision making concerning their character. The better this self-image is, the better your children's self-esteem will be.

If your child has a conflict with another child or with a teacher, help your child figure out how to solve it. Do not get directly involved unless your child is in real danger. Learning to get along with other children at school and teachers is good experience for later years. Schoolmates are like the neighbors and coworkers of the future. Teachers are like the bosses of the future. Children need to learn how to solve their own problems and to not rely on others to step in and make things "all right."

Children need to understand how to stand up for themselves without being too aggressive. They should respect the rights of others and make sure others respect their rights. Tell them that if they are not sure about the fair way to settle a dispute, they should imagine that they are an objective third party who is evaluating the situation. Conflicts to settle disputes can take a lot of time and energy. If the consequence of losing a dispute is immaterial, it may be wise to just give in and put it behind you. Favors and help should never be offered to people who provoke conflicts when they know they are in the wrong.

Children need to understand the importance of not going along with others who are doing something wrong, especially if it is illegal like stealing or vandalism. In addition, children need to understand the importance of telling their parents and their teachers when others are planning to physically hurt someone.

Chapter 5

Becoming Hard Workers Who Understand the Value of Savings

This chapter covers three basic things, listed below, that parents can do to help their children become hard workers who understand the value of savings.

- Encourage their children to work hard and save money
- Set a good example
- Explain the importance of working hard and saving money

When your children want spending money, pay them for work they do around the home. Be generous, so they will want to do it, and have set pay rates for each job. Allowances should be for living expenses you would have paid for if you were present when the purchase was made, such as lunch money.

When your children get older, encourage them to get part-time jobs that do not interfere with their schoolwork. Encourage them to save some of the money for college by matching part of it. Possibly, provide them with a car to go to work with the condition that one-half of the money earned is saved for college.

Working in a sales position, especially one that pays commissions, will be good experience dealing with customers and will help prepare your children for when salespeople try to sell things to them.

Working in a car wash, especially during cold weather, or in the kitchen of a fast food restaurant will be good experience working hard and will reinforce your children's decision to go to college.

Set a good example by working hard yourself. This does not necessarily mean working long hours. Whenever you discuss your job, do work around the home, or put time into a hobby, always make sure your children perceive you as someone who gets the job done right, without wasting time.

Make sure your children understand the following, which concerns the importance of working correctly and working hard:

- If something is worth doing, it is worth doing correctly. Sometimes the correct way to fix something is just to replace it rather than to fix it. Key point here is that whatever the decision is, it should be done correctly.

- Life is very tough without a good cash flow.

- After college, there will be no financial subsidies to their income. Possibly, you will loan them money for a down payment on a home.

  Even if you can afford to subsidize your adult children's income, it may be better to save your money to subsidize their retirement. Financial subsidies before their retirement may just lead to more money being spent on automobiles, vacations, clothes, and entertainment; it may also lessen their drive to earn a living. The exception to this is if your adult children cannot afford the necessities of life for your grandchildren. If you subsidize one of your children, make sure all your children know that you are keeping track and that everything will come out even, with interest, when your final estate is distributed. Keep your word about this in order to avoid resentment between your children after you die.

  If you have a lot of money, do not let your children know. Do not lie about it; just avoid mentioning it. If it comes up, say it is for your retirement. If your children think you are "rich," they may expect things that could spoil them, and they may be less inclined to put in the effort to become financially successful themselves.

- After college, they get full credit for their successes and take full responsibilities for their failures.

If you own your own business, your children and your business will be better off if you do not hire your adult children, as explained in the following:

- Your children may not learn to work as hard as they would have if they had to make it on their own.

- Pay and benefits your children receive in excess of what an outsider would receive could cause resentment in your children who do not work for you.

- It may be harder to keep good workers who are not family members.

- If you sell your business, you may be somewhat obligated to give money to your children who worked for you, since they will be less employable than if they had worked elsewhere.

Note: I knew an entrepreneur who came over to the USA as a teenager with nothing and started a very successful business. Unfortunately, this hardworking entrepreneur gave his children everything he never had and they never learned the lessons of hard work and frugality (two of the main keys, in my opinion, to his success).

Set a good example by not indulging in wasteful spending on yourself or your children. In the short term, indulging your children will make them happy, which will presumably make you happy. Unfortunately, this happiness will be short lived and will not be in your children's best long-term interest. The road to financial success begins with understanding the value of money, which is that money is the result of hard work and should not be wasted.

Instead of indulging your children, put the money into their college savings. Explain to your children how hard you worked for the money and how important it is to save for things that really matter. Explain about needs versus wants as covered in the Saving and Spending chapter of Book Four. Eventually, your children will need to understand everything in the Saving and Spending chapter as well as in the other chapters of Book Four.

Never tell your children that the reason for not buying something is because "you cannot afford it" or that you "do not have the money." Instead, just explain that a "better use of the money is to save it for more important things in the future," like their college education.

Children have a tendency to envy other children who have more material things. The more your children hear "cannot afford it" or "do not have the money," the more likely they will want to buy material things when they are adults to make up for their "deprived life" as children. The more your children understand the importance of saving for needs versus spending on wants, the more likely they will be financially successful adults.

If your children say that some of their friends will get cars from their parents when they turn 16 and want you to do the same for them, tell your children to remain friends with those who will get their own cars.

Chapter 6

Selecting an Occupation

Children must select their own occupation. This chapter covers helping your children select occupations that have the three attributes listed below.

- They must enjoy the type of work involved, enjoyment includes being proud of how a living is earned.
- They must be good at the type of work involved.
- Compensation must meet their needs.

If children have been encouraged and enabled to explore whatever they were interested in, excluding harmful things, and they understand the career opportunities in each of these areas, their choice for an occupation may have been narrowed down to one or more general areas. High school students should contact their guidance counselors to find out about career aptitude tests, which may reveal other occupations to consider. The parents' role in the consideration of occupations is to point out any information their children may have overlooked, such as the importance of a good cash flow.

The next step is to find out more about what the general occupations entail, in order to make sure nothing significant was overlooked. Your children must determine if the day-to-day work would be enjoyable and if they could do it well. Sources of information include family members, high school guidance counselors, libraries, encyclopedias, people already in the occupation, and schools that prepare people for the occupation.

It may not be necessary to narrow the selection of a general occupation down to a specific occupation until after the child begins formal education in the subject.

Whether the general occupation is being an attorney, engineer, or architect, the first step in each is to be enrolled in a school program that prepares students for all areas in their general occupation. As the student progresses through the school program, the choice for a specific occupation may likely become apparent. The law student may select criminal law and the engineering student may select electrical engineering. On the other hand, the architectural student may decide not to specialize. Students should keep their options open and not rush to select a specific occupation. Choices of a specific and even a general occupation should remain subject to change, even if it means that classes taken will not count toward the degree required for the new choice.

Parents should not expect or encourage their children to follow their career path. Children are more likely to follow the career path of a parent who is well respected rather than just financially successful. Well-respected parents who want their children to choose a better career than they did, need to be careful. They should possibly explain that if they had the opportunity their children have today, they would have chosen a different career.

An internship is an excellent way to get experience and to get a job offer. In order to prove themselves, interns are usually expected to work extra hard and not treat anyone as being lower than they are in the company's pecking order.

Before working in their chosen occupation, even as an intern, students should learn about the career fast track, as covered in Book One.

During their last year in school, students need to start pursuing employment in their chosen field. It is important to select a company where the student will get the necessary experience to begin building a solid career. The larger and better respected the company is, the more impressive the experience will be on a resume. Level of pay should not be an overriding consideration in deciding where to start working. Building a solid career and being one of the best in their field will result in a relatively high level of pay. Employers who try to take advantage of employees by paying less than market level wages should just be used as stepping stones in a person's career development.

It should be noted that new employees often make the mistake of thinking that all they need to do is make sure their work is as good as or slightly better than their peers' work. A much better benchmark to measure their work against is the work that was most likely done by people who later rose to the top of their field.

Chapter 7

Raising Successful Children in General

This chapter covers additional things you need to consider while raising children and ends with things you need to consider when thinking about getting married and having children.

Focus on each of your children as individuals, with their own needs, wants, desires, abilities, and everything else that makes them individuals. Focus on each as if the child was the only child you were fortunate enough to have. Avoid making comparisons between your children such as wishing one was as good a student or as athletic as another. Comparisons like this will occur to you, but you should never express them to your children or to anyone else who may repeat them to your children.

Always remember that you are on the same team as your children. The more successful they are in every aspect of life, the more successful you are as a parent. You must (1) raise each of your children to be a better person than you, and (2) "release" each child by making sure the child knows when you believe that the child is a better person than you. Without this release, the child's self-esteem can easily be locked in at a level below the child's perceived level of your self-worth. This locked-in low level of self-esteem can result in your child having the same faults that the child perceives you have.

The way you raise your children will have a major impact on how they raise your grandchildren. Make improvements to the way you were raised.

Always consider how your actions will affect your children in the long term and in the short term, as covered in the following examples:

- Attending schools in the same school system from kindergarten through high school can add a great deal of stability to children's lives.
- Attending local public schools versus private schools can be advantageous because your children will have more in common with the children in their neighborhood. Another advantage is that it is good experience associating with the different types of people that your children will live and work with the rest of their lives.
- It is good when neither parent has a job that requires frequent overnight travel and the family can all have dinner together as often as possible. At these dinners, the children should have an opportunity to bring up anything they want to discuss, so everyone feels they are part of the family. If you miss dinner with your children, try to spend some time talking to each of them individually about their day and about anything else they want to talk about.
- Children should not be allowed to stay up late on school nights or on weekends when they are young. By going to bed at the same reasonable time each night, they will develop good sleep habits. If they wake up early, they should be encouraged to read a book, work on a hobby, or play a game.
- Children who grow up in an environment where relatives gamble at family gatherings will be more likely to gamble as adults.
- Parents should set a good example by not glorifying violence or other anti-social behavior. Do not tell your children about the worst thing you did as a child because in your children's minds it will be basically acceptable for them to do the same thing and possibly worse.
- The way you drive your car will have a major impact on how your children drive.
- If you are having difficulty making a decision that affects your child, focus on what is best in the long term for your child.
- If your children think you are perfect, it will be hard for them to question your conclusions about life and form their own conclusions and opinions about life.
- Make sure your children understand that when you punish them it is not because you are trying to get even with them for making you mad.
- Look at your actions from your children's point of view. Insulting children, by saying, for example, "you are stupid," may get them to correct their actions, but to some extent, your children will believe your insults to be true.

- Make sure arguments among family members are always conducted in calm voices without getting personal or involving anger toward one another. This can be hard for children to do, but it is good experience for when they are adults. Siblings should view themselves as being on a team together, as follows:
    - Siblings should support each other so they will all succeed; the goal for each is that they all succeed.
    - Siblings should respect each other's opinions, thoughts, and feelings. If they say they disagree, they should explain why. They should not just say, "you are wrong" and end the discussion.
    - Siblings should never criticize their siblings for any problem they are having. If they are not offering to help, they should stay away from mentioning the problem.

- Always keep the end-result in mind while raising your children. You want your adult children to be self-sufficient without any financial or emotional dependency on you. Your involvement in their adult lives should be primarily limited to (1) keeping them on the successful track in life; (2) helping them become more and more self-sufficient; (3) providing appropriate advice when asked for; (4) sharing in the joy of their successes; and (5) maintaining the bond with your children that is based on emotional attachment, where you will always be there to help each other through life.

- Babies should not be picked up every time they cry and they should rarely be given a pacifier. You do not want your babies to learn that crying is the way to get what they want. This type of crying can lead to temper tantrums when they are older.

This book does not cover safety issues concerning children, other than the following list of ten items. Your pediatrician has much more information concerning the safety of your children.

- Keep babies' fingernails short so they do not scratch their eyes.

- Babies should not have access to small objects that could get caught in their throats.

- Babies should not be left unattended by tubs or pools where they could drown.

- Do not lie down and nurse a baby, when there is a chance of falling asleep and rolling over on the baby.

- Children should always be appropriately secured while riding in an automobile.

- Do not leave unattended buckets of water that a child could fall head first into; five-gallon buckets are particularly dangerous.

- Keep potential poisons (cleaning agents, insecticides, medicines, vitamins, and the like) out of children's reach.

- Children should not open the door of the home when an adult comes to the door because the children may do it when the parents are not home or are asleep.
- When you teach your children about avoiding strangers, tell them a "code word" that should not be revealed to anyone outside the family. Tell your children that if any stranger says that the children's mom or dad says for them to do anything and does not say the code word, the child should run to a safe place where there are other people. Children should be taught that if a stranger in a car starts talking to them, they should immediately drop what they have and run away, while yelling, to the nearest place with other people.
- Children should be taught never to go anywhere, especially alone, where their parents could not find them.

Do not assume that your pediatrician will notice everything about your baby and ask you all the right questions. Ask your pediatrician for a list of things to monitor. If something does not seem right or if you have a question, write it down and ask your pediatrician. For example, make sure of the following:

- Babies' hands and feet do not remain partially clenched
- Babies can follow movement with each eye, cover one eye and then the other while testing
- Babies respond to a soft voice in each ear
- By six months, babies wave their hands and bring them together
- By nine months, babies put objects in their mouths
- By 12 months, babies hold and examine objects, moving them from one hand to the other

If you want to have and raise children, be sure to consider the following about all prospective spouses before you get married:

- Do they want to have children?
- Will they be good parents? People often treat their children the way they perceive they were treated by their parents.
- Are the two of you the type of people who will commit two to three decades to properly raising children?

Note: Do not have children just because you think you are supposed to.

Index

A

absolute level in life · 50
accomplishment · 18, 20, 21, 27, 36, 70, 87, 119, 121, 122, 141, 211, 212, 229, 232, 233, 240, 311, 312
accounting rate of return tool · 203
actively managed funds · 265
activity based costing · 207, 208
actual costing · 208
adaptation · 295
additional paid-in capital · 185
administrative assistant · 107, 108
advanced degree · 118
advancement · 17, 31, 34, 58, 103, 107, 317
advertising · 19, 26, 135, 139, 145, 149, 150, 151, 155, 157, 158, 160, 162, 170, 172, 177, 215, 244, 253, 272, 279
agenda · 81, 238
American Bar Association · 290
annuity · 261, 272
art · 55, 237, 267, 268
assets · 139, 143, 146, 147, 158, 161, 165, 171, 173, 177, 178, 179, 180, 183, 184, 186, 187, 189, 191, 192, 193, 196, 198, 201, 202, 267, 268, 274, 287, 289
associations · 243
assumption · 43, 50, 74, 78, 79, 112, 142, 156, 179, 213, 214, 222, 223, 243, 250, 251, 252
ATM card · 287
attitude · 135, 225, 321
authority · 20, 22, 58, 107, 112, 116, 119, 124, 129, 166
automobile · 153, 165, 176, 255, 257, 271, 273, 274, 279, 280, 281, 292, 311, 331
automobile insurance · 257, 273
awkward situation · 99, 105

B

back-up systems · 67
bad debt · 86, 158, 159, 162, 172, 180, 185, 187, 196, 200
bad habit · 34
bailout payback tool · 202
balanced scorecard · 86
bank account · 164, 199, 256, 257, 288
bank loan · 161, 176, 184, 199
bank lock box · 199
bankruptcy · 289
belief · 213, 216, 243, 297
benchmark · 50, 117, 328
best guess/theory · 112
bonds · 176, 184, 203, 259, 261, 262, 263, 264, 265, 266
bonus · 30, 32, 64
brainstorming · 81
breakeven point · 188
breakeven time tool · 203
budgeting · 62, 249, 256
bully · 125, 304, 305
bureaucratic red tape · 46
business appraiser · 177
business broker · 171
business opportunities · 142
business plan · 156, 160

C

cameras · 147
capital financing · 203, 205
career · 13, 16, 17, 21, 32, 33, 34, 45, 55, 111, 131, 209, 293, 327, 328
career fast track · 13, 33, 34, 293, 328
cash equivalents · 259, 261, 263, 264, 266
cash flow
after tax · 201, 268
before tax · 268, 269
Certificates of Deposit (CDs) · 262
character · 97, 98, 297, 303, 322
checkbook · 147, 258
close-minded · 214, 239
COBRA · 37
coincidence · 244, 303
college · 20, 21, 22, 70, 220, 250, 251, 252, 263, 272, 307, 312, 313, 316, 319, 323, 324, 325
commercial paper · 200
commitment · 18, 41, 81, 82, 91, 116, 133, 146, 149, 160, 161, 218, 320
common stock · 178, 180, 188, 204, 205, 262, 266
communication · 22, 55, 303
compensating balance · 199
compensation · 15, 85, 126, 130, 133, 164, 165, 166, 170, 284, 327
competitive advantage · 141, 142

completion date · 36, 40, 45, 108, 122, 124
compound interest · 252
computer software · 36, 113, 220
conclusion · 78, 79, 82, 243, 244, 302, 313, 330
confidentiality agreement · 174
confiding · 37
confirm · 55, 56, 58, 74, 112, 214
conflict · 39, 53, 95, 96, 97, 98, 103, 104, 105, 113, 122, 129, 218, 235, 238, 302, 305, 315, 322
Confucius · 15
conscious mind · 219, 230, 233
contract · 90, 143, 276, 280, 283, 288
contribution margin · 149, 187, 188, 196, 197, 198
corporations
  subchapter · 166
cost measurement systems · 205, 206
cost of capital · 201, 202, 203, 204, 205
cover letter · 19, 20, 21, 23
coworker · 35, 49, 51, 97, 98, 99, 103, 105, 108, 114, 118, 119, 129, 134, 233, 236, 322
CPA · 148, 174
crash time · 64
credit card · 254, 255, 256, 257, 258, 260, 269, 283, 288, 289
credit reference · 145
critical path · 64, 65, 66
culture · 18, 129
current ratio · 187
custodial accounts · 261
customer · 21, 26, 83, 86, 89, 90, 92, 93, 117, 118, 122, 123, 140, 141, 142, 143, 144, 145, 146, 148, 149, 150, 151, 152, 153, 154, 155, 159, 161, 162, 169, 170, 176, 178, 180, 184, 185, 187, 196, 200, 207, 208, 231, 285, 323

D

debt · 173, 176, 184, 186, 189, 191, 203, 204, 205, 254, 255, 256, 257, 269, 283, 287, 289
decision · 55, 56, 64, 91, 92, 100, 104, 105, 107, 116, 118, 126, 129, 130, 132, 139, 144, 145, 156, 179, 188, 195, 196, 197, 217, 218, 219, 220, 222, 230, 241, 252, 253, 255, 269, 283, 296, 297, 302, 314, 322, 323, 324, 330
decision maker · 91, 92, 104, 116
deferred taxes · 253, 260
delegate · 123
direct report · 33, 37, 42, 43, 98, 105, 107, 117, 121, 122, 123, 124, 125, 126, 129
disability insurance · 273
discipline · 125
diversity · 116
dividends · 166, 185, 186, 191, 204, 262, 265, 266
drugs · 117
due date · 36, 42, 45, 46, 70, 73, 82, 128, 129, 162, 172, 173
due diligence · 171, 174, 175, 177, 179

E

Earnings Per Share (EPS) · 266
education · 16, 17, 21, 22, 23, 29, 36, 127, 129, 157, 254, 307, 312, 325, 327
efficiency · 86, 151, 172
efficiently · 39, 45, 61, 83, 121, 142, 230, 267, 313
Einstein, Albert · 239
email · 20, 52, 53, 55, 56, 57, 58, 59, 70, 74, 82, 84, 98, 105, 124, 125, 308
employee · 13, 18, 21, 25, 30, 35, 46, 85, 86, 104, 108, 109, 111, 113, 115, 116, 117, 118, 119, 121, 122, 123, 124, 125, 126, 127, 128, 129, 130, 131, 134, 140, 141, 142, 144, 145, 146, 147, 152, 154, 155, 157, 164, 165, 170, 175, 176, 328
employee benefits · 25
employee retirement savings
  401(k) · 30, 32, 164, 260
  403(b) · 260
  457 · 260
employer · 17, 18, 20, 26, 27, 28, 32, 33, 34, 36, 37, 47, 74, 85, 89, 107, 118, 129, 131, 132, 133, 134, 135, 139, 140, 142, 163, 253, 260, 261, 273
employment agencies · 135
Enterprise Resource Planning (ERP) Software · 140, 161
environment · 16, 18, 33, 34, 83, 87, 119, 141, 151, 153, 222, 231, 295, 296, 299, 301, 330
equipment · 36, 64, 69, 73, 93, 124, 143, 144, 157, 158, 159, 160, 167, 170, 171, 173, 176, 177, 178, 180, 184, 186, 188, 189, 191, 192, 193, 196, 198, 200, 279
equity · 176, 183, 185, 188, 189, 193, 194, 204, 205, 259, 260, 262, 277
executive recruiters · 144
expectation · 31, 36, 70, 86, 89, 93, 123, 124, 163, 179, 250, 312

F

factoring · 200
failure · 67, 74, 124, 141, 145, 217, 225, 227, 228, 243, 316, 322, 324

feedback · 108, 122
file · 40, 42, 46, 57, 105, 125, 126, 133, 164, 257, 258, 289, 290
finances · 249, 256
financial decision making · 195, 208
financial statements · 139, 143, 150, 160, 161, 174, 175, 176, 180, 183, 194, 195
  balance sheet · 160, 172, 173, 174, 175, 177, 183, 185, 193, 194
  cash flow statement · 174, 175, 183, 186, 194
  income statement · 160, 173, 174, 175, 176, 183, 185, 186, 193, 194, 195
financial transactions · 183, 194
first experience · 243
first impression · 34, 35, 130, 216, 227, 233, 238, 243, 297, 302
fixed costs · 143, 148, 188, 195, 196, 197, 208
follow up · 46, 70, 75, 146
follow-up letter · 26, 128
franchise · 140, 141, 157, 167, 177
Franklin, Benjamin · 41
fraud · 147, 285
freight · 92, 144, 145, 158, 173, 185, 190, 196, 197, 206
fundamentals of being a person · 299

G

gambling · 287, 289
GANTT Chart · 61, 62, 64
general ledger · 193, 194
generalization · 57, 242, 264, 297
Generally Accepted Accounting Principles · 194
genes · 296
genius · 216, 316
goals · 15, 17, 19, 23, 32, 33, 34, 49, 51, 55, 56, 58, 65, 74, 75, 83, 84, 86, 98, 103, 117, 132, 154, 155, 209, 211, 212, 216, 217, 218, 219, 220, 225, 230, 242, 245, 250, 313, 319, 320
going for the gold · 73
gold · 268
gossip · 50, 117
government bonds · 262
grammar · 57, 58, 308, 314
gut-feeling decision · 219

H

headcount · 47
headhunter · 144
health · 37, 159, 165, 176, 253, 271, 273, 291, 292, 303
health insurance · 37, 159, 176, 273
helping others · 296
hint · 48
hiring process · 127, 129, 130
home · 18, 20, 36, 42, 43, 134, 140, 156, 180, 230, 250, 254, 255, 257, 260, 261, 268, 271, 273, 274, 275, 276, 277, 278, 284, 285, 287, 288, 312, 316, 321, 323, 324, 332
human nature · 140
hurdle rate · 201, 205

I

income tax · 148, 158, 161, 166, 173, 174, 177, 184, 185, 186, 188, 193, 201, 257, 260, 268, 289, 290
index funds · 265
inflation · 153, 250, 251, 252, 259, 262, 274
inheritance · 254, 261
instinct · 296
insurance · 18, 37, 140, 145, 157, 158, 161, 164, 165, 166, 185, 189, 190, 192, 193, 254, 256, 257, 261, 263, 271, 272, 273, 274, 277, 279, 280, 284, 289
intern · 18, 58, 328
internal rate of return · 202, 203
International Financial Reporting Standards · 183, 194
internship · 18, 328
interview · 19, 22, 25, 26, 27, 28, 29, 34, 127, 128, 130, 132, 134, 135, 215
interview notes · 26, 28, 29
inventory · 86, 146, 147, 148, 158, 159, 160, 161, 162, 163, 167, 172, 176, 177, 179, 180, 184, 185, 186, 187, 189, 190, 191, 192, 193, 195, 196, 199, 207
inventory safety stock · 199
inventory turnover · 187
investing · 154, 167, 247, 251, 259, 260, 261, 266, 267, 272, 278
investment advisors · 267
investment grade bonds · 262
investments · 139, 153, 154, 160, 161, 162, 184, 186, 188, 191, 204, 205, 251, 254, 257, 259, 260, 261, 263, 264, 265, 266, 267, 268, 269, 278, 288
invoice · 143, 144, 146, 147, 151, 162, 163, 172, 187, 200, 279
IRA · 260
I-Savings Bonds · 262

J

job · 15, 16, 17, 18, 19, 25, 26, 27, 28, 29, 30, 31, 32, 33, 34, 35, 36, 37, 46, 48, 51, 67, 70, 75, 85, 86, 87, 89, 92, 105, 115, 116, 118, 126, 128, 130, 131, 132, 134, 135, 141, 163, 172, 205, 207, 212, 222, 226, 250, 284, 308, 317, 323, 324, 328, 330
job order cost system · 207
joint products · 197
jump-start · 13, 34

K

KPIs · 86

L

large cap (capitalization) stocks · 262
late shipments · 86, 89
laurels · 211
leaders · 119, 320
lead-time · 42, 65, 66, 86, 89, 92, 143, 152, 162, 187
lead-times · 86, 89, 152, 162, 187
lean accounting · 208
lean manufacturing · 208
lean thinking · 86, 208
learning · 13, 47, 53, 113, 115, 212, 221, 222, 299, 312, 313, 314, 315, 316, 319, 320, 322
legal matters · 165, 172, 287
legal rights · 290
liabilities · 173, 176, 177, 178, 179, 180, 183, 184, 186, 187, 189, 191, 192, 193, 194, 198, 274
life cycle costing · 208
life insurance · 165, 257, 261, 271, 272
Limited Liability Company (LLC) · 166
Limited Liability Partnership (LLP) · 166
longevity · 291
long-term financing · 160

M

manage · 45, 50, 65, 67, 117, 124, 131, 137, 145, 161, 164, 183, 195, 198, 288
manager · 93, 98, 108, 121, 124, 125, 126, 129, 131, 141, 146, 170, 266
managing cash flow · 157
managing expenses · 157
market research · 90, 149
math · 304, 309, 310, 312
measuring · 83, 311
medical benefits · 32
meeting · 27, 36, 40, 41, 42, 46, 81, 82, 84, 90, 92, 104, 122, 125, 218, 249, 264
merger and acquisition specialists · 171
mission · 85, 86, 104, 108, 122, 155
mistakes · 35, 46, 47, 51, 52, 56, 71, 109, 118, 134, 230, 232, 234, 247, 255, 297, 314, 320
modified internal rate of return tool · 202
motivate · 121, 124, 211, 307
mutual funds · 261, 262, 264, 265, 266, 268

N

negotiate · 32, 92, 95, 96, 134, 284, 315
net cash from financing · 174, 186, 188
net cash from investments · 174, 186, 188
net cash from operations · 174, 186, 188
net present value tool · 201
neural circuit · 295, 296, 297
non-value-added activities · 86, 208
normal costing · 208

O

objective · 21, 33, 47, 73, 81, 82, 83, 84, 91, 95, 124, 214, 215, 217, 232, 241, 242, 313, 322
occupation · 15, 16, 46, 222, 327, 328
open mind · 15, 74, 113, 212, 216, 245
operation cost system · 207
operational efficiencies · 86
opinion · 29, 35, 59, 97, 98, 116, 118, 174, 203, 211, 213, 215, 217, 229, 232, 233, 236, 237, 239, 281, 289, 297, 325, 330, 331
opportunity cost · 143, 148, 195, 196, 197, 254, 255
organizational chart · 33, 34, 172
organizing · 39, 42, 122, 133, 170, 249, 256, 310, 313
OSHA (Occupational Safety & Health Administration) · 170
ostracism · 119, 236
outline · 20, 57, 79
overtime · 48, 64, 128, 129, 144, 159, 163
overview · 20, 21, 26, 33, 34, 47, 53, 59, 73, 74, 78, 104, 157, 171, 216, 222, 223, 245, 314, 320

P

partnership · 157, 166, 177
payback tool · 202, 203
payroll · 140, 158, 159, 161, 163, 164, 173, 207
peer · 33, 43, 104, 105, 113, 119, 226, 230, 233, 241, 303, 313, 321, 328
perceived value · 70, 97
performance · 33, 34, 36, 83, 86, 124, 126, 131, 208, 301
performance indicators · 208
personal umbrella insurance · 274
personnel agencies · 144
perspective · 15, 234, 244, 245
PERT · 62, 63, 64, 65, 66
pet peeve · 111
petty cash · 145, 184
phone meeting · 82
preferred stock · 203, 204, 262, 266
presentation · 57, 77, 78, 79, 91, 104, 112, 134, 232
Price/Earnings ratio (P/E) · 266
proactive · 103, 225, 231
process cost system · 206, 207
product rationalization · 197
productivity · 29, 46, 108, 124, 129
profession · 23, 30, 36
professional service firm · 141, 143
proficient · 36, 47, 221, 308
profit sharing · 30
profitability index tool · 202
projecting the financial benefit · 200
projects · 27, 45, 46, 65, 67, 70, 73, 75, 81, 122, 134, 202, 312
promote · 34, 119, 130
promotion · 18, 25, 31, 34, 36, 37, 48, 98, 115, 116, 118, 119, 122, 123, 129, 131, 145, 150, 308
proofread · 47, 59, 314
property tax · 145, 166, 257
proprietary information · 90
protecting assets · 157

Q

quality · 35, 45, 73, 89, 119, 122, 144, 148, 150, 151, 152, 153, 154, 172, 177, 186, 196, 255
quick ratio · 187
quit a job · 133

R

reading · 57, 59, 73, 77, 98, 162, 295, 307, 308
real American dream · 139, 169
reality · 148, 151, 241, 243, 244, 245, 303
red flag · 52
reference · 28, 126, 133, 134, 156, 157, 186, 188, 191, 219, 293
reinforcement
    positive · 126
relative level in life · 50
report · 37, 46, 57, 74, 77, 78, 98, 117, 118, 125, 132, 133, 288
reputation · 98, 104, 130, 232, 237, 239
researching · 46
resources · 31, 36, 37, 41, 45, 64, 85, 86, 104, 105, 107, 117, 121, 124, 126, 129, 130, 142, 148, 152, 206, 312
responsibility · 75, 118, 145, 163, 319, 322
resume · 19, 20, 21, 22, 23, 26, 29, 74, 135, 157, 328
retail business · 70, 145, 154, 170
retained earnings · 185, 193, 194, 204
retirement · 18, 247, 249, 250, 251, 252, 253, 261, 264, 274, 324
return on equity · 188
roadblock · 73
romance · 119
Roth IRA · 260
routine detailed tasks · 123
routine task · 47
Rule of 72 · 252

S

sabotage · 37, 226
sales commission · 145, 185, 187, 196
sales forecast · 155, 172, 198, 201, 218
Sarbanes-Oxley Act of 2002 (SOX) · 174
saving face · 96
school · 15, 18, 20, 21, 118, 135, 233, 244, 254, 275, 302, 305, 307, 308, 310, 311, 312, 313, 316, 317, 320, 322, 327, 328, 330
schoolwork · 311, 312, 323
self-confidence · 227
self-esteem · 233, 293, 299, 302, 304, 305, 312, 319, 322, 329
self-improvement · 229
self-sufficient · 98, 230, 331
severance deal · 134
sexual harassment · 119, 164
short-term financing · 160, 199
sick day · 117

signature · 91, 147, 180, 281, 284, 288
Simplified PERT · 65, 68, 69
skill · 107, 121, 122, 134, 135, 139, 141, 221, 229, 289, 293, 300
small cap stocks · 262
small claims court · 290
sole proprietorship · 166
speculation · 213, 233
standard cost system · 206
stock out · 86, 199
stocks · 259, 261, 262, 263, 264, 265, 266
strategic collaboration · 86
strategic partner · 90
strategic planning · 151, 154
strategies · 74, 85, 86, 104, 108, 122, 154, 155, 170, 176, 230
strengths · 27, 151, 152, 154, 155
successes · 217, 226, 227, 228, 293, 322, 324, 331
supervisors · 108, 121, 124

T

task · 47, 67, 71, 74, 75, 118, 122, 124, 200
taxable · 177, 201, 265, 266, 267, 268
tax-deductible · 177, 201, 260, 268
teamwork · 83, 84, 118, 129, 289, 320
temper · 117, 331
term insurance · 271, 272
termination of employment
  firing someone · 126
  general · 119, 124, 134, 135
  layoff · 144
  resignation letter · 133
  severance agreement · 32
thought processes · 296
traditional IRA · 260
tunnel vision · 212
Twain, Mark · 236

U

U.S. Consular at the U.S. Embassy · 290
U.S. Small Business Administration · 143
unconscious mind · 219, 221, 223, 227, 230, 233
unemployment compensation · 134, 145, 163, 164
unemployment tax rate · 144

V

vacation · 31, 32, 134, 164, 254
valuable employee · 85, 117
value · 70, 85, 86, 97, 140, 142, 150, 153, 154, 165, 169, 173, 174, 175, 176, 177, 178, 180, 183, 185, 188, 189, 192, 201, 202, 203, 207, 208, 242, 253, 254, 255, 257, 262, 265, 267, 272, 273, 275, 276, 281, 311, 317, 323, 325
value-added activities · 86, 207, 208
variable costing · 208
variable costs · 143, 148, 196, 198, 208
Vienna Convention of 1963 · 290
vision · 85, 86, 104, 108, 122, 155
voice mail · 48, 98

W

warranty · 158, 180, 185, 187, 190, 255, 257, 276, 280, 281, 282, 284
weaknesses · 27, 128, 151, 152, 154, 155
Will (Last Will and Testament) · 287, 290
working capital · 161, 187, 188, 198
writing · 31, 47, 55, 56, 58, 59, 77, 79, 100, 288, 301, 308, 314
written warning · 125

www.ingramcontent.com/pod-product-compliance
Lightning Source LLC
LaVergne TN
LVHW061218100826
845148LV00004B/798

* 9 7 8 0 9 7 9 8 3 5 3 5 3 *